Global Energy Dilemmas

For Sally and Lily

Global Energy Dilemmas

Energy Security, Globalization, and Climate Change

MICHAEL J. BRADSHAW

polity

First published in 2014 by Polity Press

Polity Press
65 Bridge Street
Cambridge CB2 1UR, UK

Polity Press
350 Main Street
Malden, MA 02148, USA

ISBN-13: 978-0-7456-5064-7
ISBN-13: 978-0-7456-5065-4(pb)

A catalogue record for this book is available from the British Library.

Typeset in 9.5 on 12 pt Swift Light
by Toppan Best-set Premedia Limited
Printed and bound in Great Britain by Clays Ltd, St Ives PLC

The publisher has used its best endeavours to ensure that the URLs for external websites referred to in this book are correct and active at the time of going to press. However, the publisher has no responsibility for the websites and can make no guarantee that a site will remain live or that the content is or will remain appropriate.

Every effort has been made to trace all copyright holders, but if any have been inadvertently overlooked the publisher will be pleased to include any necessary credits in any subsequent reprint or edition.

For further information on Polity, visit our website: www.politybooks.com

Contents

Figures, Tables, and Boxes

Acronyms

BASIC	Brazil, South Africa, India and China
BRICS	Group of emerging economies consisting of Brazil, Russia, India, and China
CAIT	Climate Analysis Indicator Tools
CCS	Carbon Capture and Storage
CIBS	China, India, Brazil, and South Africa
CIS	Commonwealth of Independent States
CMEA	Council for Mutual Economic Assistance
CPE	Centrally Planned Economy
EBRD	European Bank for Reconstruction and Development
ETS	Emissions Trading System
GDP	Gross Domestic Product
IOC	International Oil Companies
LNG	Liquefied Natural Gas
MENA	Middle East and North African states
NOC	National Oil Companies
OECD	Organisation for Economic Cooperation and Development.
OPEC	Organization of the Petroleum Exporting Countries
PPP	Purchasing Power Parity
UNDP	United Nations Development Programme
UNFCCC	United Nations Framework Convention on Climate Change
WDI	World Development Indicators

Units

bcm	billion cubic metres
btu	British thermal units
mb/d	millions of barrels per day
mtCO$_2$e	metric tons of CO_2 equivalent
ppm	parts per million
tcf	trillion cubic feet
tcm	trillion cubic metres
tCO$_2$/toe	tons of carbon dioxide per ton of oil equivalent

Preface

My interest in energy issues goes back to my PhD studies at the University of British Columbia in the early 1980s. My PhD examined the relationship between East–West trade and the economic development of Siberia. The so-called "gas-for-pipe" deals that enabled the export of Siberia's natural gas to Western Europe and that became a source of disagreement between the US and Europe formed a major part of my study. At the time, Washington's concern was that Moscow would use Western Europe's growing reliance on Soviet gas imports for geopolitical gain. And 30 years later the Cold War is over, the Soviet Union is gone, and the map of Europe has been redrawn, but concerns still remain about the geopolitical manipulation of Russia's gas exports. While anxiety about energy security is not new, there are now two additional challenges that complicate the secure and affordable supply of energy. The first is the acceleration of globalization that has changed the geography of energy consumption and that is creating new sources of competition. The second is climate change that demands a dramatic reduction in the volume of greenhouse gas emissions from the global energy system to constrain global warming.

This book develops the global energy dilemmas framework to examine the interrelationship between energy security, globalization, and climate change. There is a large, and ever-expanding, literature on all three of these issues; but it is fair to say that the three knowledge communities still remain relatively isolated from one another. The emphasis in this book is upon the relationship between energy and economic development and its implications for climate change policy. This is not a detailed analysis of globalization; nor is it a study of climate change. Rather, it examines how the changing geopolitical economy of the global energy system is being driven by economic globalization, and explains how the changing geographies of the energy system are complicating climate change mitigation. A fundamental proposition of the analysis is that while the world faces a single global energy dilemma, which is explained in the introductory chapter, it is being played out in different ways across the globe. Thus, the challenges that face energy consumers in what I call the high-energy societies of the developed world are very different from those in the developing world who lack access to basic energy services. The analysis adopts a geographical perspective which maps out how the global energy dilemma varies across the major regions of the world, but which also seeks to explain how that geography complicates the interaction between energy security and climate change. Thus, geography is not just an outcome; an understanding of the spatial dimensions of the global energy dilemma is essential to overcoming the current gridlock in the negotiations on a global agreement for climate change policy.

Although the book presents a geographical analysis, it draws on a wide range of literature from a variety of disciplines. The aim is to draw together a breadth of analysis to generate new insights into the relationship of energy, economy, and environment. Thus, the originality lies in its breadth of coverage and intent to integrate analysis of some of the key challenges that confront human society today. The focus of the analysis is upon developments since 1990, which is the base year for the Kyoto Protocol, as well as the beginnings of the post-socialist transition. It also marks the beginnings of a step change in the rate of China's economic development.

I started work on this research project in the autumn of 2008, just months after the price of oil peaked at $147 a barrel, and just as the full extent of the global financial crisis was becoming apparent. These events were soon followed by the failure of the Copenhagen Summit to deliver a post-Kyoto agreement on climate change. Three further climate summits – Cancun, Durban, and Doha – have passed without agreement, as well as the Rio+20 United Nations Conference on Sustainable Development. Meanwhile, energy demand continues to grow and greenhouse gas emissions are increasing on a trajectory that will result in global warming well above the 2°C recognized as the desirable maximum. There have also been a number of events that have highlighted the vulnerability of the energy system. In January 2009, the second Russia–Ukraine gas dispute resulted in major supply disruptions in parts of Central and Southern Europe, and reinforced concerns about Russia's manipulation of energy exports for geopolitical gain. In April 2010, the blowout at BP's Macondo well in the Gulf of Mexico highlighted the environmental risks associated with deep-water oil production. Less than a year later, in March 2011, the Great East Japan Earthquake triggered a tsunami that struck the Fukushima Daiichi nuclear power station on the northeastern coast of Japan. This disaster resulted in the eventual shutdown of all of Japan's 54 nuclear reactors that together account for about a third of Japan's electricity supply. Although a small number of power stations are now coming back online, the disaster has had global consequences – first, because Japan has had to import additional supplies of fossil fuels, and, second, because it has resulted in a worldwide rethink on the role of nuclear power as a low-carbon source of electricity for the future. Also in 2011, the so-called "Arab Spring" triggered renewed concerns about the stability of the political regimes in the Middle East and North Africa, many of whom are major oil and gas exporters. The widespread unrest brought regime change in Tunisia, Egypt, and Yemen, and a civil war in Libya that culminated in the death of

Colonel Gadaffi. But the conflict in Syria continues and tensions remain as a result of Iran's nuclear ambitions. Furthermore, events in Algeria, in January 2013, have brought the world's attention to the continuing instability of much of North Africa and sub-Saharan Africa. Thus, it is clear that the traditional concerns relating to fossil-fuel energy security remain and, one could argue, continue to take precedence over the need to address climate change. Furthermore, as the unconventional oil and gas revolution gathers pace in North America – with its less than positive implications for climate change – there is now a growing realization that increased US energy self-sufficiency may leave the emerging economies of Asia more reliant on their own diplomacy (and possibly military power) to secure oil and gas imports. Equally, the consequences of the global financial crisis have resulted in a renewed obsession with economic growth on the part of the developed economies, and recession has reduced the willingness and ability of governments to make investments to address climate change at home, let alone finance low-carbon development abroad. Understandably, the emerging and developing economies remain concerned that climate change mitigation will impose economic costs on them that might damage their prospects for economic development. But all the while the gap between the politics and economics of business as usual and what the climate change scientists tell us is required to mitigate climate change continues to grow. All of this suggests a need for new thinking about the relationship of energy security, globalization, and climate change. This is the research gap that this book seeks to fill.

The analysis presented here draws on a wide range of information sources and it is necessary to say a few words about the sources of statistical data that are used. Inevitably, research on energy and climate change relies on a lot of information about reserves, production, consumption, and emissions. Equally, analysis of economic development requires information on economic performance and standards of living. But any analysis that is global in scope runs into the problem that reliable and comparable data are not available for all of the countries of the world. To minimize these problems, information has been drawn from a few key sources and the reader is advised to visit the websites of these organizations to access the most recent data. Four online databases provide the bulk of the information presented in the various tables and discussed in the text. First is the *World Bank Development Indicators* database that can be accessed at: <http://data.worldbank.org/indicator>. Second is the World Resources Institute's *Climate Analysis Indicators* (CAIT) database that was available at: <http://www.wri.org/tools/cait/>. Unfortunately, in late 2012, the CAIT website suffered a malicious attack that took the site offline and resulted in a near-total loss of its file system and database. Hopefully, the damage will be repaired, as the CAIT database was an indispensable resource for the analysis of the Kaya characteristics used in the four regional studies. Third is the OECD's online *OECD Factbook* that is available at <http://www.oecd-ilibrary.org>. The final publication is BP's *Statistical Review of World Energy* that is published on an annual basis and is available at <www.bp.com>, along with an associated workbook of historical statistics. The reference list provides further information on all the sources consulted in the conduct of this analysis.

Like the majority of the literature on energy security and climate change, reliance upon official statistics means that this analysis is overly state-centric. The tendency to see the global energy system in terms of energy-exporting and energy-importing states overstates the role of government and understates the role of companies. While the energy companies are not totally anonymous in the analysis, there is no doubt that more could be said about the role of the business sector in the provision and consumption of energy services. Equally, a lot more work needs to be done on understanding how government policy aimed at climate change mitigation can be translated into action on the part of the private sector, or in many cases state-owned enterprises. Such an approach to understanding energy and climate governance beyond a state-centric framework remains a work in progress that is essential to creating a more sustainable energy system.

The idea of "global energy dilemmas" was first conceived in the late 1990s in a first-year undergraduate course on global issues that I taught at the University of Birmingham. In my experience, good research ideas often originate in the classroom when seeking to explain complicated issues through robust frameworks. I thank all of the students at Birmingham, and Leicester, and, in the summer of 2012, the University of Oslo Social Studies Summer School for providing a sounding board for my ideas and analysis. The award of a Leverhulme Major Research Fellowship in 2007 afforded me the time to embark on a major program of research and writing that has turned the global energy dilemmas framework into the current book, and I thank the Leverhulme Trust for their support. I would also like to thank Peter Daniels, Emeritus Professor of Geography at the University of Birmingham, Mick Dunford, Professor of Economic Geography at the University of Sussex, and Jonathan Stern, Professor and Chairman of the Natural Gas Programme at the Oxford Institute for Energy Studies, all of whom supported my Leverhulme application. I also acknowledge additional study leave granted by the University of Leicester when the Fellowship ran out and the book wasn't finished. More generally, I thank my colleagues in the Department of Geography at Leicester, particularly Ann and Vanessa. Now they can all see what I have been doing for the last five years when, most of the time, I wasn't in the department.

Many individuals have helped me in thinking through this project and in writing the book. Catherine Mitchell and Jim Watson, and the participants in the Energy Security in a Multipolar World Research Cluster, provided a stimulating forum for discussing energy issues. A late introduction to the UK Energy Research Centre has also proved interesting. My fellow geographers Gavin Bridge and Stefan Bouzarovski continue to provide intellectual support in our ongoing mission to convince geographers that energy is interesting. I thank Bill Tompson for his assistance with accessing key information sources, and Benjamin Sovacool for sharing his extensive e-library of articles on energy security. I also thank Michael Klare, who I met twice during the development of this project; during that time he wrote two books in less time than it has taken me to write one! The next one won't take me as long, but it's already late. Equally, I thank those outside of academe working on energy issues who have had to suffer me convincing them that geography really matters; John Mitchell and Anthony Froggatt at Chatham House, and Cho Khong at Shell, have all been willing to listen. I have also benefited from research support to help me pull together the materials used in this analysis. I thank Saska Petrova for her help on the energy dimensions of post-socialist transition and Murtala Chindo for his help with the energy and development literature. Over the final year of the project, Charlotte Nagy-Baker assisted by doing all those jobs that authors' tend to forget, creating the list of contents, checking the bibliography, proofreading, and producing the list of acronyms, etc. All of these tasks are time-consuming and her dedication to detail is much appreciated. Thank you also to Kerry Allen, Cartographic and Design Technician in the Department of Geography at Leicester, who drew all of the figures for the book. Louise Knight and David Winters at Polity Press provided support right through the writing and production process and did not complain as deadlines frequently passed. Although apprehensive of what they might say, I thank the reviewers who provided encouragement and some critical insights just when they were needed. Finally, I thank Sally and Lily for all their love and support, and apologize for all the lost weekends; I promise that I will finally sort out my office.

CHAPTER ONE

Introduction

In 2007 the United Nation's Intergovernmental Panel on Climate Change (IPCC, 2007a: 2 and 5) concluded that "Warming of the climate system is unequivocal" and that "Most of the observed increase in global average temperatures since the mid-20th century is *very likely* [emphasis in original] due to the observed increase in anthropogenic greenhouse gases (GHG) concentrations." A year later in the introduction to their annual *World Energy Outlook*, the International Energy Agency (IEA 2008: 37) stated that "It is no exaggeration to claim that the future of human prosperity depends on how successfully we tackle two central energy challenges facing us today: securing the supply of reliable and affordable energy; and effecting a rapid transformation to a low-carbon, efficient and environmentally benign system of energy supply." This book examines the interrelationships between energy security, globalization, and climate change. It proposes that we face a global energy dilemma: *can we have secure, affordable, and equitable supplies of energy that are also environmentally benign?* The starting point for this analysis is recognition that the way the global energy dilemma plays out differs greatly around the world and that globalization is a major reason for this geographical variation in the relationship between energy security and climate change. In the world in which we live access to energy services – for heating, lighting, cooking, cooling, transforming, transporting, and so on – is essential for survival. However, as we shall see, how we satisfy those energy needs and the absolute level of energy consumption varies greatly. Consequently, there is an increasingly complex relationship between energy consumption and economic development. There is also a more straightforward relationship between the number of people on the planet and the demand for energy services; put simply, more people means more demand for energy.

In combination, population growth and economic development are resulting in an ever-increasing demand for energy and at present the largest part of that demand is being met by burning fossil fuels. According to Baumert et al. (2005: 41), almost 61 percent of total anthropogenic GHG gas emissions (and almost 75 percent of carbon dioxide [CO_2] emissions) come from energy-related activities, with the majority coming from fossil-fuel combustion. It is for this reason that energy policy is central to climate-change mitigation policies that aim to stabilize and then reduce the level of atmospheric concentrations of GHGs. John P. Holden, Science and Technology Advisor to President Obama, explains the intimate relationship between energy, economy, and environment:

> Without energy there is no economy. Without climate there is no environment. Without economy and environment there is no material wealth, no civil society, no personal or national security. And the problem is that we have been getting the energy our economy needs in ways that are wrecking the climate that our environment needs. (John P. Holdren, quoted in Ladislaw et al. 2009: 9)

This chapter provides the background needed to understand why we must confront the global energy dilemma and find ways of providing secure, affordable, and equitable access to energy supplies that do not promote further climate change or result in other forms of environmental degradation, such as oil spills, air and water scarcity and pollution, habitat destruction and the loss of biodiversity. The chapter begins by exploring the history of the fossil-fuel energy system. This is important for two reasons. First, in order to change the current system it is necessary to understand how it has developed. Second, there have already been a number of "energy transitions" within the fossil-fuel system and if we are to bring about a purposeful transition to a low carbon-energy system it is important to understand the nature of those earlier transitions. The second section examines the relationship between energy consumption and economic development, and introduces some of the key concepts and measures that are used in subsequent analysis. This is not a book about the science of climate change; however, the third section presents a brief review of our current understanding of the relationship between energy and climate change. The final section explains how the key "drivers" of population growth, economic development, and energy consumption interact to make energy strategy a key element of climate-change policy.

The Fossil-Fuel Energy System

Energy systems have five essential components: the primary energy sources that form the base of the system and that have not been subject to any conversion or transformation process, the range of technologies that are used to convert primary energy into secondary energy products and useful and usable energy, and the eventual energy services that are provided to the energy consumer (see table 1.1). It is demand for energy services that drives overall demand, but a range of different primary resources and secondary energy products can supply those services. Thus, for example, electricity can be generated on the basis of all of the primary energy resources listed in table 1.1 that comprise the current energy system. The process of decarbonization that requires that fossil fuels be replaced by low carbon sources, namely, nuclear power and renewable energy, lies at the heart of policies aimed at resolving the global energy dilemma.

TABLE 1.1 Components of the contemporary energy system

Primary energy	Secondary energy	Useful energy	Usable energy	Energy services
Fossil fuels (hard coal, brown coal, natural gas, petroleum)	Briquettes, coke, gas from coal, gasoline from coal, oil, fuel oil, vehicle fuels, liquefied gas, natural gas (processed), charcoal, biogas	Secondary energy used by the consumer (private homes, industry, small consumers) (not counting transportation losses or non-energy consumption)	Heat	Warm rooms
				Hot water
			Refrigeration	Propulsion of engines
Nuclear fuels (uranium, thorium)			Mechanical work (power)	Locomotion
Renewable energy (sun, water, biomass [wood], geothermal energy)			Chemically bound energy	Smelting aluminium
		Electric power	Light	Heating steel
	Electric power	District heat	Sound	Lighting rooms
	District heat			
	Hydrogen	Hydrogen		Communications

Source: Modified from: Wagner, H-J. (2009), *Energy: The World's Race for Resources in the 21ˢᵗ Century.* London: Haus Publishing, p. 8.

The current fossil-fuel energy system is a recent invention of human society. It was not until the seventeenth century that coal started to be substituted for wood to provide heat. Before then society was dependent on biomass and human muscle power and, following the invention of agriculture and the domestication of animals, certain animals, together with wind and water power. The resulting "somatic energy system" was basically a solar energy system managed by humans (Sieferle 2001). In this system the only important energy converters were biological ones (McNeil 2000). The system remained essentially unchanged for centuries and the development of society was linked to the fertility of arable land, access to water, and the productivity of the forest. Podobnik (2006: 21) maintains that the Industrial Revolution happened first in Britain because the increasing scarcity and cost of wood and charcoal made coal an economically viable alternative. Smil (2010: 29) adds that the falling cost of coal production was also an important part of the picture. Whatever the case, two limiting factors were that the coalmines were not located in close proximity to major markets and that mining activity was restricted by the problem of flooding. At the time, coal could only be moved short distances by horsepower and over longer distances by river, canal, and sea. Then a series of mutually reinforcing technological and social changes triggered the Industrial Revolution that fundamentally and permanently changed the relationship between energy, society, and the natural environment (Wrigley 2010).

In 1712, Thomas Newcomen invented a steam engine, which although incredibly inefficient, provided a solution to the problem of how to drain the coalmines. It was so inefficient, however, that it could only really be located at or very close to coalmines; thus, it could not provide motive power to the wider economy. That came with the further refinement of the steam engine, most famously by James Watt who patented his new steam engine in 1769. This more efficient engine gained wider application, particularly in the cotton industry. Parallel advances in ferrous metallurgy were also part of the story as they increased demand for coal to produce coke and the resultant steel provided the raw materials with which to build ever more efficient steam engines. In 1830, the first public railway from Liverpool to Manchester was opened, along which ran Stephenson's *Rocket*. The rapid expansion of the railway system provided more efficient and economic ways of moving coal and other raw materials that in turn further increased the demand for coal and made industry more mobile as it could now move away from its raw material sources, a process that spawned the industrial city. Authors such as Podobnik (2006) and Huber (2009) warn us against "energy determinism" and point out that this transition was only made possible by major changes in society. In the case of Britain, Podobnik argues that the emergence of a capitalist elite – individuals such as Matthew Boulton, the business partner of James Watt – was essential as it provided the capital needed to finance industrialization; at the same time, the expulsion of peasants from rural land provided the workforce for the new towns and factories. Thus, industrialization and urbanization went hand in hand and new cities grew to prominence, all of which drove ever-increasing demand not only for energy, but also raw materials, much of which were imported from Britain's colonies.

In 1800, Britain accounted for more than four fifths of the world's coal production and was the location of over 70 percent of the horsepower generated by steam engines, but the Industrial Revolution soon spread to Europe and then overseas to the colonies and Britain's prominence declined. According to Smil (2008), the tipping point in the transition to fossil fuels came in 1882, the year when the United States burned more oil than coal. The introduction of "town gas" as an alternative source of lighting to expensive whale oil, and also of coal and wood for heating and cooking, further increased demand for coal as the world's capitals turned to gas in 1812–25 (Davis 1984: 3). Just as coal and the steam engine were establishing themselves as the predominant energy source and prime mover, so oil emerged as a competing primary energy source. The oil age began on August 27, 1859, at Oil Creek, Pennsylvania, when "Colonel" E. L. Drake's workers penetrated 10 metres of rock and completed the world's first oil-producing well. As with coal, the industry soon spread and new centers emerged in places like Baku, the capital of modern-day Azerbaijan. Oil had a number of benefits over coal; its energy density (the amount of energy stored per unit of volume) is about 50 percent higher than standard coal, and it is also cleaner to use and easier to transport than coal. Its primacy was guaranteed at the end of the nineteenth century by the invention of the internal combustion engine. Both petrol and diesel engines fast became the prime movers of the automotive age and the lighter engines also made possible powered flight. But this did not mean that the age of coal was over. The invention of electricity and the steam turbine, which used coal to heat water to generate steam to drive turbines which generated electricity, meant that the process of electrification sustained demand for coal. Later developments and innovations saw the introduction of natural gas into the fossil-fuel energy mix, first in the United States in the 1930s and then in Europe in the 1970s. Alternatives to fossil-fuel power also emerged in the form of industrial-scale hydroelectric power and then nuclear power, the latter being used to drive steam turbines to generate electricity. Figure 1.1 shows how the global energy mix changed with the introduction of new sources of primary energy, as the resulting energy transitions brought about a relative change in the contribution of the different sources of energy, but in no case did the absolute amount of energy produced decline.

The pace and scale of the fossil-fuel energy revolution is difficult to comprehend. Grübler (2004) has estimated that, in 1800, the world's population was roughly 1 billion people and total global energy use was approximately 20 exajoules (EJs). By 1900, world energy use had increased to 50 EJs and the population to 1.6 billion people; by the end of the twentieth century, energy use had raced to 430 EJ and the population to 6.1 billion. Thus, in 200 years, the population increased sixfold and energy use twentyfold. Figure 1.2 charts this exponential growth in energy use and the associated transitions in the energy mix from a coal-based system in the nineteenth century to petroleum-based system (oil and gas) in the twentieth century. Today, the world's primary energy mix is divided between oil, gas, coal, hydro, and nuclear power.

The history of the energy system is usually described in terms of the concept of "energy transitions" that is based on the idea that a single energy source, or group of related energy sources, dominates the market during a particular period, eventually to be challenged and then replaced by a different source or group of related sources (Melosi 2010: 45; Grübler et al. 2012). From figure 1.2, we can see that the first transition involved the replacement of biomass (primarily wood) by coal as the dominant source of energy. The second transition involved the emergence of oil as the dominant energy source, which was later supplemented by natural gas. More recently, an increasingly diverse energy mix has emerged that is dominated by the three fossil fuels. According

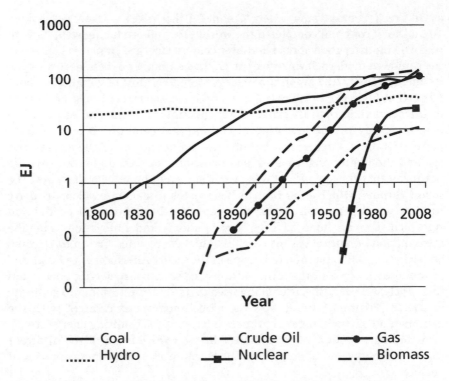

Source: Data from Smil, V. (2010), *Energy Transitions: History, Requirements, Prospects*. Denver, CO: Praeger, p. 154.

Figure 1.1 Global energy transitions, 1800–2008

to table 1.2, these three fossil fuels accounted for 83.3 percent of total global primary energy supply in 2006. This table is particularly useful as it combines commercial energy sources with biomass and waste and the latter is usually excluded in energy statistics.

The next energy transition should see those fossil fuels replaced by a variety of low carbon and renewable energy sources. However, for many years to come fossil fuels will still play an important role in the global energy mix. The other fact to consider is that this stylized history of the evolution of the global energy system is based on the experience of the developed economies. As is clear from table 1.2, there are considerable regional variations in the energy mix. In fact, one could argue that many of the low-income economies have yet to pass through the first energy transition, as biomass is still the dominant source of energy supply. Equally, some of the fastest-growing middle-income economies have an energy mix that is still dominated by coal; for example, in China in 2011 coal accounted for 70.3 percent of total primary energy consumption, and in India coal's share was 52.9 percent (BP 2012b:

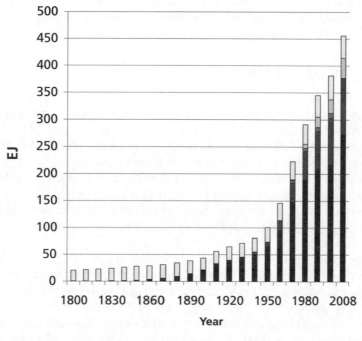

Source: Data from Smil, V. (2010), *Energy Transitions: History, Requirements, Prospects.* Denver, CO: Praeger, p. 154.

Figure 1.2 The changing scale and structure of global energy

TABLE 1.2 Regional variations in the global energy mix in 2006 (Percentage of total primary energy supply)

	Coal	Natural gas	Oil	Renewables[1]	Biomass & waste	Nuclear
World	26.6	21.0	35.7	2.8	9.8	6.3
Low income	7.3	19.1	7.8	3.1	53.8	0.1
Middle income	35.8	19.2	29.9	3.2	12.3	2.0
High income	13.9	22.9	43.7	2.5	3.4	11.0
OECD	20.5	21.9	39.7	2.8	3.8	11.1

1. Hydro, solar, wind, and geothermal energy.

Source: World Bank (2010a), *World Development Report 2010.* Washington, DC: World Bank, p. 365.

41). These regional variations suggest that there is a relationship between the level of economic development, the amount of energy consumed, and the structure of the energy mix.

Energy and Economic Development

In general, it is accepted that there is a clear positive relationship between the level of economic development in a national economy or region and the amount of energy consumed (Yeager et al. 2012). Put simply, higher levels of economic activity drive higher levels of energy consumption. This relationship between energy and economic development is captured in a measure known as *energy intensity*, which represents the ratio between the total energy consumption of a region or country to its Gross Domestic Product (GDP). It is important to remember that energy intensity is not a direct measure of energy efficiency, though improvements in efficiency obviously impact on energy intensity.

Figure 1.3 suggests a relatively straightforward relationship between energy and economic development; however, the relative position of countries, particularly the outliers, requires further investigation. Before delving into the detail, it is necessary to spend some time thinking about the exact nature and reliability of these two measures, particularly when looking at change over time and when making cross-country comparisons. The measure of energy used in calculations of energy intensity is usually primary commercial energy consumption, which by definition does not include the non-commercial use of biomass. As demonstrated by table 1.2, biomass and waste are important sources of energy in low-income economies; thus, this measure tends to underestimate the level of energy consumption in the developing world. That said, the absolute levels of energy consumption are very low compared to the developed world and therefore this has limited impact on the overall global level of energy consumption. There are also concerns about the use of GDP as a measure of the level of economic activity in a region or country. The World Energy Council (2010a: 12) maintains that it is very important to use a purchasing parity measure (PPP) of GDP that is based on the cost of a standard basket of goods and thus reduces the impact of exchange-rate distortions when converting national data into $US. This produces a more realistic measure of the level of economic activity in a given country and has the overall effect of increasing the relative level of activity in developing economies. That said, GDP is a measure of the formal economic activity that is captured by national accounting systems and, therefore, it does not include informal activity that can be very significant in many countries. The net result of these issues is that official data and the resultant measure of energy intensity may systematically understate both the level of energy consumption and economic activity in the developing world; but not to the extent that it would close the gap between the developed and developing economies. With

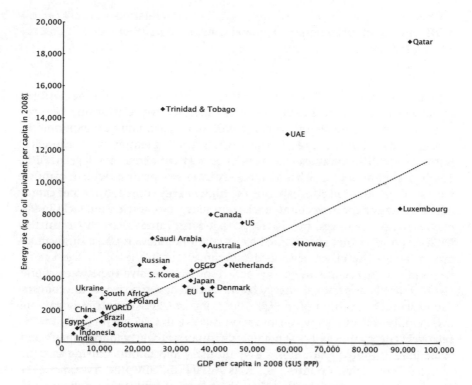

Source: World Bank Development Indicators Database.

Figure 1.3 The relationship between energy use and GDP in 2008

these caveats in mind, what do the trends in energy intensity tell us about the relationship between energy and development?

There are sufficient outliers in figure 1.3 to suggest that at a given level of energy use or economic activity there is considerable cross-country variation; nonetheless, in general, there is a fairly robust relationship between the two variables. Figure 1.3 tells us nothing about the direction of the causality in the relationship; is it high levels of economic activity that drive higher energy consumption or vice versa? A review of economic research on this issue suggests that there is no consensus on the direction of causality, but that there is a clear positive relationship between the level of electricity consumption and the rate of economic growth in a given country (Ozturk 2010: 347). One of the reasons for the lack of clarity is the fact that a range of variables influences the energy intensity of a particular country or region. Smil (2003: 72) has suggested six variables that might explain energy intensity:

- The degree of energy self-sufficiency.
- The composition of primary energy supply.

- Differences in economic structure.
- Differences in discretionary personal consumption of energy.
- Country size.
- Climate.

Returning to figure 1.3, we can use these variables to explain the position of individual countries. The three outliers that have very high levels of energy consumption – Trinidad and Tobago, UAE, and Qatar – are all exporters of energy. Qatar, for example, is the world's leading exporter of Liquefied Natural Gas (LNG), but it also has a small population and a high level of GDP. The liquefaction of LNG is itself an energy-intensive process, which, coupled with small population size, explains the high-energy consumption per capita of these energy-exporting countries. Luxembourg, by comparison, lacks indigenous energy resources, but is the most energy-intensive economy in the OECD, a position that is explained by its small population and a high standard of living. The other developed economies above the OECD average in terms of energy use are all energy- and resource-intensive economies, while the high levels of personal energy consumption and the size of the country can explain the position of the US. The group of OECD countries below the average in terms of energy consumption relative to GDP are all known to be relatively energy efficient, are net energy importers (particularly Japan), and some have a limited amount of heavy industry and manufacturing in their national economies. Countries such as Russia and Ukraine have a higher amount of energy consumption than their level of economic activity would suggest. This situation is a legacy of the Soviet centrally planned economy that was notoriously energy intensive (the reasons for this are discussed in chapter 4). In the bottom corner, we see a group of developing and emerging economies that have low levels of energy use per capita and correspondingly low levels of economic activity. However, the very large population of some of these economies means that their absolute levels of energy consumption are high. The variation along the vertical axis provides a measure of relative levels of per capita energy use. The ratio to the global average is +4:1 for North America compared to almost +2:1 for the European Union and −0.02 for sub-Saharan Africa.

By combining the analyses of energy transitions and patterns of energy intensity it is possible to suggest a simple stage model that relates energy to economic development. Elias and Victor (2005: 8) identify four stages. At an early stage of economic development, the dominance of relatively inefficient fuels and technology means that large inputs of energy are required for the production of output. The initial phase of the Industrial Revolution is representative of this stage. In the second stage, as economic development proceeds, more efficient fuels and technologies are adopted and the energy input per unit of output begins to decline. However, in the following third stage, a focus upon energy-intensive heavy industry and manufacturing may actually slow the reduction in energy intensity. As the result of de-industrialization, in the fourth stage there is a relative "de-coupling" of the relationship between energy use and economic growth. However, these so-called post-industrial economies have also benefited from the relocation of energy-intensive industries offshore and then the import of energy-intensive goods. Again, it is necessary to warn against being deterministic: this four-stage model, like the energy-transition concept, is a stylization based on the experience of the developed OECD economies, but there is no reason to assume that emerging and developing economies will follow the same path. Indeed, as explained in the following section, there is good reason to hope that they will not. Despite this health warning, BP (2012a: 13), in their *Energy Outlook to 2030*, suggest that there is a common pattern in relation to energy intensity: it increases as countries industrialize and the share of energy-intensive industry in GDP rises relative to other sectors; it then peaks and starts to decline as the nature of industry changes (from heavy and energy-intensive to lighter and higher value-added) and it becomes more energy efficient. Finally, it converges across countries as a result of energy trade, the use of common technologies, and similarities in consumption patterns.

It is true that year on year the global economy becomes more efficient at using energy to generate economic outputs. As Smil (2003: 68) has noted, it is not possible to construct a reliable historical trend for global energy intensity, but there is ample evidence of the processes that drive declining energy intensities in the developed economies. In the United States, the most energy profligate of all countries, energy intensity fell by more than half between 1949 and 2004 (US Department of Energy 2012). In the European Union (EU-25), between 1990 and 2008, total energy intensity fell at an average rate of 1.6 percent, though there are substantial national differences (European Environment Agency 2010). What these trends suggest is that once an economy reaches the post-industrial stage its energy demand tends to level off and, if it sustains economic growth, its energy intensity declines; in some cases the total amount of energy consumed is also starting to decline. But, as noted above, countries can only do this if they are able to move energy-intensive industries offshore and import energy-intensive goods instead. The production of those energy-intensive goods has relocated to countries like China and India, and is one of the reasons why they are in a more energy-intensive phase of development (Peters et al. 2011).

Given what has been said about the relationship between energy consumption and economic development, it follows that the energy intensity of countries varies in large part in relation to the level of economic development (measured as GDP) or the UNDP's Human Development Index (HDI). Just as there are huge variations in the level of wealth and income across the globe, so there are variations in the level of energy consumption. According to Gaye (2007: 2), "on average, the poorest 2.5 billion people in the world use only 0.2 toe per capita annually, while the billion richest people use 5 toe per capita a year, which is 25 times more." At present, about 2.5 billion people, mostly in developing countries, still rely on traditional biomass fuels for cooking and 1.6 billion people lack access to electricity. Thus, the lack of access to energy services – energy poverty – is seen as a key aspect of the development challenge (this is the subject of chapter 6) and it highlights the fact that the relationship between energy and development is very different across the countries and regions that comprise the global energy system.

Energy and Climate Change

From the discussion so far, it is evident that over the last two centuries there has been a dramatic change in the relationship between energy and the development of human society. The harnessing of a geological storehouse of the sun's energy via the evolution of the fossil-fuel system has enabled unimaginable advances in the quality of living for many on the planet. Unfortunately, this fossil-fueled economic miracle has come at considerable ecological cost; so much so that many scientists now describe the current era as a new geological epoch known as the "Anthropocene," as the scale of human impact on the environment is such that it is now reshaping the planet (Crutzen and Stoermer 2000; Syvitski 2012).

As explained at the beginning of this chapter, "we have been getting the energy our economy needs in ways that are wrecking the climate that our environment needs" (Holdren, in Ladislaw et al. 2009: 9). Climate change is not the only environmental problem related to energy production and consumption, but most of the others are limited to relatively small areas of the planet, though challenges such as acid rain are international in their impact. Climate change, by comparison, is global in its causes and consequences and therefore requires global action to combat it (Barnett 2007). While a minority remains skeptical, the vast majority of the scientific and policymaking community accepts that anthropogenic climate change is real, already happening, and that immediate action is required to mitigate its causes and to adapt to its consequences. This is not a book about the science of climate change; nor does it delve into the detail of climate-change policy and its economics (Stern 2007) and politics (see Giddens 2012); rather, it is concerned with the relationship between energy production and consumption, on the one hand, and economic development, on the other hand, and the ways that both contribute to climate change and are influenced by policies introduced to mitigate the causes of climate change. This approach is explained in more detail in the next chapter. For the moment, our concern is with the role of the energy system as a source of the greenhouse gases (hereafter GHGs) that are a major cause of climate change.

In their *Synthesis Report*, the IPCC (2007b: 30) defines climate change as "a change in the state of the climate that can be identified (e.g. using statistical tests) by changes in the mean and/or the variability of its properties, and that persists for an extended period, typically decades or longer. It refers to any change in climate over time, whether due to natural variability or as a result of human activity." They note that this general definition, which includes natural variations in climate, differs from that adopted by the United Nations Framework Convention on Climate Change (UNFCCC) where Article 1 states that climate change is "a change of climate which is attributed directly or indirectly to human activity that alters the composition of the global atmosphere and which is additional to nature's climate variability observed over comparable time period." Thus, the UNFCCC defines "climate change" as being anthropogenic, the result of human actions, which is seen as distinct from "climate variability" that is attributable to natural causes (Dow and Downing 2007: 15). Hereafter, the term "climate change" follows the UNFCCC convention and refers to climate change that results from human activity. The term "global warming" is often used as an alternative to "climate change," but a warming climate has quite different consequences across the globe. The IPCC (2007b: 30) concluded that "Warming of the climate is unequivocal, as is now evident from the observations of increases in global average air and ocean temperature, widespread melting of snow and ice and rising global sea levels." However, proving beyond doubt that this warming trend is a consequence of human action is a much more complicated task. The term "greenhouse effect" refers to a naturally occurring phenomenon whereby so-called GHGs retain some of the sun's radiation in the atmosphere. If it were not for this effect, the average earth temperature would be $-18°C$ rather than $+15°C$. These greenhouse gases occur in very small proportions in the atmosphere and their presence is measured in terms of parts per million (ppm) and parts per billion (ppb). Table 1.3 provides some important background information on GHGs.

As is clear from table 1.3, the human activities associated with industrialization and economic development more generally are clearly implicated as major sources of GHGs. The IPCC (2007b: 37) has concluded that "Global atmospheric concentrations of CO_2, CH_4 and N_2O have increased markedly as a result of human activities since 1750 and now far exceed pre-industrial values determined from ice cores spanning many thousands of years." In terms of the causes of these increases, they state that "global increases in CO_2 concentrations are due primarily to fossil fuel use, with land-use change providing another significant contribution." They state that it is *"very likely"* (emphasis in the original) that the observed increase in CH_4 is predominantly due to agriculture and fossil fuel use, and that the increase in N_2O concentration is primarily due to agriculture. According to their research, the global atmospheric concentration of CO_2 increased from a pre-industrial value of about 280 ppm to 379 ppm in 2005. The global concentration of CH_4 has increased from a pre-industrial value of 715 ppb to 1774 ppb in 2005 and the global concentration of N_2O increased from a pre-industrial level of about 270 ppb to 391 ppb in 2005. The rate of increase in GHG concentrations has

TABLE 1.3 Greenhouse gases: sources and warming potential

Greenhouse gases	Generated by	Global warming potential[1]
Carbon dioxide (CO$_2$)	Fossil-fuel combustion, land clearing for agriculture, cement production	1
Methane (CH$_4$)	Livestock production, extraction of fossil fuels, rice cultivation, landfills, sewage	25
Nitrous oxide (N$_2$O)	Industrial processes, fertilizer use	298
Hydrofluorocarbons (HFCs)	Leakage from refrigerators, aerosols, air conditioners	124–14,800
Perfluorocarbons (PFCs)	Aluminium production, semi-conductor industry	7,390–12,200
Sulphur hexaflouride (SF$_8$)	Electrical insulation, magnesium smelting	22,800

1. Global warming potential expresses a gas's heat-trapping power relative to carbon dioxide over a particular time period (commonly 100 years). Thus, for example, methane has 25 times the warming potential of carbon dioxide over 100 years.

Source: Adapted from McKeown and Gardner (2009), *Climate Reference Guide*. Washington, DC: World Resources Institute, pp. 1 and 3.

accelerated in recent years and the Carbon Dioxide Information Analysis Center (CDIAC 2012) reports that the average CO$_2$ concentration in 2010–11 was 390.5 ppm. Furthermore, analysis by Peters et al. (2012) suggests that the global financial crisis resulted in a short-lived reduction in the growth emissions, but they have since rebounded, largely due to economic growth in emerging economies. The notion of a "pre-industrial level" clearly identifies industrialization as the primary driver of increases in GHGs. Figure 1.4 provides a breakdown of the different sectors, showing end uses and activities associated with GHG emissions, and also details their share of global warming associated with each GHG.

It is possible to construct a fairly straightforward account of the causes of climate change. As figures 1.5 and 1.6 clearly illustrate, there is evidence that since the beginning of the Industrial Revolution there has been both a substantial increase in the global atmospheric concentration of GHGs and a general trend of global warming; furthermore, the pace and scale of these changes seems unprecedented. Unfortunately, the global ecosystem is far more complicated and there is a set of complex feedback mechanisms that

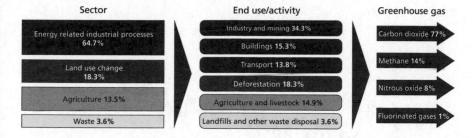

Source: World Bank (2008a), *World Bank Development Indicators 2008*. Washington, DC: World Bank, p. 123.

Figure 1.4 Greenhouse gas emissions by sector and by activity

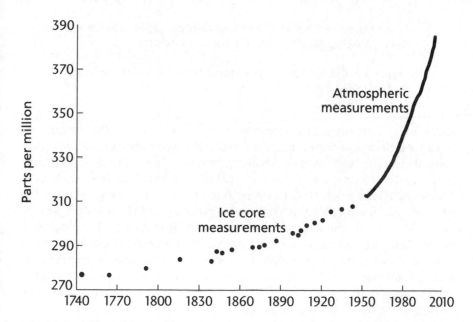

Source: Adapted from McKeown and Gardner (2009), *Climate Reference Guide*. Washington, DC: World Resources Institute, p. 5.

Figure 1.5 Changes in atmospheric concentrations of carbon dioxide, 1744–2008

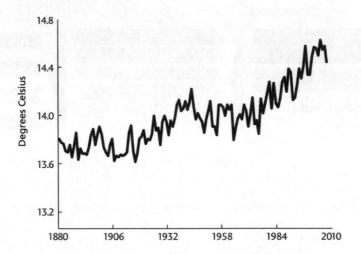

Source: Adapted from McKeown and Gardner (2009), *Climate Reference Guide*. Washington, DC: World Resources Institute, p. 5.

Figure 1.6 Changes in average global temperature at the Earth's surface, 1880–2008

make it very difficult to attribute direct causation. Additionally, the impacts of climate change are uneven and unpredictable across both time and space. Nevertheless, in 2007, in their *Summary for Policy Makers*, the IPCC (2007a: 5) was prepared to state that: "There is *very high confidence* that the net effect of human activities since 1750 has been one of warming." And: "Most of the observed increase in global average temperatures since the mid-20th century is *very likely due* to the observed increase in anthropogenic GHG concentration." Thus, we can conclude that increased demand for energy services associated with industrialization and economic development, which has largely been met by the burning of fossil fuels, has made a major contribution to the increase in the atmospheric concentrations of GHGs and to climate change and global warming in particular.

Although the exact numbers vary, it is widely acknowledged that the energy system, broadly defined, is the most important source of increases in GHG emissions, particularly CO_2 emissions. According to figure 1.4, energy-related and industrial processes account for 64.7 percent of greenhouse gas emissions. While fossil-fuel combustion accounts for the majority of this share, one should also recognize that all forms of energy supply are associated with some level of GHG emission, not least because the cement and steel used to build a nuclear power station or offshore wind farm, for example, form a source of GHG emissions. Traditionally, most of the analysis of energy and climate change has focused on the amount of CO_2 and other GHGs produced in the combustion process; however, increasingly, there is a concern to calculate the "full life-cycle" carbon footprint associated with particular energy sources. This is because it is the total amount of GHGs emitted in the provision of a particular energy service that matters, and a failure to carry out such comprehensive carbon-accounting can result in misleading claims about the "low carbon" characteristics of a particular energy source. This issue has gained prominence because of the rapid growth of shale gas production in the United States (discussed in chapter 3). For our current purposes, it is sufficient to note that when it comes to the three fossil fuels there are significant fundamental variations in the amount of CO_2 emitted when they are burnt. According to the IPCC, on average conventional coal produces 92.0 gCO_2/MJ of energy produced (that is grams of carbon dioxide emitted per mega joule of energy produced), while conventional oil produces 76.3 gCO_2/MJ, and conventional gas 52.4 gCO_2/MJ (Metz et al. 2007: 264). Thinking back to our earlier discussions of energy intensity and energy transitions, it is clear that it is not only the absolute amount of energy consumed by a country or region that matters, but also the energy mix – that is, the share of the different types of fossil fuel and other types of energy source. If we return to figure 1.2, we can see that as the total amount of energy consumed by the global economy increased and as the energy mix changed from coal to oil to gas, so the level of carbon intensity of each new source declined. The problem is that the absolute level of energy consumption and the associated levels of CO_2 emissions continue to increase. But, as table 1.2 illustrates, there remain substantial regional variations in energy mix, which means there are also regional variations in the carbon intensity of energy production. The global ecosystem does not discriminate against the geographical origins of CO_2; equally, GHGs remain in the atmosphere and contribute to climate change long after the initial emissions (in most cases for a century or more, though about half of the carbon historically emitted is stored in natural carbon sinks, which are themselves being compromised by deforestation and land use change), and thus the issue of cumulative emissions is important. The IEA (2008: 179) points out that the non-OECD (the less industrialized) economies today account for 55 percent of the world's emissions of energy-related CO_2, but, over the period since 1890 as a whole, their responsibility is only 42 percent. Put another way, the developed world is responsible for the majority of the energy-related CO_2 emissions since 1890, and the United States alone is responsible for 28 percent of historical emissions. As we shall see in chapter 2, the history, dynamics, and geography of the carbon intensity of energy production are key factors in the relationship between energy, economic development, and climate-change policy.

In the context of climate change, it is not just the absolute levels of energy consumption or the relationship between energy and economic development that matter; the *carbon intensity of energy use*, that is, the amount of carbon dioxide emitted per unit of energy used, and the *carbon intensity of economic activity*, that is, the amount of carbon dioxide per unit of economic output (GDP), are also key considerations. Equally, the level of *carbon dioxide emissions per capita* is an important indicator in climate change policymaking. The carbon intensity of energy use is closely related to the way in which a particular country or region obtains its energy services (the carbon intensity of electricity is a closely related indicator). Reliance on more carbon-intensive primary energy sources, such as coal, results in a higher level of carbon intensity of energy use than the use of natural gas. Obviously, reliance upon less carbon-intensive sources of energy, such as renewables and nuclear power, has the effect of reducing the carbon intensity of energy use. Thus, as we shall see, "decarbonizing" the sources of energy supply is a key target of climate change policy. As noted above, there are marked differences in energy mix across countries and regions, and it follows that there are similar variations in the carbon intensity of energy use. In its *International Energy Outlook 2010*, the US Energy Information Agency (IEIA: 2010) provided information on regional trends in the carbon intensity of energy use in terms of metric tonnes of CO_2 per billion BTUs of energy consumed. In the case of the OECD, carbon intensity fell from 57.7 in 2000 to 55.7 in 2007. In the non-OECD, the carbon intensity increased very slightly from 64.0 in 2000 to 64.2 in 2007; however, there are some interesting regional variations here. In non-OECD Europe/Eurasia, carbon intensity fell from 63.0 to 56.3, while in non-OECD Asia, it fell slightly, but at a much higher absolute level, from 74.3 in 2000 to 74.1 in 2007. The substantial fall in Europe/Eurasia is a consequence of the collapse of the Soviet Union and the closure of much of the smokestack heavy industry associated with Soviet-style industrialization (this is the subject of chapter 4); while the high absolute levels in Asia reflect the higher levels of dependence on coal in the dominant economies of China and, more recently, India (which is discussed in chapter 5).

There is generally an inverse relationship between per capita income and emission intensity, that is, the higher the level of income, the lower the emission intensity; but a country's economic structure, geography, and energy choices are also important factors influencing their emission intensity. Since 1990, there has been a general trend of falling levels of CO_2 per unit of GDP. That said, the Middle East is the one region that bucks the trend (this is discussed in chapter 5). In absolute terms, China is currently one of the world's leading CO_2 emitters per unit of GDP, at just below double the world average. This can be explained by both its reliance on carbon-intensive sources of energy supply – principally coal – and the fact that it accounts for a large share of the world's industrial and manufacturing output. By comparison, when measured on a per capita basis, in 2007 China only ranked 59th with 4.6 tons of CO_2 per capita, compared to the United States which was ranked 7th with emissions of 19.0 tons per capita.

Standing back from the numbers, while it is true that both the energy intensity and carbon intensity (of both energy use and economic output) show general improving trends, the absolute levels of energy demand and carbon emissions – notwithstanding the impact of the global financial crisis – continue to grow. And all the projections show that both energy demand and carbon dioxide emissions will be substantially higher in the future unless drastic action is taken now to stabilize and then reduce energy demand and carbon dioxide emissions (Anderson and Bows 2012). To do this, it is necessary to understand the underlying socio-economic processes that are driving energy and emissions growth and that seem to confound effective international agreement on climate-change policy. With that in mind, the final section explains the centrality of energy policy to climate change mitigation.

Putting it all Together: The Kaya Identity

It is easy to be overwhelmed by the scale and complexity of the global energy dilemma; fortunately, the so-called "Kaya Identity" provides an elegant and relatively simple way of explaining the interrelationships that have been discussed above. Its intellectual origins lie in the so-called IPAT equation, developed by Ehrlich, Holdren, and Commoner (Commoner 1972), which sees the environmental impact (I) as the production of: population (P), affluence (A), and technology (T) (Chertow 2011). The Kaya Identity was developed by the Japanese energy economist Yoichi Kaya and has been very influential in the modeling of future energy demand and carbon emissions. It plays a core role in the IPCC emissions scenarios and is also used in the EIA's *International Energy Outlook*. A simple version of the identity is presented below in Box 1.1. The EIA (2010: 129) describes the identity as: "an intuitive approach to the interpretation of historical trends and future projections of energy-related carbon dioxide emissions." Figure 1.7 illustrates their use of the formula to project future emissions at a global scale. The analysis is based on their "2010 Reference Case" that assumes no new climate policies; they project worldwide increases in output and relatively moderate population growth, and the

---

Box 1.1 The Kaya Identity

$CO_2 = (CO_2/E) \times (E \times GDP) \times (GDP/Pop) \times Pop$
CO_2 = total energy related carbon dioxide emissions
E   = energy consumption
GDP = level of economic activity
Pop = population

Put simply:
CO_2 Emissions = Carbon Intensity × Energy intensity × GDP per capita × Population

Source: EIA (2010)

findings suggest that these two drivers will overwhelm projected improvements in energy intensity and carbon intensity, with a resultant continuing growth in carbon dioxide emissions through to 2035. Raupach et al. (2007) have conducted a somewhat similar analysis, but looking back at regional trends in the global economy since 1990. They found that no region was decarbonizing its energy supply and that the growth rate of emissions was strongest in the rapidly developing economies, particularly China with its high dependence on coal in its energy mix.

The Kaya Identity explains why energy strategy is so important to climate-change mitigation. Of the four Kaya factors – population, economic output, carbon intensity of energy use, and energy intensity – it is only the energy-related elements that are subject to the influence of policymakers. As Rivers and Jaccard (2009: 289) note: "No government has yet tried to slow population or economic growth, or to redirect economic activity, as part of its climate policy." It is true that countries such as China have adopted policies to control population growth, but not as a response to climate change (the issue of population and climate change in the context of developing economies is discussed in detail in chapter 6). When it comes to economic output, the opposite is the case, as all governments seek to promote economic growth and increased output. Environmentalists decry this obsession with growth, but the hard reality is that forgoing economic growth to protect the environment is a political non-starter. This is what Pielke (2010: 59) calls the "Iron Law." It states that there are limits to what individuals and society more generally are willing to pay to achieve environmental objectives: "experience shows quite clearly that when environmental and economic objectives are placed into opposition with one another in public and political forums, it is economic goals that win out." Thus, any policy aimed at reducing carbon emissions by forgoing economic growth or imposing high costs on individuals would be deemed politically unacceptable; even though the Stern review tells us that by taking early action the costs of climate-change mitigation are much lower, by postponing action we increase the eventual cost and scale of damage done (Stern 2007). The remaining policy levers are then energy intensity and the carbon intensity of energy use. In a critique of the current approach of international climate policy that is based on emission, the reduction targets set by the Kyoto Protocol, the so-called "Hartwell Paper" (2010) uses the Kaya Identity to argue that climate policy should be focused on the levers of energy intensity and carbon intensity. This means promoting technological change that brings about substantial improvements in energy efficiency and thus a reduction in the energy intensity – the amount of energy use per unit of output – and the diversification of the energy system beyond fossil fuels to meet growing energy demands from lower carbon alternatives, which would decarbonize the energy system and reduce the carbon intensity of energy use. Following the logic of the Kaya Identity, the net result would be a reduction in carbon dioxide emissions from energy-related activity. But

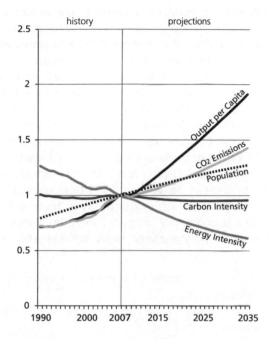

Source: EIA (2010), *International Energy Outlook 2010*. Washington, DC: EIA, p. 8.

Figure 1.7 EIA analysis of impacts of the four Kaya factors on world carbon dioxide emissions, 1990–2035 (index: 2007 = 1.0)

it is also important to remember that carbon dioxide is not the only GHG; nor is energy-related activity the only source of anthropogenic GHG emissions. Nonetheless, the twin goals of improved energy efficiency and decarbonization of the energy system are at the heart of most national energy policies in relation to climate change.

Conclusions: The Triple Challenge

At the beginning of this chapter it was suggested that we face a global energy dilemma: *can we have secure, affordable, and equitable supplies of energy that are also environmentally benign?* The discussion in this chapter has explained how we have come to be where we are today. Since the Industrial Revolution, economic development and population growth (and urbanization) have driven ever-increasing demands for energy services that have largely been satisfied by combustion of fossil fuels. Their combustion has made a major contribution to a substantial increase in atmospheric concentrations of GHGs, particularly carbon dioxide, which is now proven to be changing the climate in ways beyond that which might naturally be expected. In response to this problem of anthropogenic climate change, it is now recognized that we must stabilize and then substantially reduce the levels of GHG emissions. With respect to energy-related carbon dioxide emissions, the Kaya Identity suggests that the key policy drivers are related to reductions in energy intensity and carbon intensity. However, this chapter has not yet reflected on the fact that the dangers of climate change are not the only reason for reducing our reliance on fossil fuels. As we shall see in the next chapter, fossil fuels are finite non-renewable resources and they are proving increasingly expensive, as well as geopolitically and environmentally challenging, to deliver to consumers in a secure and affordable manner. The net result is that there is a second, equally persuasive, driver in favor of an energy transition away from fossil fuels, and that is energy security, which is discussed in more detail in the next chapter. In sum, this introductory chapter concludes that to overcome the global energy dilemma, policymakers must address and reconcile three challenges:

- To improve *energy intensity*, that is, to reduce the amount of energy used per unit of economic output.
- To reduce the *carbon intensity* of energy supply, that is, the amount of CO_2 produced per unit of energy supplied.
- To achieve the above in ways that are *secure, affordable, and equitable* (and that do not threaten economic growth).

CHAPTER TWO

The Global Energy Dilemmas Nexus

In the past decade, energy issues have come to the fore, and growing concerns about energy security and the environmental impacts of fossil fuels have heightened public and media interest and attracted the attention of politicians. Unfortunately, there is ample evidence to suggest that public understanding of the issues is limited, as is their trust of politicians (Happer et al. 2012; Boykoff and Smith 2010). It is hoped that the global energy dilemma approach can aid by synthesizing a wide range of research and presenting it in a novel manner that enables dialogue between specialist knowledge communities, civil society, and the business and policy world. This chapter is divided into four sections, each addressing a key dimension of the global energy dilemmas nexus. The first section considers the major challenges facing global energy security. The second section moves beyond the traditional concerns about security of supply to examine the various dimensions of energy scarcity. The third section then turns to the relationship between energy security and climate change, exploring the need for a "new energy paradigm." The final section explains how globalization is the missing link that explains the tensions between energy security and climate-change policy. The chapter concludes by combining the discussions of energy, globalization, and climate change to present the conceptual framework that organizes the analysis that follows.

Challenges to Global Energy Security

In recent years, a number of significant events and issues have combined to generate increased uncertainty about the future of global energy security. In the aftermath of the 2008 global financial crisis, after a dramatic dip, oil prices are back at historically high levels. In part, this is due to continuing concerns about the exhaustion of easily accessible supplies of conventional oil, but, as we shall see, new sources of demand are also a key part of the story. Equally, the gas disputes between Russia and Ukraine in 2006 and 2009 served to highlight how energy can still be used to geopolitical purpose. The Macondo disaster in the Gulf of Mexico, in 2010, was a stark reminder of the environmental consequences of extending the frontiers of oil and gas production; while the events at the Fukushima nuclear power plant in Japan, following the earthquake and tsunami in March 2011, highlight the vulnerability of the energy infrastructure to natural disasters. Most recently, the civil unrest across the Middle East and North Africa, in the so-called "Arab Spring" of 2011, have all raised new concerns about the relationship between oil wealth and autocracy, while Iran's nuclear ambitions and the civil war in Syria threaten to further destabilize the region. This chapter is primarily focused on those energy security concerns that stem from the changing geographies of production and consumption (Bradshaw 2009a). The point is that the dominance of the international oil companies over the oil-exporting developing economies was gradually eroded as oil reserves were nationalized, and then shattered in the early 1970s when the manipulation of oil supplies by OPEC for geopolitical purpose triggered an energy crisis and economic recession. This led to the formation of the International Energy Agency (IEA) and the creation of a strategic reserve among OECD states to ward against short-term supply disruptions (more on this below). Until recently, the IEA (2007: 160) defined energy security as the "adequate, affordable and reliable supplies of energy," but the consequences of globalization and the policy imperatives of climate-change mitigation have added considerable complexity to the contemporary notion of energy security.

There is now a voluminous literature of policy statements, think-tank reports, and academic books and papers on the topic of energy security (see Sovacool 2011 for a comprehensive assessment). On its website, the IEA now defines energy security as "The uninterrupted physical availability [of energy] at a price which is affordable, while respecting environmental concerns." In relation to its member-states, the European Commission (CEC 2010: 2) suggests that "A common energy policy has evolved around the common objective to ensure the uninterrupted physical availability of energy products and services on the market, at a price which is affordable for all consumers (private and industrial), while contributing to the EU's wider social and climate goals." In the United States, energy security is a central concern of the Energy Independence and Security Act of 2007, which aims to reduce dependence on energy imports through the promotion of energy efficiency and the development of domestic renewable energy supplies. All of these definitions view energy security from the perspective of energy-importing states with the emphasis on security of supply at affordable prices. But this begs the questions, whose security and whose affordability?

From the viewpoint of energy-exporting states, energy security is about security of demand and obtaining a "fair" price for their energy resources. But what is a "fair" price? The vast majority of energy-importing states would rather rely on market mechanisms to balance supply with demand to set the "market price," but energy prices are volatile, and oil and gas companies and the governments of energy-exporting states – many of whom own national oil companies – want to ensure that there will be a sufficient market for their exports at a price that will cover their investments in production and transportation infrastructure, as well as provide a level of return (rent) to enable them to cover their social costs. An added complication, and one that OPEC is at pains to point out, is that the "price at the pump" is determined by the level of taxation or subsidy in a particular country as much as the price of crude oil. In 2009, following a dramatic fall in oil prices triggered by the global financial crisis, the rulers of Saudi Arabia expressed the view that between $70 and $80 a barrel was a fair price, but social unrest across the Arab world in 2011 means that they now need to spend even more to placate their people, and a fair price is now seen as around $90 a barrel (see chapter 5). Some oil-exporting countries, such as Saudi Arabia and the Gulf States, understand that if the price of oil rises too high it will trigger an economic slowdown, which has the effect of reducing the demand for oil, and consequently its price; but there are hardliners in OPEC, such as Iraq and Venezuela, who seem concerned just to maximize their export income and are happy to keep oil prices high regardless of the longer-term consequences. An added complication is that natural gas is traded on a regional basis with a variety of different pricing and contractual mechanisms, some of which are indexed to oil, but others not (Stern 2012). The shale gas revolution in the US, discussed in chapter 3, has destabilized the pricing of natural gas and created uncertainty about the future of oil indexation and long-term contracts. As we shall see in later chapters, many energy-exporting states have had problems dealing with the volatility of energy prices and with the destabilizing impact of the high rents associated with energy exports. The more one examines the contemporary challenges to global energy security, the more it becomes apparent that the simple definition of "secure and affordable supplies of energy" is no longer fit for the purpose of describing the situation that the world now confronts. Sovacool and Brown (2010: 79), on the basis of a comprehensive review of the literature, conclude that "notions of energy security are either so narrow that they tell us little about comprehensive energy challenges or so broad that they lack precision or coherence." Chester (2010: 893) describes energy security as an "inherently slippery" concept, while Valentine (2011) describes it as "fuzzy." Perhaps it is the scale of analysis that is important here in generating all this confusion? There are clearly global energy security challenges – which are discussed below – but they play themselves out in particular ways in the context of individual regional organizations (EU, IEA, OPEC, etc.) and countries. On the basis of their review, Sovacool and Brown (2010: 81) propose that energy security should be based on four interconnected factors: availability, affordability, efficiency, and environmental stewardship. The first two reflect the traditional concerns of importing states, but the second two reflect the new challenges that face the global energy system – the prospect of constraints on the physical supply of energy and thus the need to reduce demand and use it more efficiently, and the contribution of fossil fuels to climate change. The following section examines these new challenges in greater detail, focusing on events since 1990 and forecasts to the mid-2030s.

"Peak Oil" and "The End of Easy Oil"

There is a small but increasingly vociferous group of academics, policymakers, and industry analysts who subscribe to the view that the physical volume or rate of global oil production is about to peak and thereafter production will decline quite rapidly, with profound consequences for the global economy. This line of thinking is described as "peak oil" and is based on the pioneering work of the geophysicist M. King Hubbert, who worked for Shell as a geologist. In 1956, he used his simple model of a depletion curve, a bell-shaped distribution with symmetrical increases and decreases before and after peak production, to accurately predict the peaking of US oil production in the early 1970s (Deffeyes 2001; Hemmingsen 2010). The current concern with peak oil dates back to 1998 when Colin J. Campbell and Jean H. Laherrère (1998) published an article in *Scientific American*, entitled "The End of Cheap Oil," that predicted global oil production would start to decline in 2010. Since then, the debate has gained momentum and the activities of the peak-oil supporters can be followed via the website of the Association for the Study of Peak Oil and Gas (ASPO) (<http://www.peakoil.net>). In a UK context, the UK Industry Task Force on Peak Oil (ITPOES) represents a group of British companies that are concerned because threats to energy security are not receiving the attention they merit. They have produced two reports (ITPOES 2008, 2010) and are now working with the UK Government's Department of Energy and Climate Change (DECC) on peak-oil threat assessment and contingency planning. The banner on ASPO's home page quotes Colin Campbell, a founding figure of the Association, who states that "The term Peak oil refers to the maximum rate of the production of oil in any area under consideration recognising that it is a finite natural resource, subject to depletion." The total amount of hydrocarbons on the planet today is the resource base, but this is not the amount available for human exploitation. From an energy-security perspective, the most important component of the resource base is the "proven reserve." According to BP (2009: 6), the "proven reserve" is "generally taken to be those quantities that geological and engineering information indicates with reasonable certainty can be recovered in the future from known reserves under existing economic and operating conditions." The level of proven reserves is neither stable nor absolute. At any given moment, whether or not a particular deposit or field is developed is conditional upon the price that the resource commands (and projections of future price), the technology available, and the political, legal, and fiscal conditions in the host country. Increasingly, the geopolitical, social, and environmental impacts of resource exploitation are also becoming determining issues – together these represent the "above-the-ground" issues that shape resource availability.

Critics of peak oil point out that we have no way of knowing the full extent of proven reserves and thus our estimates of total recoverable production cannot be certain. They are confident of the ability of the oil industry to find new reserves of oil and invest in bringing it to market (Helm 2011). The oil and gas industry now points to the rapid growth of unconventional oil and gas production as an example of how new reserves can be created through competition and technological innovation (BP 2013: 5). Confidence in sustained high prices can open up reserves in high-cost locations, as well as bring unconventional sources of oil and gas to market. For example, price hikes in the 1970s made viable the exploitation of oil reserves in the relatively high-cost locations of Alaska and the North Sea, thus increasing OECD production and reducing the level of dependence on OPEC. Most recently, high oil prices have made the exploitation of non-conventional oil reserves, such as the Canadian oil sands, economically viable. However, CERES (2010: 2) maintains that the oil sands are the world's most expensive source of new oil and require a price between $65 and $95 to make economic sense. Including unconventional oil and gas reserves in our reserve estimates can make a huge difference, but those resources may be more "conditional" than conventional oil and gas (more on this later in relation to oil sands and shale gas). Equally, a fall in price can bring about a reduction of investment in high-cost and/or high-risk fields. Technological change can also increase resource availability; the current surge in the production of non-conventional shale gas and shale oil in the United States is a case in point, as are the technological advances that enable oil and gas to be produced from ever-deeper water offshore; for an optimistic view, see Maugeri (2012) and Morse et al. (2012). Obviously, the macro-economic situation also affects energy demand and price. The IEA (2009: 135) estimates that as a result of the global financial crisis, global upstream oil and gas investment budgets for 2009 were cut by around 19 percent ($90 billion) over 2008 levels, and that the oil sands development in Canada accounted for the bulk of the postponed oil. There has since been a rebound with substantial new investment now going into fossil-fuels production worldwide. However, it should be evident from this discussion that the numerous "above-the-ground" factors shape the current and future availability of oil and gas, as much, if not more than, the "below-the-ground" geological concerns of the peak-oil campaigners.

The advocates of "peak oil" accept the growing importance of the "above-ground factors," but still maintain that the current tightness of oil supply reflects the fundamental fact that the global oil industry is about to or will soon reach peak production and that thereafter there will be a substantial decline in achievable levels of production (Hirsch et al. 2005). Bridge (2011: 311) eloquently summarizes their view: "peak oil proclaims a particular form of 'energy crisis' that is global in scope, geological in origin, and which takes the form of a permanent reduction in the rate at which conventional oil can be extracted." Not surprisingly, the notion of "peak oil" is highly contested because, as noted above, knowledge of the extent of reserves is limited and subject to constant revision, and the level of production is contingent upon so many "above-the-ground" factors (Mills 2008; Clarke 2007). There are also very strong vested interests in maintaining a belief in the continued abundance of affordable hydrocarbons. That said, we should not continue to believe blindly that there is still plenty of easy oil to find or that technological change will continue to improve exploration and enhance recovery. Sustaining fossil-fuel production will come at a cost, both economically and environmentally. The current hype surrounding shale gas is an obvious example; it may be the case that there are substantial reserves, though even that is subject to dispute (McGlade et al. 2012), but that does not mean that we should develop them (Broderick et al. 2011). Ultimately, it is recognized by all that the end of the hydrocarbon age will come long before the world physically runs out of reserves. The UK Energy Research Centre has conducted a thorough review of the oil depletion literature and concludes that "the date of peak production can be estimated to lie between 2009 and 2031" (Sorrel et al. 2010: ix) and that "a peak of conventional oil production before 2030 appears likely and there is a significant risk of a peak before 2020" (p. x), which is now within less than a decade.

In the past, the IEA confidently predicted ever-increasing levels of global oil production. However, in their *World Energy Outlook 2008* (IEA 2008: 42), while maintaining that global oil resources are still plentiful, they warned for the first time that there could be no guarantee that new reserves would be exploited quickly enough to meet the level of demand projected in their "Reference Scenario" (business as usual or BAU). Together with IOCs such as BP, Shell, and Total, the IEA has become a proponent of the notion of "the end of easy oil." Put simply, the line of reasoning is that there is no physical shortage of oil reserves; the problem is that new production is increasingly more difficult to access, more costly to extract, and will take more time to reach the market. A further refinement of the argument is that it is reserves of light crude oil that are increasingly in short supply (Tertzakian 2007: 3), a situation that is aggravated when existing production is compromised by political disputes, civil unrest, and even armed conflict, as in the recent uprising in Libya. As a result, it is increasingly challenging to match supply with demand, and the market responds very quickly to signs of unrest and supply disruption. In their *Energy Scenarios to 2050*, Shell (2008: 8) predicted that by as early as 2015 "growth in the production of easily accessible oil and gas will not match the projected rate of demand." By contrast, the influential consulting company IHS-Cambridge Energy Research Associates maintains that oil production will be around 115 million barrels per day (mb/d) in 2030, with no evidence of a peak in supply before then (IHS-CERA 2009). Thereafter, they maintain there will be an "undulating plateau," rather than a peak and decline in production (this view is heavily dependent on production from non-conventional sources such as oil sands, shale oil, and biofuels).

The following analysis of energy futures uses four sources of information: the US Government's Energy Information Administration (EIA 2011a), which publishes an annual *International Energy Outlook*; the International Energy Agency's *World Energy Outlook* (IEA 2011a) that is published annually; Exxon Mobil's (2012) *The Outlook for Energy: A View to 2040*; and BP's (2012a) *Energy Outlook 2030*. With the exception of the IEA's *World Energy Outlook*, all of these sources are freely available, but it should be remembered that each serves its own internal purposes and should be read as a particular view on the energy future. The scenarios in these publications are based on models that make particular assumptions about the key drivers of future demand, and they are widely used by both the academic and policymaking communities (for a discussion of the limitations of energy forecasting, see Smil 2003: 121–80; and Jaccard 2005: 31–55). In the case of the EIA, their analysis is based on their "Reference Scenarios" which reflect what would happen if current trends continued and there were no changes in government policies; the EIA then presents two other scenarios which reflect differing rates of economic growth. Recently, the IEA changed the name of its central scenario to "New Policies," which reflects the implementation of all planned new policies. Finally, the IEA have produced a "450 scenario," which reflects the changes needed to keep atmospheric CO_2 concentrations to 450 ppm. Thus, when reading these various reports, it is important to pay attention to the scenarios and their underlying assumptions. The interest here is with views concerning the changing role of fossil fuels in the global energy mix and the changing geography of energy supply and demand.

The EIA (2011a: 1–2) reference scenario predicts total liquids demand (oil and condensate) to be 97.6 mb/d (million barrels a day) in 2020, rising to 112.2 mb/d by 2035. To meet this increasing demand, the IEA expects "liquids production" (including both conventional and unconventional liquid supplies) to increase by 26.6 mb/d from 2008 to 2035. Both the IEA and EIA predict that fossil fuels will still dominate the global primary fuel mix in 2030. According to the IEA's (2011a: 69–71) *World Energy Outlook 2011*, between 2009 and 2035 global oil demand will increase, and overall the share of fossil fuels in the global energy mix will only fall slightly from 81 percent of primary energy demand in 2009 to 80 percent in 2035. However, the IEA's (2011a: 103) "New Policies Scenario" forecasts a more modest increase in crude oil production from 87 mb/d in 2008 to 99 mb/d in 2035. A large part of the difference between the EIA's and IEA's projections for future production lies in the wider notion of "liquids" used by the EIA, as opposed to the IEA's focus on crude oil. This is an important distinction as it highlights the key role that will be played by unconventional production in bridging the gap between conventional production and growing demand, especially in North America. Exxon Mobil's (2012: 42) *Outlook for Energy 2040* places even greater emphasis on the role of unconventional sources in meeting global liquids demand. They forecast that global liquids demand will increase by 30 percent over the next 30 years and that by 2040 conventional crude oil will account for 60 percent of total liquids supply, down from 80 percent in 2010. According to Exxon Mobil (2012: 1), in 2040, hydrocarbons will still account for 80 percent of total energy consumption. The final set of forecasts comes from BP's (2012a) *Energy Outlook 2030*. They forecast that total global energy consumption will increase by 39 percent between 2010 and 2030. Although they see oil as the slowest-growing fuel over the next 20 years, global liquids demand will exceed 103 mb/d by 2030. In terms of the overall energy mix, the three fossil fuels will converge on a market share of 26–28 percent each, which will mean that they still account for over 80 percent of consumption. Overall, these four sets of scenarios suggest that fossil fuels will remain the dominant source of energy – over 80 percent – over the next 20–30 years and that oil production will continue to grow, though an increasing share of that production will come from unconventional sources. None of this suggests a looming crisis in fossil-fuel production, but these are only forecasts and they could easily be wrong!

Not surprisingly, the advocates of peak oil consider these estimates to be totally unrealistic. Aleklett at al. (2010) maintain that the IEA has significantly overstated the prospects for future oil production and that it puts far too much faith in production from "fields yet to be discovered." Consequently, they believe that world oil supply in 2030 could be as low as 75 mb/d, which is significantly lower than current production and well below the 100 mb/d discussed above. In sum, while there is no consensus, there *are* real doubts about the ability of conventional oil production to match demand in the future and, increasingly, it appears that future demand can only be met by relying on unconventional liquids that bring with them a new set of environmental problems, discussed later in the context of North America (chapter 3).

The Globalization of Energy Demand

When in 2009 Daniel Yergin, the author of the Pulitzer Prize-winning book on the history of the oil industry, *The Prize*, was asked to reflect on what had changed to the oil industry since the first edition of his book was published in 1991, he identified four defining characteristics of this "new age of oil": first, "that oil has developed a split personality," and is now both a physical commodity and a financial asset; second, the globalization of demand and the surge in oil demand driven by economic growth in emerging markets; third, "the rise of climate change as a political factor shaping decisions on how we will use oil, and how much of it in the future"; fourth, "the drive for new technologies that could dramatically affect oil along with the rest of the energy portfolio." But he concluded that "what is decisively new is the globalization of demand" (Yergin 2009).

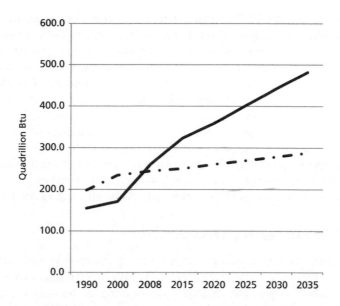

Source: EIA (2011a), *International Energy Outlook 2011*. Washington, DC: EIA, p. 9.

Figure 2.1 Past and projected energy demand OECD and non-OECD

According to the *BP Statistical Review of World Energy June 2009* (BP 2009), in 2008, non-OECD primary energy demand surpassed OECD demand for the first time. The main driver behind this change was the fact that the non-OECD contribution to global economic growth had almost doubled since the 1990s to over 40 percent by 2013, with most of this increase happening since the turn of the century (Rühl 2008: 4). Furthermore, the impact of this shift in the locus of economic dynamism had a disproportionate impact on energy demand, as economic growth in the developing world is far more energy intensive than in the OECD economies. Consequently, over the past decade, the developing world contributed approximately 90 percent of the growth in total energy demand, with the non-OECD contribution to energy growth exceeding that of the OECD every year since 2000 (Rühl 2009: 2). Thus, in a relatively short period of time, there has been a dramatic shift in global energy demand and all of the scenarios discussed above conclude that this pattern is set to continue (figure 2.1).

The EIA's (2011a: 9) reference case forecasts that the non-OECD countries will consume 38 percent more energy than the OECD countries by 2020 and 67 percent by 2035, with China and India as the main locus of growth, followed by the Middle East. As a consequence, the non-OECD economies will account for almost all of the future growth in energy demand and, by 2035, they will account for 62.7 percent of world energy consumption. The key drivers underlying this growth are discussed later, but for the moment we can simply identify them as population increase and economic growth, with the associated processes of urbanization and industrialization (including an expansion of international trade). Furthermore, much of this additional demand is likely to be met by coal-fired electricity generation, with the non-OECD Asia accounting for 90 percent of the increase in coal use (EIA 2009: 4). At the same time, growing demand for transportation services means that non-OECD Asia will also account for the majority of the growth in demand for oil (Schipper et al. 2001). This geography of new demand growth will have a major impact on energy trade and will also result in substantial new financial flows from energy importers to energy exporters (El-Gamal and Jaffe 2010).

Dimensions of Energy Scarcity

The dynamics described above suggest that guaranteeing the secure and affordable supply of energy, and particularly oil supply, is going to be increasingly difficult. However, rather than just focusing on security of supply, in the contemporary context it makes more sense to consider the various dimensions of energy *scarcity* that now confront us. The geographer Judith Rees (1991: 6) has suggested four different dimensions to resource scarcity, all of which can be applied to energy resources to generate different types of energy security challenge. The first dimension is that of *physical scarcity*, the exhaustion of available reserves of particular energy resources. By definition, this is a particular concern for non-renewable fossil-fuel supply; but, for example, it also affects the supply of uranium for nuclear power stations, rare-earth metals for some forms of renewable energy, and lithium for batteries. As discussed above, the peak oil position is that the global oil industry will soon hit peak levels of production and that thereafter there could be substantial declines in production, which, set against continuing demand growth, will result in high prices driven by scarcity. While many see this as an extreme position, there is a growing consensus that it will be increasingly difficult to match demand with supply and that physical scarcity, particularly of lighter grades of crude oil, will become a reality. In such a situation, demand reduction becomes an essential means of managing scarcity.

The second dimension is that of *geopolitical scarcity*. One case of this is the situation whereby an energy-exporting country or group of countries uses energy as a geopolitical weapon to promote their own foreign-policy interests. The OPEC oil embargo in 1973 is the most obvious example; the early twenty-first-century conflicts between Russia and Ukraine over deliveries of gas are another. A similar difficulty arises if military conflict, either inter-state or civil war, interrupts the production and export of energy resources. Examples include the impact of the revolution in Iran in 1978/79 and the impact of the two Gulf Wars on oil production in Iraq, or more recently the civil war in

Libya. A different case is where there is a relative shift in the location of low-cost energy production to "hostile" or unstable blocs of nations. This is certainly the way that the US perceives the OECD's reliance on OPEC oil supplies. Writing before he was elected to his first term, President Barack Obama observed that:

> A large portion of the $800 million we spend on foreign oil every day goes to some of the world's most volatile regimes – Saudi Arabia, Nigeria, Venezuela, and, indirectly at least, Iran. It doesn't matter whether they are despotic regimes with nuclear intentions or havens for madrassas that plant the seeds of terror in young minds – they get our money because we need their oil. (2006: 168)

This is a situation that could be exacerbated in the near future by the decline of conventional oil production in the OECD, uncertainty over Russian oil production, and by increasing demand competition from the emerging and developing worlds. It is these pressures that have led authors such as Michael Klare (2008) to predict a future of resource wars, unless we can reduce our reliance on fossil fuels.

The third dimension is that of *economic scarcity* and this follows on from both physical and geopolitical scarcity, whereby insufficient production is available relative to demand and the price increases, resulting in shortages for those consumers who cannot afford to pay. Historically, there have been periods of oil price fluctuation, often in response to specific events, but the period since the early 1970s has been one of volatility in crude oil prices (figure 2.2).

To mitigate the negative effects of sudden oil supply shortages and the impacts on price, the IEA emergency response mechanism requires IEA member-states to hold oil stocks equivalent to at least 90 days of net oil imports. In the event of a major supply disruption, the member-states will then release stocks, restrain demand, and take other measures as needed. At the end of 2010, the total stocks in IEA countries totaled some 4.2 billion barrels (IEA 2011b: 7). In June 2011, the 28 IEA counties agreed to place 60 million barrels of oil on the market to offset the disruption in supply caused by unrest in Libya. Before that, oil stocks had been released twice in response to supply shortages, once during the 1991 Gulf War and in 2005 after Hurricane Katrina\Rita in the Gulf of Mexico. The US Strategic Petroleum Reserve amounts to less than 40 days' supply as the US consumes 19 million barrel a day. Such mechanisms can address short-term supply shocks, but they cannot deal with the long-term stresses caused by stagnating global supply and continuing demand growth. Sustained high-energy prices also cause economic hardship for individuals, households, regions, and countries that are particularly dependent on imported fossil fuels. In such a situation the rich economies and households can outbid the poor, resulting in problems of energy poverty for the less well off. Developing countries and poorer households alike have to spend more of their available income on purchasing

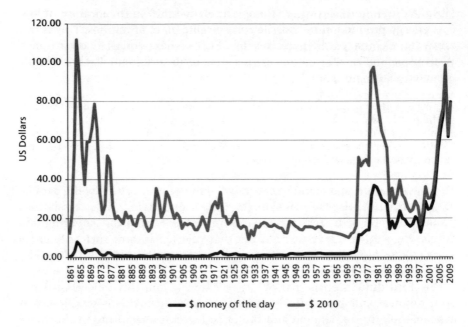

Source: BP (2011), *Statistical Review of World Energy 2011*. London: BP, p. 16.

Figure 2.2 Historical trends in the world for crude oil price, 1861–2010

energy services. There is evidence that because of their higher levels of reliance on oil – in 2010 oil accounted for 41.7 percent of total primary energy consumption in Africa, compared to 31.0 percent in Europe and Eurasia (BP 2011: 41) – developing economies are likely to be more vulnerable to high oil prices. Barnett (2008: 1) reports that a $10 rise in the price of oil causes GDP to fall by 1.2 percent in Kenya, 2.8 percent in the Philippines, and by 2.8 percent in Jamaica.

The conventional economic explanation of resource price volatility is that high prices stimulate increased investment in new production, which, in turn, rebalances supply with demand. However, such a solution is not available if there is a physical shortage of low-cost reserves to invest in. This could be due to geological reasons – the peak-oil argument – or because of problems of access to new reserves – as a consequence of resource nationalism whereby resource-holding governments deny foreign oil and gas companies access to develop reserves. In such a case, energy prices could escalate on a permanent basis to cover the higher costs of new investment. This is the end of the easy oil scenario discussed earlier. Historically, the global business cycle and the oil and gas investment cycle have not been synchronized with high oil prices stimulating new investment in production, which then comes on to the market when the economy is in a downturn (in which high energy prices are often implicated) and demand is stagnant. This exacerbates the problem of oversupply and further depresses prices. This in turn results in a reduction in new investment, such that when growth returns and demand picks up there is insufficient supply. After a prolonged period of low prices, in 1999 *The Economist* magazine famously proclaimed that the world was "drowning in oil"; at the time, the oil price was $10 a barrel and they predicted that it could fall as low as $5 a barrel. What followed was almost a decade of oil price increase, peaking in July 2008 at $148 a barrel. What happened? IHS-CERA (2009: 9) linked the 2008 "price-spike" to "an array of political and economic factors" that includes the rise of emerging markets, financial speculation, and constraints on "catching-up" in developing new capacity. The 2008 global financial crisis and subsequent recession brought a dramatic reduction in demand and, yet again, a reduction in investment. In December 2008, the oil price fell to $32 a barrel. The price soon recovered and, in 2009, the average annual spot price of crude oil was 64.66 $US per barrel (in 2011 dollars), in 2011 it averaged $111.26 and, until August 2012, it averaged $110.89 (Bolton 2012: 12–13). The future price of oil is impossible to predict with any certainty, but going forward appears to be unchartered territory as the forecasts suggest that demand will continue to grow, particularly in emerging markets, while production struggles to keep pace (Rubin 2009). This is prompting concerns about a global supply crunch, resulting in sustained high prices and concerns about economic scarcity. It remains unclear what oil price the global economy can sustain without triggering economic recession and demand destruction. A further complication is the fact that high oil and gas prices are good for promoting energy efficiency, notwithstanding that the rebound effect means that efficiency gains often promote increased consumption, as well as the development of renewable sources of energy supply. Thus, to avoid a hard landing, a balance needs to be struck between an oil price that stimulates both new investment in oil production and investment in efficiency and renewables. Of course, in the longer run, it should be the low-carbon energy transition that drives fossil demand destruction, but for this to happen sufficient incentives need to be in place, such as a global carbon tax, to discourage a return to high-carbon energy sources. In the OECD, there are already signs that this is happening as oil demand has peaked (the reasons for this are discussed in chapter 3) but, as discussed above, at a global scale this is more than matched by the level of demand growth in the non-OECD countries, hence economic scarcity and price volatility remain very real concerns.

The final dimension is *environmental scarcity*. Here Rees (1991) identified a number of different cases and it is important to appreciate that the environmental impacts of energy production are not just related to climate change (Emberson et al. 2012). First, there is the situation where energy production and consumption generate pollution loads that exceed the "absorptive" capacity of the environment, causing health and amenity problems. Here we can think of the classic industrial city dominated by coal-fired smoke stacks billowing out fumes that create local air-pollution problems as well as acid rain downwind for hundreds of miles. Today, those same conditions can be found in many of the cities of the emerging world, particularly where coal dominates the energy mix. China, for example, is home to 20 of the world's 30 most polluted cities. In the EU, strict air-pollution legislation is forcing polluting coal-fired power stations out of operation or requiring them to fit expensive pollution-abatement technologies; but this is not affordable or a priority in many developing economies where meeting energy demand takes priority over health and amenity. Energy production also results in significant cumulative long-term damage to the environment. Historically, the collection of firewood resulted in widespread deforestation across Europe and, where not properly managed, this remains a problem in many developing countries. A more obvious contemporary case is that of the oil spills associated with the production and transportation of crude oil, some of which are catastrophic in scale and impact. There are large areas of the world that are constantly under threat to such disruption, such as the Gulf of Mexico, the Baltic Sea, and the North Sea. There are also areas where large-scale environmental degradation goes hand in hand with oil and gas production, for example, the West Siberian lowlands in Russia, the Niger Delta in Nigeria, and Northern Alberta in Canada. In such areas, fossil-fuel exploitation results in the loss of plant and animal species (biodiversity) and of landscape amenity (particularly for the indigenous populations who reside there). Again, such disruption is not confined to fossil-fuel production; hydroelectric dams and biofuel plantations can be equally damaging (Hoff 2011: 18–24). Finally, there is the situation where pollution results in the disruption of biogeochemical cycles that threaten the sustainability of life on earth; here we are talking about the carbon cycle and global climate change.

Actual and potential environmental impacts promote energy scarcity because they may result in societal decisions to forgo developing energy resources in particular places, thus constraining the future supply of energy. Equally, they may require that we reduce the consumption of particular types of energy source – fossil fuels – because of their impact on the environment. Two examples illustrate the case. First is the question of Arctic oil and gas exploration. According to a survey by the United States Geological Survey (USGS 2008: 4): "The total mean undiscovered conventional oil and gas resources of the Arctic are estimated to be approximately 90 billion barrels of oil (12.3 billion tons), 1,669 trillion cubic feet (467 billion cubic meters of gas) of natural gas and 44 billion (6 billion tons) barrels of natural gas liquids." Not surprisingly, the circumpolar states are anxious to claim those reserves and the oil companies want to exploit them. Ironically, such exploration is only made possible in part by the retreat of the Arctic ice, brought about by climate change; but operating conditions remain extremely demanding and such oil and gas will be expensive to produce (Galkina 2012). The Arctic ecosystem is particularly vulnerable to climate change, added to which we currently have no effective means of dealing with oil spills under ice (Bachman 2010). Thus, developing Arctic oil and gas resources (and consuming them in the South) would aggravate the impact of climate change on the region and also expose it to the dangers of oil spills; consequently, there is a strong ecological argument to place a moratorium on oil and gas exploration in the Arctic. However, such a move would potentially constrain future oil and gas production and thus contribute to physical and economic scarcity. The second case is climate-change policy that requires us to reduce our consumption of fossil fuels to stabilize and then reduce GHG emissions. As noted earlier, this has a potentially positive impact on energy scarcity, as it will promote increased energy efficiency and fossil demand destruction that may reduce the pressure to develop new oil and gas reserves in remote costly and environmentally fragile locations. However, reducing the amount of fossil fuels that we consume to meet carbon reduction targets, particularly if we fail to improve energy efficiency sufficiently, places greater emphasis on the timely expansion of nuclear, hydroelectricity, and renewable sources of energy. Nuclear power itself poses a different set of environmental problems and, post-Fukushima, there are many who feel that these are far greater than the benefits it might bring as a low-carbon source of electricity. Thus, talk of a nuclear renaissance as a response to climate change has been rejected by many governments, most notably Germany. Japan itself is also contemplating an energy future with no nuclear power. At the same time, we are far from certain what kinds of new environmental problems will be associated with a substantial expansion of renewable energy. The experience of first-generation biofuels suggests that the unforeseen ecological costs are potentially more damaging than the supposed climate-change mitigation benefits. Clearly, what is required is a rigorous assessment of the environmental impacts of all energy sources, conventional and unconventional, non-renewable and renewable.

Scarcity Rather than Security

A focus on energy scarcity, rather than some simplistic notion of energy security, serves to demonstrate the complexity of the situation that we face. Bridge (2011: 321) aptly sums this up when he states: "Any transition away from fossil fuels, therefore, will be historically unique in that the transition will be towards lower quality, more costly resources and largely as a political response to recognition of the incumbent energy system's social and environmental costs." The current fossil-fuel system may not be sustainable; but simply stating that the solution lies in a transition to a low-carbon energy system fails to recognize, first, that we are only just beginning to identify the energy security challenges associated with that transition, and, second, that the nature of the transition varies greatly across the globe. At the same time, it is certainly not proven that a low-carbon energy system will be any more secure than the current fossil-fuel system; rather, the dimensions of insecurity and scarcity will be different and, despite what the politicians might say, it may inevitably result in more costly energy services, with obvious implications for economic scarcity and equity. At present, we face the worst of both worlds as we seek to address the energy security challenges associated with increasing fossil-fuel scarcity, while at the same time orchestrating a transition to a lower-carbon environmentally benign energy system.

Climate Change and the New Energy Paradigm

While many of the energy security concerns that are discussed above share common characteristics with the situation in the 1970s, there are two elements of the current situation that are new: the impact of climate change on energy policy and the global shift in energy demand growth. As noted in chapter 1, anthropogenic climate change has forced the issue of CO_2 emissions on to the energy policy agenda. As explained in the previous chapter, energy is central to climate-change policy for the simple reason that the combustion of hydrocarbons to supply energy services is the single most significant source of CO_2 emissions. The science suggests that even if we could secure the fossil fuels needed to meet future demands for energy services, the earth's ecosystem cannot sustain the associated increases in the level of CO_2 concentrations without triggering catastrophic climate change (Kharecha and Hansen 2008; Anderson and Bows 2012). The paradoxical nature of the current energy security and climate-change debate is described by Homer-Dixon and Garrison (2009: 20) as the "best-case and worst-case scenario": "The best we can hope for is that we don't run out of cheap oil, and the worst we have to fear is that we will continue to burn fossil fuels, including oil, as we've burned them in the past." The scale of the challenge posed by climate change has led some to suggest that there is now a "New Energy Paradigm" where, according to Helm (2007: 34), the central question is "how to design a new energy policy with security of supply and climate change at the core." In a similar vein, Chevalier (2009: 2) talks about a "New Energy Crisis" that "is not related to high oil prices or the exhaustion of oil and gas reserves. The new energy crisis comes from the recent intrusion of climate change into energy economics and geopolitics." The reality is that we are simultaneously thinking in terms of an "old" energy crisis, which is associated with the fossil-fuel energy system that will still be with us for many years to come, and a "new" energy crisis, which is related to the increasingly pressing need to transform the energy system to reduce carbon emissions. It is the two in combination with the globalization of demand that creates the "New Energy

Paradigm" that requires us to rethink the interrelationships between energy, economy, and environment.

A Low-Carbon Energy Revolution

Anticipating the Copenhagen UN Climate Change Summit in December 2009 (hereafter Copenhagen Summit), the IEA's *World Energy Outlook 2009* focused on the changes to the global energy system needed to stabilize atmospheric CO_2 concentrations to 450 ppm, which would limit to 50 percent the probability of a 2°C global temperature increase. The aim of limiting warming to 2°C was subsequently enshrined in the Copenhagen Accord. The IEA (2009: 44) Report stated that: "Continuing on today's energy path, without any change in government policy, would mean rapidly increasing dependence on fossil fuels, with alarming consequences for climate change and energy security." The IEA maintains that "limiting temperature rise to 2°C requires a low-carbon energy revolution." End-use energy efficiency is seen as the largest contributor to CO_2 abatement in 2030, with big reductions in the role of coal-based electricity generation and bigger contributions from nuclear power and renewable energy. They also see carbon capture and storage (CCS), which has yet to be proven on a commercial scale, contributing a 10 percent reduction in emissions in 2030 compared to today. In the transportation sector, where dependence on oil is greatest, improved fuel economy, the use of biofuels, and hybrid and electric vehicles will lead to a big reduction in demand. As a result, global oil demand would be 89.25 mb/d in 2030, which is slightly higher than it is today (still higher than the level of production predicted by the peak-oil camp, but lower than the 100 mb/d level predicted in the scenarios discussed earlier). However, even in the 450-scenario, fossil fuels still account for 68 percent of world primary energy demand in 2030, but the share of zero-carbon fuels increases from 19 percent in 2007 to 32 percent. This low(er)-carbon energy revolution comes at considerable cost; the 450-scenario required $10.5 trillion more investment in energy infrastructure and energy-related capital stock globally than in the reference scenario. Clearly, the new energy paradigm and associated low-carbon revolution require a major political commitment from the international community and individual states. It also requires a pace of technological change unmatched in human history (Kramer and Haigh 2009). The legacy and equity issues, discussed below, associated with carbon emissions mean that the global North (principally the member-states of the OECD) must lead the way, if for no other reason than the fact that they are responsible for the vast majority of the anthropogenic GHG gas emissions currently in the atmosphere (Parks and Roberts 2008). But it is also the case that the non-OECD countries, particularly the emerging economies, will have to limit (mitigate) CO_2 emissions to achieve the 450-target (Wheeler and Ummel 2007). In other words, the non-OECD cannot follow the fossil-fueled energy intensive path to modernization experienced by the developed world.

The Geography of Past and Future Carbon Emissions

The Copenhagen Summit in Denmark in 2009 involved 193 countries, and the Doha Summit in Qatar in late 2012 involved 195 countries, but high levels of energy consumption and their related CO_2 emissions are currently concentrated in a relatively small number of countries. It is well understood that the 35 percent increase in atmospheric CO_2 concentrations that has been observed since the beginning of the Industrial Revolution is largely due to the burning of fossil fuels and from deforestation that has enriched the developed world; as a result, the geography of energy-related carbon emissions displays a high level of concentration. As figure 2.3 illustrates, the top 15 emitters accounted for 85 percent of emissions between 1990 and 2007, while five countries alone were responsible for 60 percent of emissions (the 27 EU member-states are counted as a single unit for the purpose of the climate-change negotiations). Looking at these top 15, it is possible to identify "old emitters," the members of the OECD/EU (plus the core

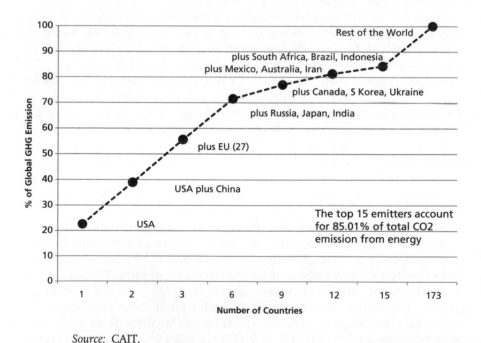

Source: CAIT.

Figure 2.3 Cumulative carbon dioxide emissions, 1990–2007

remnants of the USSR – Russia and Ukraine) and "new emitters," such as China, India, and Brazil. The Kyoto Protocol committed 37 industrialized economies and the European Community (so-called Annex 1 countries) to reducing their emissions by an average of 5 percent against 1990 levels over the five-year period of 2008–12. Annex 1 captures the emissions from the developed world, but does not include the new emitters. As indicated above, the dynamics of future energy demand and potential carbon emissions for these two groups are quite different, hence the importance attached to bringing the likes of China and India into any post-Kyoto climate-change agreement (Cranston and Hammond 2010). The Durban Summit failed to deliver a post-Kyoto agreement on emissions reductions; instead, it was agreed that an agreement would be reached by 2015 on a new regime, which would include both the developed and the developing world, to be implemented by 2020. The "Durban Platform" provided the possibility of extending the current Kyoto Protocol to 2020, while the "Doha Climate Gateway" agreed an amendment to extend the Kyoto Protocol from the beginning of 2013 to 2020 to achieve an 18 percent reduction over 1990 levels (countries have until 2014 to review their further commitments to emission reductions). However, as the US, Canada, Japan, New Zealand, and Russia have already withdrawn from the Protocol, the remaining countries probably only account for about 15 percent of global emissions. Despite all this talk, the harsh reality is that the world is now in the climate policy doldrums, reliant on national policies, without a truly global commitment to reduce emissions. It is also the case that global emissions continue to grow at alarming rates despite all of the good intentions of the UNFCCC.

Given the role of fossil-fuel combustion in climate change, it is no surprise that both the IEA and EIA project significant increases in the levels of non-OECD CO_2 emissions. The IEA (2011a: 140–1) suggests that between 2008 and 2035 OECD emissions will increase only 0.2 percent per year on average, while non-OECD emissions will increase at 10 times that rate – 2 percent a year, and over that period non-OECD Asia alone will account for 74 percent of the growth in global carbon emissions. Under the IEA's (2011a: 100) New Policies Scenario, the non-OECD countries account for all of the projected growth in energy-related carbon emissions between 2009 and 2035, and the net result is that global energy-related CO_2 emission will grow by 20 percent, a trajectory that is consistent with a long-term rise in average global temperature of 3.5°C. What is just as worrying is that the IEA (2011a: 69) maintain that "45 percent of those emissions in 2035 are already locked-in as a result of investments in capital stock which either exists now or is under construction and will still be operating in 2035." This means that drastic action is required if the world is to avert a level of global warming above 2°C. A recent study of emissions scenarios concludes: "Unless large and concerted global mitigation efforts are initiated soon, the goal of remaining below 2°C will soon become unachievable" (Peters et al. 2013: 6). Time is running out.

It is important to restate that these scenarios are not a prediction of what is most likely to happen; rather, if anything, they demonstrate the consequences of inaction. Nonetheless, it is safe to assume that if current trends are left unchecked, the twin specters of resource wars and catastrophic climate change become far more likely. This analysis demonstrates that while the legacies of the past oblige the OECD countries to take the lead in reducing CO_2 emissions, the dynamics of the recent past and the likely future require energy and climate-change policies to address the needs of the emerging and developing worlds, particularly in terms of finance and technology transfer, as it is they – through a combination of economic development and population growth – who will be demanding an increasing share of global energy services and generating the largest share of future CO_2 emissions. Thus, meeting growing energy demand with low-carbon energy sources in the global South is a key development challenge (which is discussed in chapter 6).

Globalization as the Missing Link

If we return to the Kaya Identity discussed at the end of the previous chapter, carbon emissions from energy were seen as a function of population, economic output, the energy intensity of that output, and the carbon intensity of the energy consumed. It was noted that controlling population growth and restricting economic development were not effective policy options for reducing carbon emissions, hence the focus on energy intensity and carbon emissions (Pielke 2010). However, it follows that the rate of population and economic growth are the key drivers behind the increase in energy demand and carbon emissions. In other words, the energy and carbon consequences of the globalization of energy demand are key challenges to climate-change negotiations, yet for some reason the climate-change literature remains divorced from work on globalization and, at the same time, the literature on energy security does not address the impact of globalization. As O'Brien (2006: 3) has observed: "Climate change, for example, is being addressed as a pollution problem divorced from its relationship to contemporary economic structures, development paths, and powerful interests." Furthermore, Leichenko and O'Brien (2008: 9) note that "within both academic literature and policy realms, globalization is generally viewed as separate and distinct from global environmental change, with each process having its own set of driving factors, each creating uneven outcomes, and each requiring different types of policy response." As events at the Copenhagen Summit, and since, at Cancun, Durban, and Doha, have made clear, the reality is that globalization is centre stage in the current impasse over a post-Kyoto climate-change agreement, as the global South sees the North's demand that they must also constrain emissions as a threat to their future economic prosperity.

The Resurgence of Asia and the Rise of the Emerging Markets

There is a huge literature on economic globalization and it is not intended to review it here (see Dicken 2004, 2011; Hirst et al. 2009; Murray 2006); rather, the focus is on the role of processes of economic globalization as key drivers of the demand for energy services (and as a consequence carbon emissions). For the purposes of this discussion, economic globalization is defined as: "a set of processes whereby production and consumption activities shift from the local or national scale to the global scale" (O'Brien and Leichenko 2000: 225). At the heart of these globalization processes is "the widening, deepening and speeding up of global interconnectedness" (Held et al. 1999: 14). In his seminal text on the economic geography of globalization, Dicken (2011: 3) observes "that many of the things we use in our daily lives are derived from an increasingly complex geography of production, distribution and consumption, whose scale has become, if not totally global, at least vastly more elastic."

Dicken (2011: 16) maintains that two features have characterized the global economy since 1950: the first is the increased volatility of economic growth (which is closely related to energy price volatility); the second is the growing interconnectedness between different parts of the world. It is telling that during this period international trade has grown faster than economic output and that foreign direct investment has grown faster than trade. The result is increasing specialization and interdependence and growing structural imbalances in the global economy, as evidenced by the huge trade surpluses of China and the energy-exporting economies, and the balance of payments and debt problems of many of the OECD states. The net result is a shift in economic power toward Asia. Much of the globalization literature sees this as a new phenomenon, but historians will point out that this represents a return to Asia after a period of Western dominance. In 1700, Asia's share of global trade was 62 percent and the West's was 23 percent; by 1950, the share of the West had risen to 60 percent and Asia's share had fallen to 19 percent (Dicken 2011: 16). Venables (2006: 62) suggests that it is possible to identify four phases in the development of the global economy: the initial dominance of Asia, followed by the rapid growth of Europe during and after the Industrial Revolution, then the rise of North America and, most recently, the resurgence of Asia. Between 1950 and 2001, the Asian economies increased their per capita GDP and narrowed the gap relative to the West (Maddison 2002). The postwar resurgence of Asia itself involves a number of different stages, starting with the reconstruction of Japan and then the emergence of the Newly Industrializing Economies (NICs), followed by the dramatic growth of China, and now the potential for similar development in India. Growing involvement in international trade has been a cornerstone of this growth and the World Trade Organization (WTO and UNEP 2009: xi) notes that the share of world GDP that is accounted for by international trade increased from 5.5

percent in 1950 to 21 percent in 2007 and that the volume of trade had increased 32-fold. Since 1990, the developing world's share of international trade flows has increased from 30 percent in 1995 to an estimated 45 percent in 2010 (World Bank 2011a: xi), and China alone accounted for 32 percent of global exports and 22 percent of imports (WTO 2011: 36). This growth in trade has been made possible by changes in transportation and communication technologies that have reduced the friction of distance as part of the cost of production. The vast majority of international trade is transported by sea – 90 percent when calculated by weight and 70 percent by value, and international shipping accounts for 2.7 percent of global CO_2 emissions (IMO 2009: 7). Containerization, which now accounts for 90 percent of world trade, has dramatically increased the efficiency of international transportation. Falling transport costs have enabled multinational companies to seek out sources of lower-cost labour, prompting what has been called the "new international division of labour." As a cumulative consequence of these changes, the World Bank (2011a: xi) has concluded that "The world economy is in the midst of a transformative change" and that "one of the most visible outcomes of this transformation is the rise of a number of dynamic emerging market economies." Those emerging economies include the so-called "BRIC" members of Brazil, Russia, India, and China, plus the likes of Indonesia and South Africa. The net result is that "a new world order with a more diffuse distribution of economic power is emerging." It is this that is driving the globalization of energy demand discussed earlier. Recent research on a consumption-based approach to carbon accounting makes clear the carbon consequences of the expansion of international trade (Peters et al. 2011). Put simply, the apparent reduction in carbon emissions by the developed economies is in part accounted for by the export of energy and carbon-intensive activities to emerging economies, such as China (Malm 2012). The net result of this "offshoring" of emissions is that industrialization in the emerging economies is driven by production of energy- and carbon-intensive exports for consumers in the developed economies, contributing to high levels of energy consumption and carbon emissions. If, however, the carbon emissions associated with that consumption are ascribed to the point of consumption, rather than production, then the apparent emission reductions in the developed economies are reversed. As noted above, while the atmosphere does not discriminate in terms of the location of emissions, the important point is that globalization and the expansion of international trade undermines the logic of a production-based approach to carbon accounting, such as the Kyoto process. It also highlights that consumers in the developing economies are implicated in the energy and emissions growth of the emerging economies. As my Apple iPod Classic clearly states on its back: "Designed in California and assembled in China."

However you measure it, behind the numbers it is the creation of global production networks and the related increase in international trade that is driving new economic activity that, in turn, is promoting economic development in the emerging economies of the world. Furthermore, economic development and population growth, and the associated processes of industrialization and urbanization, are increasing demands for energy services in places previously beyond the reach of global production networks. In many instances, these networks create high-energy export-oriented enclaves, sometimes formalized as Special Economic Zones or Export Processing Zones, aimed at satisfying consumer demand in developed and emerging markets. These enclaves are not restricted to manufacturing; they are also a feature in the service sector and agribusiness. Witness the emergence of call centres in places like India to provide 24/7 customer support worldwide. Wealthy consumers across the globe benefit from an "endless summer" as high-value agricultural products are produced in places like East Africa and Central America and then airfreighted to supermarkets year round. This activity generates wealth (and consumes energy), though the multinational corporations that orchestrate this process retain much of it. As they develop, these emerging economies themselves become major markets and energy consumers in their own right. In terms of our earlier discussion of energy and development, many of these economies are experiencing rapid rates of economic growth and high levels of energy intensity (and also carbon intensity). But economic globalization is a highly uneven and increasingly contested process that generates winners and losers, both within states and between states. According to Venables (2006: 62), the ratio of per capita incomes of the richest to poorest nations increased from 8:1 in 1870 to 50:1 in 2000. The fact that there are still over 1.6 billion people in the world today without access to electricity is stark proof of the highly uneven nature of these processes and the existence of what Dicken (2011) calls the "persistent periphery."

Global Trends in Population Growth and Urbanization

The rate of population growth is another key factor in determining future energy demand. At a simple level, more people means more demand; but it is obviously more complicated than that, as the future standard of living of each new citizen is vitally important. Jared Diamond (2005: 495) calculated that the estimated 1 billion people who live in the developed world (which includes most of you reading this book) have a relative per capita consumption rate of 32. By comparison, most of the other 5–6 billion people living in the developing world have a relative per capita consumption well below 32, with most being close to one. Put another way, the average American consumes 32 times more resources than the average Kenyan. Thus, when forecasting energy demand, it matters greatly where those future generations are born as that determines to a large extent their per capita consumption rates. The consequences of this are dramatically illustrated by Laurence Smith, who asks what would happen if tomorrow we woke up and everyone on the planet had the same per capita consumption rate as the 1 billion people in the developed world? According to Smith (2011: 17): "It would be as if the world's population suddenly went from under 7 billion today to 72 billion." According to the World Bank (2011b), from 1981 to 2005 (the most recent year for which comprehensive estimates are available), the number of people living on less than $1.25 a day (based on purchasing parity data in 2005) has fallen from 1.9 to 1.4 billion (the total in 2005 was 6.46 billion, so roughly 25 percent of the world population was living in extreme poverty). Clearly, no one would deny those in the developing world the right to improved living standards; the problem is that the planet simply cannot sustain the resultant increases in per capita consumption rates. Factoring in a 2050 population of 9.2 billion, Smith (2011: 17) estimates that if everyone then had a per capita consumption rate of 32, the resource demands would be equivalent to a population of 105 billion!

The UN produces estimates of future population growth and urbanization (see table 2.1). The UN's latest *world population prospects* project forward to 2100, which is well beyond our timeframe of 2030–50 (detailed information on these projections can be obtained from the UN Populations Division: <http://esa.un.org/unpd/wpp/index.htm>). Table 2.1 is based on their projections to 2050 and demonstrates that Asia will remain the most populous major area in the world, with Africa gaining ground as its population is

TABLE 2.1 Current and future demographic trends

	Total population (millions) (2010)	Percent of total 2010	Projected population (millions) (2050)	Percent of total 2050	Percent urban (2010)	Projected percent urban (2050)
World	6,908.7	100.0	9,150.0	100.0	50	68.7
Africa	1,033.0	14.9	1,998.5	21.8	40	61.6
Asia	4,166.7	60.3	5,231.5	57.2	42	64.7
Europe	732.8	10.6	691.0	7.6	73	84.3
Latin America & Caribbean	588.6	8.5	729.2	8.0	80	88.8
North America	351.7	5.1	448.5	4.9	82	90.1
Oceania	38.8	0.6	51.3	0.5	70	74.8

Source: United Nations Population Fund (2010), *State of the World Population 2010*. New York: UNPF, p. 105; and United Nations Department of Economic and Social Affairs/Population Division (2010), *World Urbanization Prospects: The 2009 Revision Highlights*, New York: UN, p. 9.

expected to more than triple to 3.6 billion by 2100. Asia's population is expected to peak at 5.2 billion in 2052. The combined population of the other major regions (the Americas, Europe, and Oceania), which amounts to 1.7 billion people in 2011, is projected to peak at 2.0 billion in 2060 and then decline slowly. As a result of these changes, Asia's share of world population will decline from 60 percent today to 55 percent by 2050, and Africa will increase from 15 percent today to 24 percent in 2050. At the same time, Europe and North America's combined share of world population has fallen from 28.2 percent in 1950 to 16.7 percent in 2010, and is projected to be 12.5 percent in 2050. All of this makes clear there are dramatic changes taking place, which will have a profound impact on future energy demand and carbon emissions, which is reflected in the scenarios discussed earlier. At present we are most concerned with the rise of the Asian economies, which is largely going hand in hand with economic growth and improved living standards. The number of people living under extreme poverty in the East Asia and Pacific region has fallen by 50 percent since 1990, with China alone lifting 500 million people out of poverty (World Bank 2011b). Africa presents the greatest challenge as it hosts many of the world's least developed economies. What is abundantly clear is that at a global scale the population component of the Kaya Identity is increasingly driven by demographic trends in Asia and Africa.

As a recent report from the World Bank (2010b: 15) notes: "Cities consume as much as 80 per cent of energy production worldwide and account for a roughly equal share of global greenhouse gas emissions." The same report calculates the total GHG emissions of the 50 largest cities, which together are ranked third after the US and China; the C40 Cities, a group of large cities committed to tackling climate change, would be ranked fourth. For the moment, we can simply assume that people living in cities tend to consume more energy and emit more carbon than people living in rural locations. Thus, it is not just projected population increases that matter, but also the future levels of urbanization. During 2009, the world's population became predominantly urban with more than 50 percent of us living in urban areas. As table 2.1 demonstrates, there is still considerable regional variation in the level of urbanization and there are also variations within countries. The UN's 2009 revisions to its *World Urbanization Prospects* (UN 2010) estimate that by 2050 the world's urban population will increase to 6.3 billion (it was 3.5 billion in 2009). This means that the urban areas are forecast to absorb all of the population growth expected over the next 40 years, as well as continue to draw in people from rural areas. The energy and climate implications are obvious. By 2050, the level of urbanization in the more developed regions of the world is projected to be 86.2 percent and, in the less developed regions, 65.9 percent (UN 2010: 4). The number of "megacities" (over 10 million inhabitants) will increase from 21 today to 29 in 2025, at which point they will account for 10.3 percent of the world's population. As a reference point, in

1975 there were only three megacities: New York, Tokyo, and Mexico. By 2025, there will be 16 megacities located in Asia, six in Latin America, three in Africa, and two each in North America and Europe. Again the implications are clear: not only is the centre of the world's population shifting South and East, but it is also becoming increasingly dominated by cities. This makes initiatives like C40 all the more important and suggests an alternative governance structure to the state-centred Kyoto-style negotiations (Bulkeley and Betsill 2003).

Conclusion: the Global Energy Dilemmas Nexus

The bulk of this chapter has been concerned with the nature of contemporary challenges to energy security; but it has also examined the complex interrelationship between energy security, globalization, and climate-change policy that underlies the idea that the global energy dilemma reflects a "New Energy Crisis" that requires a "New Energy Paradigm." This book presents a geographical analysis of how the global energy dilemma is played out in different ways across the globe. In this analysis, the Kaya Identity is used to summarize the interaction between the key drivers that link energy consumption to carbon emissions. The *global energy dilemma nexus* is presented to bring together the processes, consequences, and issues behind global energy security, economic globalization, and climate-change policy. Such an approach adds value and insight because it focuses on the underlying processes driving the geographies of energy demand and carbon emissions that are the essential components of the Kaya Identity. Furthermore, it stresses the highly uneven and dynamic nature of the tectonic shifts currently taking place in the global political economy that are confounding global agreement on climate-change policy.

The central proposition of this book is that the nature of the energy dilemma facing a particular region, state, or world region is shaped by the interplay of energy security concerns (both security of supply and security of demand), the processes of economic globalization (and the associated drivers of economic and population growth, industrialization and urbanization) and climate-change policy, and also by its "position" in the global political economy (after Sheppard 2002). The typology presented in table 2.2 stresses the interplay between the relative position of a particular region or state in the global economy, including its energy endowment and status as energy-rich or energy-poor and energy importer or exporter. The aim here is to provide a starting point for examining the energy dilemmas nexus on the basis of groups of countries that face similar challenges. To support this argument a sample of countries is identified in each category. It is understood that there is considerable variation amongst the states and regions within each grouping and that some states might occupy multiple positions in the typology. Furthermore, the division between energy-rich and energy-poor is

TABLE 2.2 Global energy dilemmas: a typology

	Energy-Rich/Exporting	Energy-Poor/Importing
Sustaining Affluence (chapter 3)	Australia, Canada, Norway	US, Japan, Germany
Legacies and Liberalization (chapter 4)	Russia, Azerbaijan, Kazakhstan	Poland, Czech Republic, Ukraine
Fueling Growth (chapter 5)	Saudi Arabia, UAE, Indonesia	China, India, South Africa
Energizing Development (chapter 6)	Nigeria, Venezuela, Ecuador	Jamaica, Kenya, Philippines

Note: The countries listed in each category are for illustrative purposes only.

also more of a continuum, as no county in the world is totally energy-independent and none is totally energy-poor. The purpose is to illustrate the broad contours of how the energy dilemma nexus plays itself out in different ways across the globe, thus defying a "one-size-fits-all" approach to the dual challenges of energy security and climate change. It also provides a framework that organizes the rest of the book.

The typology presented in table 2.2 divides the world on the basis of the nature of the energy dilemma that they face: chapter 3, "Sustaining Affluence," focuses on the situation in the OECD; chapter 4, "Legacies and Liberalization," examines the post-socialist states of Central Europe and the former Soviet Union; chapter 5, "Fueling Growth," considers the case of the rapidly growing emerging economies; chapter 6, "Energizing Development," examines three key issues that shape the research and policy agenda in the global South in relation to energy, energy access, population and climate change, and the so-called "Resource Curse." A final chapter pulls together the findings of the analysis and considers the governance challenges that must be overcome to address the dual global concerns of energy security and climate change in an era of accelerated globalization.

CHAPTER THREE

Sustaining Affluence
Energy Dilemmas in
High-Energy Societies

Introduction

This chapter deals with the energy dilemmas that face the wealthiest billion or so people on the planet. These inhabitants of the so-called "developed world" account for 14.1 percent of the world's population, yet their economies produced 47.6 percent of global income in 2009, consumed 42.2 percent of total global energy usage in 2008, and were responsible for 39 percent of global energy-related CO_2 emissions in 2007. The Industrial Revolution first took hold in these countries and it is their subsequent development that accounts for the majority of the anthropogenic GHGs in the atmosphere today. In other words, it is their energy demands, and those of their ancestors, that have created the fossil-fuel energy system that is the root cause of climate change today. Because of this, many believe that the developed world has a moral responsibility to drastically cut its carbon emissions to create the "emissions headroom" needed for the rest of the world to develop without causing catastrophic climate change. Consequently, energy and climate-change policies in the developed world must aim to stabilize and then dramatically reduce GHG emissions.

As explained at the end of the previous chapter, for the purposes of this analysis the countries of the world are organized into four groupings based on the different energy dilemmas that they face. Unfortunately, this does not map directly on to the regional divisions used by international organizations that publish the socio-economic data that underpins this analysis. A certain amount of summary data has been reworked using the regionalization scheme detailed in Annex 1, but in this chapter the OECD is used as short-hand for high-energy societies. This is not entirely satisfactory as it now includes six post-socialist economies – the Czech Republic, Estonia, Hungary Poland, Slovenia, and the Slovak Republic – that are considered in chapter 4, and three emerging economies – Chile, Mexico, and Turkey – that are considered in chapter 5. However, the combined economic weight of these member-states is modest, accounting for just over 10 percent of the OECD's GDP in 2008. The essential "Kaya characteristics" of the remaining 26 member-states are presented in table 3.1. Historically, it is these states that have been the driving force behind the various energy transitions described in chapter 1

TABLE 3.1 Kaya characteristics of high-energy societies

	CO_2 per capita 2007[1]	Population (,000s) 2010	GNI per capita 2009[2]	Energy intensity 2008[3]	Carbon intensity of energy use[4]
Australia	17.7	22,327.2	38,510	5.69	3.23
Austria	8.3	8,381.8	38,400	9.08	2.17
Belgium	9.7	10,866.6	36,640	6.13	1.93
Canada	16.9	34,173.9	37,280	4.48	2.17
Cyprus	9.6	879.7	30,160	8.06	3.40
Denmark	9.1	5,565.0	38,310	9.86	2.64
Finland	12.1	5,362.6	35,910	5.07	1.79
France	6.0	64,876.6	33,940	7.36	1.44
Germany	9.6	81,635.6	36,840	8.27	2.47
Greece	8.8	11,329.2	28,500	10.02	3.30
Iceland	7.5	318.5	29,950	2.21	0.49
Ireland	10.2	4,451.3	33,030	11.60	3.10
Israel	9.3	7,577.0	27,010	8.55	3.12
Italy	7.9	60,574.5	31,910	9.57	2.59
Japan	9.8	127,380.0	32,880	8.06	2.47
Korea	10.4	48,875.0	27,250	5.47	2.33
Luxembourg	22.6	506.6	59,580	8.68	2.64
Netherlands	10.6	16,622.6	39,690	7.86	2.28
New Zealand	7.7	4,370.7	28,050	6.32	2.16
Norway	9.1	4,882.9	55,410	7.89	1.45
Portugal	5.5	10,641.7	24,050	9.65	2.37
Spain	8.0	46,217.4	31,480	9.30	2.58
Sweden	5.4	9,394.1	37,810	6.39	0.95
Switzerland	5.0	7,790.0	47,090	10.91	1.72
United Kingdom	8.8	62,246.6	35,620	10.03	2.51
United States	19.3	309,712.0	45,640	5.77	2.49
OECD	11.0	1,234,995.4	33,936	6.38	na

Continued

TABLE 3.1 Continued

	CO_2 per capita 2007[1]	Population (,000s) 2010	GNI per capita 2009[2]	Energy intensity 2008[3]	Carbon intensity of energy use[4]
EU (27)	8.0	502,096.4	31,609	8.13	2.31
World	4.6	6,855,208.8	10,580	5.46	na

Notes on indicators
1. Carbon dioxide emissions are those stemming from the burning of fossil fuels and the manufacture of cement. They include carbon dioxide produced during consumption of solid, liquid, and gas fuels, and gas flaring. The data are metric tonnes per capita.
2. GNI per capita, based on purchasing power parity (PPP). PPP GNI is gross national income (GNI) converted to international dollars using purchasing power parity rates. An international dollar has the same purchasing power over GNI as a US dollar has in the United States. GNI is the sum of value added by all resident producers plus any product taxes (less subsidies) not included in the valuation of output plus net receipts of primary income (compensation of employees and property income) from abroad. Data are in current international dollars.
3. GDP per unit of energy use (constant 2005 PPP $ per kg of oil equivalent).
4. Tonnes of CO_2 emitted divided by tonnes of oil-equivalent energy consumed.

Sources: WDI and CAIT.

and, as evidenced below, although there is some variance between them, they all share the same essential characteristics of being mature, economically developed economies, with low levels of population growth, high levels of urbanization, high levels of per capita energy consumption, a high degree of reliance on fossil fuels and, in the majority of cases, a high level of fossil-fuel import dependence.

A Changing Relationship between Energy and Economy

High-energy consumption is synonymous with the levels of economic activity and personal consumption that characterize the world's developed economies. However, over the last three decades there has been a significant change in the relationship between energy, economy, and society that was triggered by the energy crisis of the 1970s. At that time, the sudden rise in energy costs and the resultant global recession were key factors behind the dual processes of de-industrialization and economic restructuring. Rising energy costs also resulted in energy conservation and efficiency becoming a higher priority in economic decision-making. Much of the heavy industry and manufacturing activity that had been the basis of earlier economic growth moved offshore as falling transport costs made it economic to seek out sources of cheaper labor, the harbinger of what we now know as economic globalization. As noted in the previous chapter, the OECD countries still consume energy and labor-intensive products; it is just that these now tend to be produced elsewhere. Thus, at a global scale, the overall level of energy consumption and carbon emissions continues to grow. The Swiss Institute for Integrated Economic Research (2011: 8) suggests that the notion that the developed economies have broken the link between energy-demand growth and energy growth is largely illusory, and they maintain that "If one includes energy transfers embedded in imports of raw materials and finished goods, no economy in the world demonstrates a disconnect between energy and GDP." Notwithstanding this caveat, taking the UK as an example, the share of total value added contributed by industry has fallen from 42.6 percent in 1970 to 23.6 percent in 2008. At the same time, the share of services (including the public sector) has increased from 54.6 percent in 1970 to 75.2 percent in 2008 (Department of Energy and Climate Change 2011: 165). Across the OECD, by the end of the 1990s services accounted for 69 percent of value added, while the share of manufacturing had fallen to about 19 percent (OECD 2005: 7). The service and knowledge-based sectors of the OECD economies have experienced rapid growth, resulting in the rise of the so-called post-industrial economy. Of course, this is a generalization about a complex set of processes that had many motivations and that produced both winners and losers across OECD member-states and the regions within those states. The processes of economic restructuring have produced a new spatial division of labor that has seen new growth sectors, some regions have been able to reinvent themselves, and new growth centers have emerged. As a result, over the past 30 years there has been a dramatic change in both the structure and the geography of economic activity in the OECD and this has had profound implications for the relationship between energy consumption and economic growth.

As figure 3.1 shows, since 1980 there has been a decrease in both the energy intensity of the economy and the carbon intensity of energy use in the OECD. However, the rate of decline of energy intensity has been much greater than the decline in the carbon intensity of energy use. This decline in energy intensity is due to a variety of factors. Again, using the UK as an example, the energy intensity of GDP fell 43 percent between 1970 and 2010. The UK Department of Energy and Climate Change (2011: 164–5) suggests that this is for four reasons: first, improvements in energy efficiency; second, saturation in the ownership levels and improved efficiency of the main domestic appliances; third, the unresponsiveness of certain industrial uses, such as space heating, to long-run output growth; and, fourth, a structural shift away from energy-intensive activities (such as steelmaking) toward low-energy industries (such as services). The share of industry in UK energy consumption fell from 43 percent in 1970 to 18 percent in 2010, but the share of the service sector remained unchanged at 12 percent. The largest growth was seen in the transportation sector, which increased from 19 percent in 1970 to 37 percent of total UK energy consumption in 2010. The share of the domestic sector has remained relatively stable around the 30 percent mark since 1980. From an

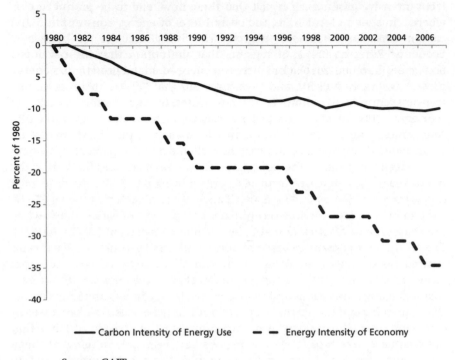

Source: CAIT.

Figure 3.1 OECD change in energy intensity of GDP and carbon intensity of energy use, 1980–2007

energy security and climate-change perspective, this means that domestic consumer behavior and the transportation sector are the obvious targets for conservation and efficiency measures, along with conversion to low-carbon energy supplies.

Over this period, the absolute level of energy consumption has not declined as both the populations and the economies of the OECD region have continued to grow. According to OECD data (all data are from the OECD's online Factbook 2011a), the total population of the OECD region increased by 23 percent, but during the same period total world population grew by 51.8 percent. Consequently, the OECD's share of world population actually fell from 21.7 percent in 1980 to 17.6 percent in 2008. Between 1980 and 2008, the OECD's total primary energy supply grew by 34.1 percent, compared to a global increase of 66.5 percent. As a result, in 2008 the OECD accounted for 45 percent of global energy supply, compared to 56 percent in 1980. These trends tell us two things: first, that the OECD is responsible for a large part of global economic output and consumes a large amount of energy relative to its share of global population, a fact that is clear from table 3.1; second, that while in absolute terms the OECD's share of energy consumption and economic activity remains high and is still growing at a modest rate, the recent trend is for the non-OECD to grow even faster, thus reducing the OECD's relative global standing and potentially its influence over energy exporters (Mitchell 2010). Comparative time series data are not available for GDP, but a recent OECD study (Arnal and Förster 2010: 16) reports that the region's share of world GDP has fallen from 79.9 percent in 1980 to 67.4 percent in 2008. All the indications are that the OECD's relative global weighting will continue to decline as the bulk of future population, as well as economic and energy demand growth, will lie outside the region.

Fossil Fuels Remain Dominant

The process of economic restructuring discussed above has been paralleled by a change in the energy mix in most OECD countries, which explains the modest fall in the carbon intensity of energy use in figure 3.1. However, within the OECD there are significant differences in energy mix, particularly in terms of the role of coal, gas, and nuclear power, and in some cases renewable energy. In most OECD countries, electricity generation has moved away from oil and coal toward gas, and in some cases nuclear power. Most recently, there has been an increasing role for renewable energy sources. Figures from BP's *Statistical Review of World Energy for 2012* (BP 2012b: 41) show that on average in 2011: oil accounted for 37.9 percent of the OECD's total primary energy supply, natural gas 25.1 percent, coal 19.8 percent, nuclear power 8.7 percent, hydroelectric power 5.7 percent, and renewables only 2.7 percent. There were some notable differences between countries. Natural gas accounted for 36.4 percent in the UK, reflecting the dash for gas based on North Sea reserves. In France, nuclear power accounted for 41.2 percent of total primary energy, and in Norway hydroelectric power's share was 63.4 percent. The leaders in terms of renewables are Denmark, where they account for 18.2 percent of total primary energy, and Portugal, where their share is 11.5 percent. In general, we can say that the OECD countries are characterized by a diversified energy mix that is dominated by fossil fuels that, on average, currently account for 82.8 percent of total primary energy consumption. Oil remains essential to the transportation sector and to many industrial processes. Thus, access to secure and affordable supplies of fossil fuels remains essential to the economic prosperity of the OECD.

Increasing Import Dependence

In the immediate aftermath of the energy crisis in the early 1970s, oil demand fell and the OECD sought to boost indigenous oil production in areas such as Alaska, the Gulf of Mexico, and the North Sea. The net result was a steady decline in oil-import dependence. In the early 1980s, falling demand due to

Source: BP (2011), *Statistical Review of World Energy 2011*. London: BP, pp. 8–9.

Figure 3.2 OECD oil balance, 1970–2010

recession and increased production resulted in the level of import dependence falling below 50 percent for a short period of time. However, as is clear from figure 3.2, OECD production was soon unable to keep pace with growing demand, and import dependency has risen ever since. According to BP data (2012b: 6 and 8), in 2011 the OECD accounted for 21.7 percent of global oil production, and held 14.2 percent of total oil reserves, while OPEC accounted for 42.4 percent of oil production and held 72.4 percent of total oil reserves. The situation for the EU is particularly precarious, as in 2011 it accounted for 2.0 percent of global oil production and held a mere 0.4 percent of global oil reserves, yet it accounted for 15.9 percent of global oil consumption. Looking forward, the situation changes if we include increased production from Canadian tar sands and shale oil in the US, but for the moment we can conclude that the OECD will struggle to maintain current levels of conventional oil production. Consequently, increased import dependence and a growing reliance upon OPEC suppliers seem inevitable, unless OECD oil production can be increased or demand can be substantially reduced. The situa-

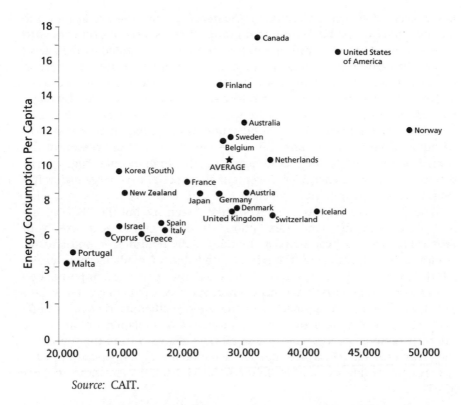

Source: CAIT.

Figure 3.3 The relationship between energy and economy in high-income and high-energy societies (2007)

tion with natural gas is rather different because it is still traded on the basis of regional markets, but as we shall see below, some perceive the level of EU dependence on Russian gas as a major cause for concern.

Although the high-energy societies of the OECD share common characteristics and face a common energy dilemma in relation to security of supply and climate-change policy, the priorities of individual countries differ and there is a limit to the insight that can be gained from analyzing aggregate data. Figure 3.3 shows the relationship between energy consumption per capita and GDP per capita for the countries listed in table 3.1. To draw out the distinctions between the countries, two outliers have been removed, Iceland and Luxembourg. Iceland, with its northerly location and abundant geothermal energy, has a very high level of energy consumption, a high level of income, and a small population. Luxembourg has a high income and a small population. Without these outliers, it is possible to identify three groups of countries. In the bottom left-hand corner are the less developed members of the group, who have lower levels of GDP and correspondingly lower levels of energy consumption. Clustered around the average are the member-states of the EU. Within that group, there is a set of countries with a lower level of energy consumption than would be suggested by their level of GDP. This group also includes Japan. In the top right-hand area of the graph lie Canada, the United States, and Norway. Norway occupies a special place as a high-income energy exporter, a role that Australia increasingly also plays. Canada's position reflects its relative specialization in high-energy resource processing and exports, including oil sands, which explains its decision to withdraw from the Kyoto Protocol at the end of 2011. The position of the United States reflects its pre-eminence as the high-income, high-energy society. It is a major energy producer, but its appetite for energy makes it a substantial energy importer.

So far this discussion has focused on energy security, but the OECD economies were, with one notable exception, the key signatories to the Kyoto Protocol (the Annex I countries) and made legally binding commitments to reduce their GHG emissions (though, as noted above, Canada has now legally left the Protocol). The imperatives of climate-change policy can impose added cost and uncertainty to the delivery of energy services. To gain greater insight into the variations in approaches to the energy dilemma that faces high-income, high-energy societies, the remainder of this chapter examines the interplay between energy security and climate change within the context of the US and the EU (27), which together accounted for 33.4 percent of global energy demand in 2010 and 35.3 percent of global GHG emissions in 2007 (CAIT).

The United States: Energy Independence and Climate Change Intransigence

Any discussion of energy security and climate change in high-energy societies must start with the US, which is the world's largest economy and, until recently, the leading consumer of energy and emitter of GHGs (a position now held by China). But its importance lies not just in its aggregate contribution to energy security and climate-change concerns, but also in its very high per capita levels of wealth, energy consumption, and carbon emissions that place it in stark contrast to the rest of the world, particularly to those who live in the global South. The US is home to 5 percent of the world's population, who consume more than 20 percent of the world's energy. According to data from CAIT, in 2007 the per capita level of CO_2 emissions in the US was 24.2 tonnes, compared to a world average of 5.5 tonnes. The per capita level of energy consumption, measured in terms of tonnes of oil equivalent per person, was 7.8 tonnes in the US, compared to a world average of 1.8 tonnes. Finally, the average income per capita in the US was $43,031, compared to a world average of $9,449. Obviously these are national averages that do not capture the wide variations in income, energy consumption, and carbon emissions that exist within the US; nevertheless, the US is the ultimate high-energy society. A secure and affordable supply of energy, particularly gasoline, is essential to the American way of life. The physical fabric of the US is a direct result of high levels of automobile ownership and cheap gasoline. Compared to the other G7 states, the US has the lowest overall gasoline prices and the lowest tax take at the pump (OPEC 2010). Thus, policies that seek to reduce energy consumption and increase energy costs are bound to meet with resistance from both US politicians and the wider population (see Pielke 2010).

Essential Characteristics of the US Energy System

A recent study by the US National Academy of Sciences (Committee on America's Energy Future 2009) on *America's Energy Futures* identified five essential characteristics of its energy system. First, the US relies very heavily on the burning of fossil fuels to meet its demand for energy services. In 2011, fossil fuels accounted for 86.4 percent of total US primary energy consumption, which compares to an OECD average of 82.3 percent (BP 2012b: 41). Second, the US has high levels of GHG emissions, both in absolute and relative terms. In 2010, total US GHG emissions were 6,821.8 million metric tons of CO_2 equivalent, and overall emissions have increased by 10.5 percent between 1990 and 2010 (US EPA 2012: ES-4). In 2008–09, emissions fell by 6.1 percent, due to the impact of economic recession and the switching of some power generation from coal to gas, but they rebounded, growing by 3.3 percent in 2009–10, due to increased economic activity. In 2011, they fell by 2.4 percent, despite positive economic growth. The US Environmental Protection Agency (US EPA 2012: ES-7) reports that since 1990, on average, fossil-fuel consumption has accounted for 78 percent of total GHG emissions, with the level increasing from 77 percent in 1990 to 79 percent in 2010. In 2010, fossil-fuel combustion accounted for 94.4 percent of total US CO_2 emissions. Thus, there is a clear need to align energy strategy with climate-change policy. Within the category of fossil-fuel combustion, power generation and transportation are by the far the most significant sources of emissions, accounting for 39.1 percent and 31.2 percent respectively. In the US, coal is still the most common fuel used to generate electricity. In 2010, 45 percent of the country's electricity generation capacity was coal-based, followed by natural gas at 23 percent and nuclear at 20 percent. Hydroelectric power accounted for 6 percent and other renewables 4 percent (all data are from the EIA website). There are substantial variations in energy mix between states, but that is beyond our consideration here. The US is second only to China in terms of the amount of electricity generated by coal; yet it is China, rather than the US, that is criticized for its heavy reliance on coal-fired power generation. That said, the share of coal is trending downward from 52 percent in 2005 to 43 percent in 2011. The shale gas revolution, which is discussed below, is a major reason

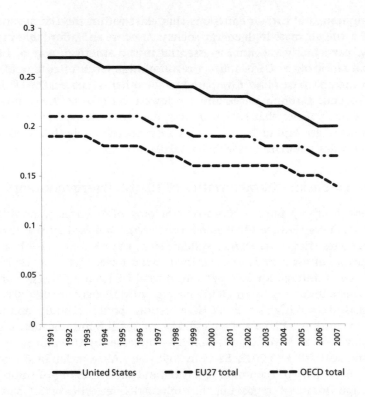

Source: OECD (2011a), *Factbook 2010: Economic, Environmental and Social Statistics.* Paris: OECD. At: <http://www.oecd-ilibrary.org/economics/oecd-factbook_18147364>

Figure 3.4 Total primary energy supply per unit of GDP: US, OECD and EU (tonnes of oil equivalent per thousand 2000 US dollars of GDP, PPPs)

for this as the share of gas in power generation is increasing, which in large part explains the fall in carbon dioxide emissions identified above. The third essential characteristic of the US energy system, which is graphically illustrated in figure 3.4, is that, despite declines in energy intensity, the US lags behind the EU and the OECD average when it comes to turning energy into economic output.

The fourth characteristic is that the US transportation system is completely dependent on oil. In 2008, the transportation sector accounted for 71 percent of US oil consumption and 31 percent of CO_2 emissions (WRI 2011: iv). Thus, it is the energy demands of the transportation sector that are a major cause of US dependence on imported oil. Smil (2011: 713) maintains that the excessive demand of the US transportation sector does not result from climatic difference or the size of the country, but rather what he sees as the "indefensibly low average efficiency of the U.S. vehicular fleet," plus the virtual absence of diesel vehicles and the absence of modern intercity trains. Consequently, one obvious solution to growing oil import dependency lies in improving vehicle efficiency and the domestic transportation system. This is well recognized by policymakers and environmentalist alike. In 2007, President George W. Bush called for the US to reduce its gasoline usage by 20 percent by 2017 – the so-called "Twenty in Ten" initiative. This was to be achieved by increasing the production of renewable and alternative fuels and by improving the fuel economy of the vehicle fleet. With an abundance of shale gas, there are now efforts to develop natural gas as a transportation fuel to enable the reduction of oil-import dependence.

The fifth and final characteristic of the US energy system is that it is aging and in need of substantial renewal. In their report, the Committee on America's Energy Future (2009: 13) noted that conventional domestic oil and gas reserves are fast depleting, that the currently operating fleet of nuclear power stations was built in the 1970s and 1980s, and that many of the coal-fired plants are even older; and, finally, that the transmission and distribution systems contain infrastructure and technologies from the 1950s. They estimated that renewing and replacing these assets would take decades and cost several trillion dollars. This is a common problem across the OECD, as much of the postwar energy infrastructure is now reaching the end of its life and starting to fail; witness the increasing incidence of blackouts. In the current economic climate, financing the renewal of energy infrastructure is a daunting task, but there is also a major opportunity here to cast off the old fossil-fuel and carbon-intensive system, and to invest in low(er)-carbon energy sources and smarter and more efficient distribution systems. A further consequence of such an approach, based on increased efficiency and renewable energy, is that US oil demand would fall, thus reducing the level of oil-import dependence.

The Pursuit of Energy Independence

Every US President, since Nixon in the 1970s, has been concerned about energy security. Domestic oil production peaked in 1970, while demand continued to increase. Thus, until recently, the US was becoming more and more reliant on imported oil, and by 2005 the level of import dependence had increased to 60.3 percent. However, thanks to reduced demand and increased domestic production, in 2011 the share of net imports was 45.0 percent (EIA 2012a). Contrary to popular belief, 52 percent of US oil imports currently originate in the western hemisphere, with only about 22 percent now coming from the Persian Gulf. According to the EIA (2012a), in 2011 the five biggest suppliers of crude oil and petroleum products to the US were: Canada (29.0 percent), Saudi Arabia (14.0 percent), Venezuela (11.0 percent), Nigeria (10.0 percent), and Mexico (8.0 percent). In 1977, some 70 percent of US petroleum imports came from OPEC countries; in 2011, about 52 percent of imports came from OPEC, and within that imports from West Africa – Nigeria and Angola – have increased at the expense of the Persian Gulf. Nonetheless, because of the nature of the global oil market, the US is sensitive to any development that threatens the secure supply of crude oil to global markets. Thus, the promotion of a freely functioning global oil market is a key element of US foreign policy (Kalicki and Goldwyn 2005).

Even though the US itself has reduced its reliance on the region, since World War II it has protected oil production in the Middle East, particularly in Saudi Arabia (Bromley 2005; Klare 2005; Simmons 2005). Initially, US oil companies played a key role; but when the oil-rich states nationalized their industries the US government became the key guarantor of security. Following the invasion of Afghanistan by the Soviet Union in 1989, US President Jimmy Carter made the US position clear in a statement now known as the "Carter Doctrine": "Any attempt by any outside force to gain control of the Persian Gulf region will be regarded as an assault on the vital interests of the United States of America, and such an assault will be repelled by any means necessary, including military force" (Carter 1980). During the Iraq–Iran conflict in the 1980s, the US "reflagged" Kuwaiti ships with the American flag and escorted them through the Persian Gulf (Klare 2002: 22). In August 1990, Iraq invaded Kuwait. After negotiations and UN resolutions failed, on January 17, 1991, a US-led international coalition attacked Iraq. By the end of February 1991, Iraq had been defeated, but Saddam Hussein remained in power and sanctions were imposed that limited the amount of oil that Iraq could export. In March 2003, 12 years and 21 days after the end of the first Gulf War, the Iraq War began. This time, in the wake of the 9/11 terrorist attacks, the justification for war was far less clear-cut; not surprisingly, many maintained that it was "all about oil" (Harvey 2003; Jhaveri 2004; Klare 2005; Noreng 2006; Rutledge 2006). Others argued there was no evidence that this was the case (Noël 2006). Whatever the reality, the fact is that the Iraq War and its aftermath denied global markets access to significant amounts of oil, as do the continuing sanctions against Iran, thus reducing global energy security by constraining global oil supply. In 2010, a third of the world's total crude oil exports passed through the Straits of Hormuz; thus, Iran's threat to close this shipping route would have a dramatic impact on the global oil supply (Emmerson and Stevens 2012).

In his 2006 State of the Nation address, President George W. Bush (2006) famously declared that "America is addicted to oil, which is often from unstable parts of the world." He pledged to replace more than 75 percent of US oil imports from the Middle East by 2025, something that would be relatively easy to achieve by reducing the overall level of imports from that area and increasing imports from Canada's oil sands and from Africa. The key issue is not so much that the US imports a lot of oil, which it does, but that its politicians perceive that it comes from unstable states, which undermines US foreign-policy interests (Council on Foreign Relations 2006). Some argue that the US uses its oil-import dependence to justify its actions to guarantee the uninterrupted supply of oil to world markets on behalf of importing countries. As a result, they reason, it has little interest in reducing its level of oil imports as that would make such actions even more difficult to justify (Le Billion and El Khatib 2004; Rice and Tyner 2011). Policy advisors in the US have been increasingly concerned that oil production may soon peak or plateau (Hirsch et al. 2005) – an issue that was discussed in chapter 2 – and some observers maintain that US military strategy is now focused on the need to prosecute "resource wars" to maintain access to vital industrial raw materials (Klare 2012). There is no doubt that the US military and intelligence community see energy security as a key issue, not least because the military itself is a major consumer of energy (US DoD 2011). These strategic concerns have resulted in a renewed conviction to address energy security. The Bush administration in its two energy bills favored technological solutions and also planned to drill for more oil and gas at home, in protected areas such as the Arctic National Wildlife Reserve in Alaska and the continental shelf (Cleveland and Kaufmann 2003). Thus, there was a two-track strategy of seeking to increase domestic oil and gas production to reduce import dependence, on the one hand, while harnessing technology to improve energy efficiency (including a very modest target of improved vehicle efficiency) and to promote the development of alternative energy sources, on the other hand. What none of this aimed to do was force Americans to change their lifestyles or pay more for their energy, both of which are necessary to reduce energy-related GHG emissions.

In his first inaugural address, President Barrack Obama (2009) noted "each day brings further evidence that the ways we use energy strengthen our adversaries and threaten our planet." He went on to say "We will harness the sun and the winds and the soil to fuel our cars and run our factories." It is clear from these statements that there is actually far more continuity than change here when it comes to a comparison with the energy strategy of the Bush administration. As we shall see below, despite his electoral promises of a climate-change Bill and a cap and trade system, President Obama's administration has continued the two-track strategy of seeking to increase domestic oil and gas production and promoting efficiency and technological solutions, the latter as part of a "Green New Deal." Undoubtedly, the global financial crisis has made the situation more complex as politicians in Washington are unwilling to take measures that might increase energy costs and impact on economic recovery. Equally, the Macondo disaster in the Gulf of Mexico in the summer of 2010 further complicated things, as the federal government had just approved new exploration licenses on the continental shelf when the disaster happened. It cancelled those licenses, but has since approved oil and gas drilling in the Arctic offshore of Alaska.

Unconventional Solutions and Extreme Energy

As noted above, a key element of US energy strategy has been to increase domestic oil and gas production. This approach is increasing tensions between energy security and environmental security, as both technological change and high oil and gas prices have driven the development of unconventional sources of oil and gas that contribute to national energy security, but that also threaten the environment. The two most significant developments at present are the rapid growth in unconventional shale oil and gas production and increased imports of oil produced from the Albertan oil sands. Both of these developments have consequences for climate-change policy in North America and beyond.

The Shale Gas Revolution

In a short period of time the prospects for natural gas production in the US have been transformed by the application of technologies that have enabled the production of unconventional gas. At present, commercial production of unconventional gas comes from three sources: "tight gas" where the gas is trapped in sandstone, coal-bed methane (CBM) where the gas is associated with coal deposits, and shale gas where the gas is found in shale deposits. All three sources of unconventional gas have been produced in the US for a number of years, but it is shale gas that is experiencing a rapid increase in significance.

The first shale gas well was drilled by William Hart back in 1821. Thus, it has been known for a long time that there are substantial shale gas deposits; what was missing was the technology to make shale gas a commercial proposition. In 2001, shale gas production accounted for less than 2 percent of total US dry gas production, by 2010 its share had increased to almost 23 percent, and the EIA (2011b) predicts that by 2035 its share could be 46 percent, with a further 22 percent coming from tight gas and 7 percent from CBM. Most recently, the EIA (2012b) reported that, in 2011, 94 percent of the natural gas consumed in the US was produced domestically. Reserve estimates for US natural gas continue to increase as more geological prospecting is conducted. In 2011, the EIA (2011b) put US natural gas reserves at 2,543 trillion cubic feet (tcf), of which shale resources account for 862 tcf; this reserve estimate is twice what it was in 2010. At 2010 rates of US consumption, there are now sufficient gas reserves in the US to last 100 years and further additions to reserves are to be expected. However, the EIA (2012b) makes clear that there is a good deal of uncertainty surrounding future levels of unconventional oil and gas production, but their reference case suggests that by 2035 oil-import dependence could fall to 36 percent, and there are already plans in place to export LNG within a matter of years.

What has enabled this rapid growth in shale gas production? The combination of lateral drilling techniques with improved geological prospecting and the development of hydraulic fracturing (the use of water, sand, and drilling liquids to break up or fracture the gas-bearing shale rocks) has enabled the rapid expansion of shale gas production (see Yergin 2011: 323–32, for a brief description of the historical background). This so-called "shale gas revolution," or "shale gale" as Daniel Yergin calls it, has taken place within the context of dwindling domestic conventional reserves and in the 2004–8 period expectation of higher gas prices in the future and the availability of credit. At the same time, early shale gas operations benefited from tax credits and a regulatory loophole in the Energy Policy Act 2005 that exempted hydraulic fracturing operations from the Safe Drinking Water Act. The nature of the sub-soil law in the US, which ascribes mineral rights to the landowner, as opposed to the state, also provides an incentive for landowners to allow shale gas drilling on their landholdings. A final set of factors relate to the fact that the US has a well-developed national natural gas pipeline system and a mature oil and gas service sector with a large number of drilling rigs at its disposal; thus, the infrastructure is in place to drill the necessary wells and to get gas to market (see Gény 2010; Stevens 2010, 2012; WEC 2010b). The latter is important because small independent oil and gas companies and oilfield service companies dominated the early phase of shale gas development. As the potential for shale gas production became recognized, the oil majors rapidly became involved in the sector. In late 2009, Exxon Mobil paid $41 billion for XTO Energy Inc. a major player in US shale gas production. Other oil companies, including BP, Statoil, Total, and ENI, have since bought assets in the sector, and companies from emerging economies such as China and India are also seeking entry into the industry, largely with the aim of learning about shale gas technologies so they can deploy these at home. If all of this seems too good to be true, perhaps it is; there are growing concerns about the sustainability of shale gas production in the US, and questions about the transferability of the US experience abroad.

Shale gas has a more intrusive footprint than conventional gas. The development of a shale gas play requires the drilling of a large number of wells to maintain production, as the flow from individual wells declines quickly. The hydraulic fracturing process itself requires large amount of fresh water, while the latest "slickwater fracturing techniques," which are less water intensive than early practices, can still use up to 5 million gallons of water per well. This water is injected under pressure with special additives and sand. Only about a third to a quarter returns to the surface as "flow back water," which is contaminated. At the same time, the production process releases "produced water" that is usually saline, and both these waste waters have to be dealt with (see WEC 2010b for a discussion of the production process). Thus, shale gas production is a water-intensive process that raises a number of environmental concerns. It is fair to say that the technologies are rapidly evolving to improve efficiency and reduce environmental impact. For example, the use of "pad" drilling techniques allows a number of wells to be drilled from a single location, thus reducing the number of drilling operations needed in a given area to maintain production. Equally, it is now possible to recycle up to 80 percent of the water used. Nonetheless, each drilling pad requires a lot of heavy equipment to be moved in and out of the area, causing considerable local congestion. As a result of all of these issues, there is a growing opposition to shale gas in the US and now in Europe.

The shale gas industry has not helped itself by being far from transparent about the nature of its operations, particularly the issue of the chemicals that are used in hydraulic fracturing. There is a growing list of environmental problems that are now associated with the expansion of shale gas production, which will become increasingly acute as production moves into more populated areas and protected watersheds. Environmental groups in the US are waging a campaign against the industry, and films such as "Gaslands," where people are shown setting fire to their tap water, have added to the distrust and opposition. In March 2011, President Obama instructed Secretary of Energy Steven Chu to form a subcommittee of the Secretary of Energy Advisory Board to make recommendations to address the safety and environmental performance of shale gas production. The committee published its second and final report in November 2011 (SEAB 2011: 1) and made 20 recommendations that if implemented "would assure that the nation's considerable shale gas resources are being developed responsibly, in a way that protects human health and the environment and is most beneficial to the nation." The prevailing sentiment seems to be that if managed correctly, using the most up-to-date technologies and best practice, the environmental issues associated with shale gas production are no more significant than other forms of oil and gas production. Of course, for most environmentalists this is a case of damning with faint praise and the problem is that there are many instances where poorly managed shale gas operations have caused significant environmental problems. In 2011, the IEA published a report entitled *A Golden Age of Gas?* that presented a scenario whereby gas played a more significant role in satisfying future energy demand; the report was subsequently included in their *World Energy Outlook 2011* (IEA 2011c). Abundant reserves of unconventional gas play an important part in their scenario, and in 2012 they published a further supplement entitled *Golden Rules for a Golden Age of Gas*, in which they present seven rules that if adhered to would minimize the environmental and social impacts of unconventional gas development; they maintain that these measures would only add 7 percent to the cost of the average shale gas well. The rules are thus key preconditions for the realization of a golden age of gas. Clearly, the future prospect for unconventional gas is a key uncertainty, not just in the US, but elsewhere in the world where it is seen as a possible solution to energy security concerns, but it is worth noting that the IEA's *Golden Age of Gas* scenario results in 3.5°C warming by 2035.

In the US, the combination of depressed demand due to the economic crisis and a rapid increase in the volume of shale gas production has driven down gas prices, which is good news for consumers. It seems the case that shale gas could keep gas prices low in the US for some time to come. Those investing in the industry presumably hope that a combination of technological improvements driving down price (which could be threatened by regulatory burden) and an increased demand will sustain profitability. There is already evidence that cheap shale gas has forced coal out of the power-generation mix, which has environmental benefits. However, there is research that maintains that because of methane leakage associated with unconventional gas, the GHGs produced per unit of energy could be significantly higher than conventional gas and possibly higher than coal (Howarth et al. 2011). Contrasting research finds that gas production based on the Marcellus shale adds only 3 percent more emissions than the average conventional gas (Jiang et al. 2011). The IEA (2011c: 64) maintains that in the best-case scenario, shale gas from production through to use (well-to-burner) emissions are only 3.5 percent higher than conventional gas and around 12 percent higher in the worst case. This is clearly an area that requires further research. In a wider context, a study in the UK by the Tyndal Centre for Climate Change Research (Broderick et al. 2011: 5) questions whether increased shale gas production would actually displace other fossil fuels. They conclude "it is difficult to envisage any situation other than shale gas largely being used *in addition* to other fossil fuel reserves and adding a further carbon burden." It is noteworthy that the IEA (2011c) sees coal-fired power generation in the US increasing 25 percent between 2009 and 2035, with its share of the total generation mix falling from 45 to 43 percent, while at the same time, the share of gas-fired power generation only increases from 23 percent to 25 percent in 2035. Whatever the environmental costs, it is already apparent that the shale gas revolution has had a positive impact on US energy security as increased domestic gas production has dramatically reduced the need for imported LNG. This has released a large amount of LNG planned for the US on to global markets, which in turn has made additional LNG available to the EU and the Asia-Pacific region. This has been a boon for Japan, as it has had to source additional LNG in the aftermath of the crisis at the Fukushima nuclear power station and in 2010–11 its LNG imports grew by 12 percent (Hosoe 2012). Although the North American gas market is now essentially self-contained, the low price of US gas stands in stark contrast to the price paid for pipeline gas by European consumers and LNG by consumers in Japan. The Japanese government now wishes to benefit from shale gas and is seeking to buy what it hopes will be cheaper LNG from the US. At the same time, the European Commission is taking action against Gazprom in relation to the high and variable prices that it charges consumers in Europe.

Thus, the shale gas revolution in the US is destabilizing price formation in the global gas industry.

For the moment, in the US at least, it would seem to be the case that energy security concerns are trumping those of environmental security and that the shale gas gale continues to blow and is now being sustained by the expansion of shale oil production. The surprising rebound in domestic oil production has the potential to redraw the geopolitical map as the US becomes far less dependent on imported oil. The problem is that it is only in retrospect that we will be able to assess if an expansion of unconventional fossil-fuel use in the US has become more part of the problem of climate change than part of the solution of global energy security concerns.

Extreme Energy: The Case of the Albertan Oil Sands

Just as there is a growing debate about shale gas and shale oil in the US, so there are also growing concerns about the environmental consequences of increased US imports from Alberta's oil sands. Again, this represents a classic trade-off between energy security and environmental security. Canada is now the leading source of crude oil imports into the US; in 2010, it supplied 1.9 mb/d or 22 percent of total US crude oil imports (EIA 2012a). About half of Canada's daily oil production of 2.9 mb/d comes from oil sands, and these represent 97 percent of Canada's oil reserves. Oil sands (also known as tar sands) consist of bitumen, unconventional petroleum that is heavy, thick, and viscous, which is naturally found blended with clay, sand, and water. Canada's oil sand reserves are located in the western province of Alberta, where they occupy 140,000 square kilometres (an area that is larger than the UK), much of which is boreal forest, which is a globally significant carbon sink. According to the government of Alberta (2011), some 169.9 billion barrels of crude oil could be recovered by using current technologies under current conditions. This places Canada third after Saudi Arabia and Venezuela in terms of its share of global oil reserves (conventional and unconventional combined). Thus, the oil sands have the potential to make Alberta one of the most important oil-producing regions in the world. However, there is a problem: getting oil sands to market is a very costly process, both economically and in terms of the impact on the environment.

The Albertan oil sands are "mined" using two techniques. For deposits that lie close to the surface (down to 75 metres), the so-called "open pit" process is used, which involves stripping away the surface to reveal the deposits which are then mined in a fashion similar to open-cast coal mining. To produce one barrel of oil requires two tonnes of material to be mined (WWF and The Co-operative Bank 2008: 6). The deeper deposits require the use of the "in-situ" process that involves drilling down into the deposit and then injecting steam to melt the bitumen so that it can move to the surface. The "in-situ" process is less intrusive on the landscape, but it does involve the construction of facilities to generate the steam – which requires substantial amounts of energy from natural gas – to recover the bitumen. Only about 3 percent of the reserves are suited to "open-pit" mining, but they have been the focus of the early phases of oil sands production. Images of monster trucks digging out millions of tons of earth to feed the upgraders and refineries that turn bitumen into synthetic crude oil, or inject gas condensate into it so it will flow in pipelines, are now commonplace, as are the huge tailing ponds that store the contaminated water that is a by-product of the process. There is no getting away from the fact that producing crude oil from oil sands is far more water, energy, and land intensive than conventional oil production. It is the most obvious example of what Michael Klare (2009, 2012) has termed "Xtreme energy." Therefore, it is not surprising that plans to substantially expand oil sands production and to increase oil exports to the US, and possibly China, are proving extremely controversial, not just in Canada, but also in the US and globally as the environmental impact of the substantial expansion of oil sands production has major implications for climate-change policy.

The government of Alberta (Alberta Department of Energy 2012) and the Canadian federal government are mounting campaigns to convince the world that it is possible to expand oil sands production in a responsible and sustainable manner. The key issues relate to the destruction of the boreal forest associated with oil sands operations, the large amounts of water drawn from the Athabasca river system, the large amounts of natural gas used to enable extraction and to upgrade and refine the raw bitumen, sourcing the condensate needed to make the oil transportable, and the large amounts of waste water and air pollution generated by the production process. Finally, the area impacted by oil sands production is also the ancestral homeland of indigenous peoples; their way of life and health and safety are already compromised, and they are taking legal action to try and stop the expansion of oil sands production. A study by the Royal Society of Canada (2010) into the environmental and health impacts of Canada's oil sands industry refutes claims about the detrimental impacts of current oil sands production, but the tenor of the report makes it clear that the rapid expansion of production could outpace the environmental and regulatory capacity of the Albertan and Canadian governments. All of the work on the oil sands accepts that with current technologies in-situ mining is more energy intensive and therefore emits more greenhouse gases than open-pit mining, and that both forms of production are more emission intensive than conventional oil production. Thus, if the planned expansion of the oil sands goes ahead it will have a more substantial environmental footprint, and it will also require the construction of a gas pipeline down the Mackenzie Valley as well as additional pipelines to deliver crude oil to markets in the US and possibly China. The latter is linked to the so-called Northern Gateway pipeline system to the coast of British Columbia that would export oil and import condensate. The high cost

of developing oil sands also means that it needs a high oil price to be profitable. Technological improvements are reducing the cost of production, as
well as its resource and carbon intensity, but increased regulatory requirements and the imposition of a carbon tax by the Albertan government have
increased costs. There are widely differing estimates of the "break even" point
for oil sands and it differs for open-pit and in-situ production. A report by
CERES (2010: 3) suggested that a price approaching $100 a barrel would be
necessary to make the expansion of oil sands production profitable, which
adds additional conditionality and uncertainty to the prospects for increased
production.

The line being adopted by the government of Alberta (2011) is to maintain
that oil sands expansion can be managed responsibly and that the GHG emissions are not substantially higher than some other sources of crude oil, such
as heavy oil from Venezuela and Nigeria. Why does this matter? It matters
because both the US and EU have enacted legislation that might prohibit the
import of crude oil from sources with high GHG emissions. For example, the
US Energy Independence and Security Act 2007 prohibits federal agencies
from purchasing "alternative fuels" with life-cycle greenhouse emissions
greater than those of conventional oil. Environmental groups claim that oil
sands are an "alternative fuel"; those supporting increased oil sands imports
argue that they are not. If the type of low-carbon fuel standards enacted by
the state of California were to be adopted by the federal government they
would almost certainly stop oil sands expansion, but that does not seem likely
to happen any time soon. Instead the focus of attention has turned to the
need to build additional pipeline capacity to move Albertan crude oil to
refineries in the Gulf of Mexico, that have until now relied on heavy oil
imported from Mexico and Venezuela, the former being in decline and the
latter considered geopolitically unreliable.

Pipeline Protests

The Keystone XL pipeline, an expansion of the existing Keystone pipeline
system, has become the focus of the conflict over oil sands imports. Because
the pipeline crosses international borders, a presidential permit is required
and the US Secretary of State has to decide whether or not the project is in
the national interest. The request for a permit was made in September 2008.
The project provoked a substantial NGO campaign that focused on the environmental impact of the 1,700 mile pipeline itself, but also questioned the
supposed economic benefits of the project, pointing to the fact that the refineries in the Gulf would export much of their output. They also questioned
the wisdom of promoting an expansion of oil sands production that would
result in large-scale environmental degradation and substantial increases in
GHG emissions. In the end, the Obama administration fudged the issue by
agreeing to review the route of the pipeline in response to the concerns of

environmental activists and officials in Nebraska about the impact of the pipeline in the sensitive Sand Hills region. This delayed the final decision until well after the presidential elections in November 2012; this and other energy-related issues were a key area of debate in the presidential campaign, with the latest energy report from the White House (2012) stressing the increase in domestic oil and gas production under the current administration. Environmental groups in the US are now lobbying the new Obama administration not to approve a revised pipeline route. Although the willingness of the Albertan and Canadian governments to permit the expansion of oil sands production is a national issue for Canada, the climate-change consequences are seen as an issue of global significance. Those in favor of the project point to the energy security benefits of displacing imports from less "reliable" sources with increased imports from Canada (Levi 2009), but because oil is a globally traded product such imports will do little directly to reduce the price of oil and oil products to consumers. However, it is possible to envisage a future of North American energy self-sufficiency based on unconventional fossil-fuels production that would break the assumption that a low-carbon energy transition in the US is necessary to improve energy security.

Climate Change Policy by Stealth

One reason why the Keystone XL pipeline has become such an issue is because it gives environmental groups in the US an opportunity to vent their frustration about the lack of progress on a federal climate-change Bill. In 1997, the US Senate voted that the US should not be a signatory to the Kyoto Protocol and in March 2001 George W. Bush decided not to submit the Kyoto Protocol to the US Senate for ratification. Since then the US has lacked a coherent climate-change policy at the federal level. The US did ratify the UNFCCC in 1992 and takes part in the climate-change negotiations and meets its international obligations; however, its failure to sign up to an emissions reductions target under the Kyoto Protocol sets it aside from the vast majority of the developed economies and the 190 countries that have ratified the agreement to date. Two issues shaped the decision in 2001 and still remain in the way of US agreement to legally binding targets: first, insistence that rapidly industrializing economies such as China and India should be subject to reduction targets; second, that in the absence of a wider agreement, such measures would have a detrimental effect on US economic competitiveness. When President Barrack Obama came into office in January 2009 it was hoped that this would mark a change in direction; in the election campaign he had promised to implement an economy-wide cap-and-trade program to reduce GHG emissions by 80 percent by 2050, an ambition that would match that of the EU. He also pledged to make the US a global leader on climate change, and at the Copenhagen Conference in late 2008 the US pledged a 17 percent reduction on 2005 emission levels by 2020, dependent on passing domestic legislation. In its first term, the Obama administration has been unable to deliver the required domestic legislation. President Obama did not attend the Rio+20 Earth Summit and climate change did not figure as a key issue in the 2012 presidential elections. However, President Obama has since identified climate change as one of his priorities for his second term. In his second inaugural address, President Obama said: "We will respond to the threat of climate change, knowing that the failure to do so would betray our children and future generations . . . The path towards sustainable energy sources will be long and sometimes difficult. But America cannot resist this transition; we must lead it." Despite the lofty rhetoric, the reality is that the political gridlock discussed below still remains and it is difficult to see a direct assault in the form of federal carbon reduction policy being successful.

In June 2009, the US House of Representatives (Congress) did pass comprehensive energy and climate legislation in the form of the American Clean Energy and Security Act of 2009, which included a cap and trade policy; but the US Senate did not pass the legislation. However, that does not mean that the federal government has not enacted legislation that has the effect of reducing GHG emissions. Even under the Bush administration, measures such as the Energy Independence and Security Act of 2007 were taken to improve energy efficiency, promote conservation, and promote alternate and low-carbon sources of energy; but they were promoted in the name of energy security, rather than climate change. In 2007, the US Supreme Court ruled that the Environmental Protection Agency (EPA) had the authority to regulate GHG emissions as "air pollutants" under the Clean Air Act, though this did not apply to existing stationary source polluters, such as power stations. In 2010, the EPA used this authority to seek improvements in emissions from light-duty vehicles (which includes the infamous sport utility vehicles or SUVs); the legislation requires an improvement in average fuel economy from 29.2 mpg in model year 2010 to 35.5 mpg in 2016 (PEW Center 2011). This would reduce GHG emissions and save consumers money. The EPA is also seeking to address GHG emissions from major new stationary sources, but there are moves afoot by politicians from both parties to strip the EPA of these powers. The American Recovery and Reinvestment Act of 2009, introduced to stimulate the economy in the aftermath of the 2008 financial crisis, included $80 billion in funding, tax expenditures, and load guarantees for climate- and clean-energy-related purposes. The Obama administration's Blueprint for a Secure Energy Future (White House 2011), first launched in March 2011, outlined a three-part strategy: to develop and secure America's energy supplies; to provide consumers with choices to reduce costs and save energy; and to innovate a clean-energy future. The document includes numerous measures that would have the effect of reducing GHG emissions, but again these are not presented as climate-change policy. This seems tacit admission that in the current political and economic situation a comprehensive federal climate change policy is not on the agenda.

A Bottom-Up Approach to Climate-Change Policy

A failure to enact climate-change policy at the federal level has been countered by an active engagement with the issue at the state and municipal level and also by the business community. A review of state and local action in 2009–10 conducted by the World Resources Institute (2010) reported that more than half of US states, covering a majority of the US population, were taking steps to reduce their CO_2 emissions; 24 states had developed comprehensive climate plans, 26 states had set economy-wide reduction targets of some form, and 23 states were in the process of developing and implementing mandatory regional CO_2 trading markets. Finally, to date, 1,054 mayors have signed the US Conference of Mayors Climate Change Protection Agreement to reduce emissions in line with the Kyoto Protocol targets of 20 percent below 2005 levels by 2012 (7 percent below 1990 levels). These initiatives are of great significance. An earlier assessment of bottom-up climate-change mitigation policy in the US concluded that if all of the existing subnational initiatives as of September 2007 had been realized, the US could stabilize emissions at their 2010 levels by the year 2020. It is worth remembering that Texas emits twice the amount of GHGs as Spain and that California's emissions exceed those of Italy.

While all of the activity at the sub-state level is laudable, effective climate-change governance in the US still requires that the federal government provide a comprehensive framework (Selin and VanDeveer 2010). The US National Academy of Sciences Committee on America's Climate Choices (2011) Report on *America's Climate Choices* concluded that the US lacks a framework of national goals and policies to help coordinate and expand climate-change actions. Furthermore, they suggest that the US needs a creditable national emissions reduction policy with an emissions budget that would set a quantitative limit on domestic GHG emissions, and suggest a budget that would reduce 1990 levels by 80–90 percent by 2050. This level of emissions reduction is simply not going to be achieved by a bottom-up approach; thus, the legislative stalemate in Washington leaves a substantial gap between what is required and what is being done. At the same time, despite the bottom-up activities, the international perception is that the US is not providing the necessary international leadership on climate change. However, it is difficult for US negotiators to take the lead in international discussions when they know that the necessary domestic legislation is lacking. Although many of the measures required to curb emissions are being taken in the name of energy security, the bottom line is that the energy isolationism and climate intransigence of the US remains one of the major barriers to a new global agreement on climate change. This is a position that is likely to be amplified by the recent rebound in domestic fossil-fuel production.

The European Union: 20/20/20 Vision

Taken together, the 27 member-states of the European Union (EU) form the world's largest energy market with over 500 million consumers, ranked second only to the US in terms of their share of global GHG emissions between 1990 and 2007 (in absolute terms, in 2007, the EU-27 were ranked third in terms of CO_2 emissions with 13.96 percent of the global total). Furthermore, the EU has actively sought to provide global leadership on climate-change policy and has introduced legally binding measures to reduce GHG emissions, to improve energy efficiency, and to promote renewable energy, as well as implementing the world's first "cap and trade" system to reduce carbon emissions (Lund 2012). Two of the founding Treaties of the EU, the European Coal and Steel Community (ECSC), created by the Treaty of Paris in 1951, and the European Atomic Agency Community (EURATOM), created in 1957, have energy issues at the heart. They focused on the dominant issues of the time, the need to coordinate postwar reconstruction through the development of the coal and steel industries of Western Europe and the promise of the peaceful use of nuclear power. The ECSC has been absorbed into the structures of the EU, but EURATOM retains its independent identity.

Developing a European Energy Strategy

Despite the centrality of energy issues in the early days of the EU, control over energy policy remains an area of national competence and is an enduring source of tension between the national interests of member-states, on the one hand, and the desire of the European Commission to shape the EU-wide energy strategy, on the other. Over the last 20 years, the European Commission has been able to use policy imperatives such as the creation of the single market in the 1990s, and more recently the need to coordinate climate-change policy, to try to impose its energy vision on the member-states. At the same time, growing concerns about security of supply and the prospect of growing import dependence have provided further impetus for the development of the EU energy strategy. The Treaty of Lisbon, which entered into force at the beginning of 2009, contains Article 194 which lays out the aims of an EU energy policy accordingly:

> in the context of the establishment and functioning of the internal market and with regard for the need to preserve and improve the environment, Union policy on energy shall aim, in a spirit of solidarity between member states, to:
> (a) ensure the functioning of the energy market;
> (b) ensure security of energy supply in the Union;

(c) promote energy efficiency and energy saving and the development of new and renewable forms of energy;
(d) promote the interconnection of energy networks.

The Article affirms the goals that have been promoted by the European Commission in its various policy documents, going back to the 2005 Green Paper *A European Strategy for Sustainable, Competitive and Secure Energy*. If there is an EU energy policy it is built around the three "E's: energy security, economic competitiveness and environmental sustainability." However, there are obvious tensions between the three dimensions of this policy framework. For example, it is widely recognized, though often denied by politicians, that meeting climate-change targets and promoting new and renewable forms of energy will increase the price of energy to consumers and industry, which might damage the global economic competitiveness of the EU (remember that this same issue has blocked a federal agreement on climate policy in the US). Another example is the Large Combustion Plant Directive which aims to reduce air pollution problems, but which will force member-states to shut down their older coal-fired power stations after 2016. An EU energy strategy must balance the Union's needs with the interests of individual member-states and their energy companies; it must also strike a balance between state intervention and the market. This is no easy matter and there are plenty of examples of member-states failing to operate in the spirit of solidarity by seeking national solutions to their energy concerns. Some would see Germany's support for the Nordstream pipeline as a case in point (more on this below). Equally, Germany's decision to close some nuclear power stations and phase out nuclear power early was taken without any consultation; decisions over member-states' energy mix remain a national competence. More recently, Poland's reliance on domestic coal production and its concerns about reliance on imported Russian gas have translated into vocal opposition to EU climate policy. Differing national attitudes toward shale gas development may become a new source of conflict should the EU seek to impose supranational regulation on drilling operations. Nevertheless, the EU and its member-states have entered into a number of legally binding policies that are shaping national and EU-wide energy strategies. In January 2008, the European Commission (CEC 2008) proposed the Energy and Climate package with "20-20-20 by 2020 goals," which translated means: a reduction in greenhouse gas emissions to 20 percent below 1990 levels (which would be increased to 30 percent in the context of a global agreement on climate); a 20 percent share of renewables in final energy consumption; and a 20 percent reduction in primary energy use by 2020. Critics see this as an arbitrary and contradictory set of targets that are driven by political expediency (Helm 2009). In 2009, the European Council and the European Parliament agreed the so-called "Third Package" to complete the integration of the EU gas and electricity market. In late 2010, the European Commission (CEC 2010: 2) published

Energy 2020: A Strategy for Competitive, Sustainable and Secure Energy, which stated that:

> A common EU energy policy has evolved around the common objective to ensure the uninterrupted physical availability of energy products and services on the market, at a price which is affordable for all consumers (private and industrial), while contributing to the EU's wider social and climate goals.

The document warned that "Europe's energy systems are adapting too slowly, while the scale of the challenges grows." The Commission also has plans to part-fund some of the key infrastructure projects that are needed to improve the "connectedness" of the EU energy system (Buchan 2011). The European Commission (CEC 2011) published a communication, "On security of supply and international cooperation," *The EU Energy Policy: Engaging with Partners beyond Our Borders*, which makes the case for a unified approach when dealing with third-party energy suppliers. This is the first time that the member-states have allowed the Commission to speak on their behalf in external energy negotiations. The EU currently imports over 50 percent of its energy needs, and the level of import dependency could increase to 70 percent by 2030 (Van Rompuy 2011). The communication identified the following priorities: building up the external dimension of the internal market; strengthening partnerships for secure, sustainable, and competitive energy; improving access to sustainable energy for developing countries; and better promoting EU policies beyond its borders. The latest initiative of the European Commission is its 2050 Roadmap that explains the various ways that the EU can achieve an 80 percent reduction in GHGs by 2050. Thus, one cannot fault the Commission for its ambition; the problem is that the member-states have other priorities at the moment in relation to the Eurozone and the need for economic recovery. It is also the case that the EU's 2050 strategy, like that of the OECD countries more generally, is dependent on significant improvements in energy efficiency, which are proving difficult to deliver, and key technologies such as Carbon Capture and Storage (CCS) that have yet to be proven as commercially viable.

The Geopolitics of Russian Gas-Import Dependence

For more than 30 years, Russia, and before it the Soviet Union, was a reliable supplier of energy to Europe; however, after the fall of the Berlin Wall in 1989 and the collapse of the Soviet Union in 1991, the political map was redrawn and new transit states were created between Russia and its European markets (see figure 3.5). This new cartographic reality has created a condition of "transit insecurity" whereby disputes between Russia and Belarus, Moldova, and Ukraine have disrupted oil and gas exports to Europe (Yafimava 2011). The most serious of those disruptions, the Russia–Ukraine gas crises of 2006 and 2009, served to demonstrate how vulnerable some EU member-states are

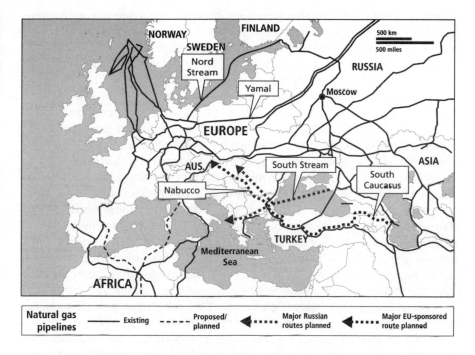

Figure 3.5 European gas pipelines

to supply disruption. A close examination of the levels of dependence on Russian gas reveals considerable variation and continued existence of what Noël (2009: 13) describes as an "iron curtain" in terms of reliance upon Russian energy supplies. The new member-states of Central Europe are the most vulnerable to supply disruption. According to Noël, the average rate of dependence on Russia was 60 percent of total gas imports, compared to 20 percent for the EU-15. However, the EU-15 accounts for over 80 percent of Russian gas imports and the seven biggest gas markets are all in the EU-15. Thus, Gazprom's most important customers are Germany, Italy, Austria, France, and the Netherlands, in that order. All of these countries have a diverse energy mix with Russian gas imports making a modest contribution to total primary energy consumption. They were forewarned of the 2009 dispute and had adequate gas storage. By contrast, the new member-states of Central Europe have much higher levels of dependence on Russian gas in their primary energy supply, and had limited access to storage or to alternative sources of gas supply. For those already poorly disposed to Russia and to Gazprom, the gas dispute was seen as a demonstration of how the Kremlin uses its energy relations to geopolitical ends, in this case punishing Ukraine for electing an anti-Moscow government. A more level-headed analysis sees this primarily as a commercial and legal dispute over non-payment that was mismanaged by both parties (Pirani et al. 2009). Whatever the motivation, the disputes were a public relations disaster for Gazprom, damaging its reputation as a secure source of gas supply for European customers. For the EU, the disputes highlighted the lack of solidarity between member-states and the lack of interconnectedness of key energy infrastructures. The European Commission has since introduced measures to promote improved gas security. However, it would now seem that there is a difference of opinion within the EU about the reliability and desirability of Russian gas imports. On the one hand, there are those who see Ukraine as the problem in the recent disputes, largely the governments and business interests in Gazprom's major markets in the EU – Germany, France, Italy, and the Netherlands – who are happy to partner in projects that bypass Ukraine. On the other hand, there are those who see Russia as the problem – mainly the countries of Central Europe which are minor players for Gazprom, but which have high levels of dependence on Russian gas and have also been subject to Gazprom's downstream acquisitions activity (these issues are discussed in more detail in the next chapter). For analysts like Pierre Noël, the solution is to create an effective internal gas market to deal with the problem of dependence, rather than engage in energy diplomacy with Russia. That said, many politicians in the EU are happy to use the specter of increased reliance on Russian gas to promote alternative energy sources, such as renewables, new nuclear, LNG, and, most recently, shale gas. The reality is that EU dependence on Russian gas imports has actually fallen significantly from 50–60 percent in the 1980s to around 40 percent now. Furthermore, the global economic crisis has dampened global energy demand and that, together with the impact of shale gas in the US, has the potential to reduce further the market power of Russian gas exports to the EU (Medlock et al. 2011). This has provided some breathing space and EU member-states are now using market opportunities, such as the availability of LNG and the prospects of shale gas production, to diversify further their sources of gas supply.

Pipedreams and Security of Demand

Whatever the rights and wrongs of the gas disputes, past and present, fundamental differences do remain between the EU and Russia when it comes to energy policy, not least because Russia will not ratify the Energy Charter Treaty, which aims to create a regime for energy management and transit security (Boussena and Locatelli 2011). Russia sees such measures as market liberalization and diversification of supply as threats to its position in EU markets, which they are. Through Gazprom, Russia has chosen to make substantial investments in new pipelines to bypass Ukraine – Nordstream and South Stream – and guarantee transit security to its most important European customers. Gazprom's differential treatment of its European customers is now the subject of a DG Competition anti-trust case, instigated by a complaint from Lithuania about the price it was being charged by Gazprom, which is further souring relations between the EU and Russia (Riley 2012). The new reality is that if Gazprom wishes to maintain its market share in the EU it will need to change the way that it does its business with its commercial partners in the EU. In an effort to diversify its sources of gas supply, the EU is now supporting the development of a "Southern Corridor" that would bring pipeline gas – upwards of 20 percent of demand – from Central Asia (Turkmenistan), the Caucasus (Azerbaijan), and even the Middle East (Iran) to markets in Southern Europe, which are particularly dependent on Russian gas supplies. Various projects are being proposed, including the Nabucco pipeline (named after the opera by Verdi), with the clear aim of reducing dependence on pipeline gas imports from Russia. Perhaps not unreasonably, Russia counters that these developments serve to reduce the security of demand that Gazprom requires to justify substantial new investments in gas fields, such as the Stokhman project in the Barents Sea that is currently suspended, and on the Yamal Peninsula in Western Siberia. This line of argument does not explain why Gazprom is willing to spend billions on expensive new bypass pipelines – Nordstream and South Stream – rather than reach an agreement with Ukraine to modernize the existing pipeline infrastructure, which would be the commercially logical thing to do. The real danger for the EU lies in the fact that gas-import dependence is set to increase as domestic production continues to decline (as does that of Norway); thus, if the energy and climate policies that would reduce future gas demand fail to deliver quickly enough, then some EU countries may find themselves having to turn to Russia to access additional gas supplies. Current analysis of shale gas potential in Europe suggests that while it could compensate for some of the decline in indigenous conventional gas production, gas-import reliance would still be in the region of 60 percent (Pearson et al. 2012). It should also be remembered that EU customers already have long-term contracts in place with Gazprom for the import of 180–200 bcm of gas, most of which stretch beyond 2025 and some beyond 2030 (Pirani et al. 2009: 59). Thus, Russia will remain the EU's most important source of gas imports for years to come. In this context, a more constructive dialogue between Russia and the EU is in the interests of both parties.

On Target for Kyoto and Beyond?

One of the reasons for considering the EU-15 as separate from the newer member-states in Central Europe is that they negotiated as a single party in the Kyoto process and agreed as a group to reduce their GHG emissions by 8 percent by 2012, compared to 1990 levels. They then distributed responsibility for that target amongst themselves on the basis of the principle of "burden-sharing agreement." The idea at the time was not to constrain the future economic development of the less-developed member-states, which had modest reductions or were allowed to increase their emissions (see table 3.1). As a result, the more developed economies were given higher targets and contributed the largest share of the EU-15 reductions. Thus, for example, Germany has a target of −21.0 percent, which equates to a reduction of 259 mtCO$_2$e, which was almost 76 percent of the total reduction to be achieved in total. The UK has a target of −12.5 percent, which accounts for 28.4 percent of total reductions (remember that some states are allowed to increase their emissions). Of course, Germany includes the former East German länder who experienced the same economic restructuring that resulted in substantial energy consumption and emission reductions experienced in Central Europe (discussed in the next chapter).

In their most recent assessment, the European Environment Agency (EEA) (2012: 8) concludes that, at the end of 2011, "The EU-15 is on track towards . . . [its] 8 per cent reduction target, compared to the base-year levels under the Kyoto Protocol." Here, there is no need to delve into the complexity of the EU's carbon accounting system, or the performance of individual member-states. However, it is clear that a combination of economic restructuring, some efficiency savings, fuel switching, and, most recently, economic recession, have probably accounted for the bulk of the emissions reductions, rather than widespread behavioral change and a commitment to a low-carbon economy. At the same time, the goalposts have also moved, as the EU is now committed to reducing carbon emissions by 20 percent, compared to 1990. The EEA (2012: 59) assessment concludes that at present, on the basis of current measures, the EU is just below the 2020 target, with a 19 percent reduction projected. It is clear that to achieve the longer-term target of an 80 percent reduction by 2050, more needs to be done to decarbonize the energy mix and also to promote energy efficiency; the problem is that all of this will cost a substantial amount of money at a time when the Eurozone's finances are stretched to the extreme.

A Market for Carbon Emissions

Since February 2010, the European Commission has had a Directorate-General for Climate Action (DG CLIMA). According to its website: "It leads international negotiations on climate, helps the EU to deal with the consequences of climate change and to meet its targets to 2020, as well as develops and implements the EU Emissions Trading System (ETS)." The ETS is an EU policy that aims to reduce emissions by setting a ceiling on the total emissions of the industries that it covers. The EU's GHG target is divided in two between the sectors covered by the ETS – power generation and industry covering about 45 percent of total emissions – and the rest. The ETS carbon budget is then divided between the member-states, and then individual installations – now over 12,000 in 30 countries – are given a carbon allowance in EUAs (1 tonne of Carbon Dioxide = 1 EUA). If they exceed their emissions cap, they then have to purchase an additional allowance from a market created by other installations that have excess EUAs to sell. The result is a trade in emissions, hence the idea of "cap and trade" (the alternative is a carbon tax). The theory is that the market decides the value of carbon credits, but the price of carbon has been quite volatile – between less than $10 and $40 a tonne of CO_2 – and there has been a persistent problem of surplus allowances, most recently aggravated by the recession. The ETS is now nearing the end of its second phase and there have clearly been teething problems. In Phase 1, far too many permits were given away, resulting in windfall profits for some and a thin market. With each phase, the total emissions cap has been reduced and, in Phase 2, credits from the Kyoto Protocol's Clean Development Mechanism (CDM) and Joint Initiatives (JI) were introduced into the scheme. By 2020, the overall level of emissions for installations covered by the scheme will be 21 percent lower than 1990. Critics of the scheme argue that the carbon price has been too low to really influence behavior and that it has not resulted in any net additional emissions reductions (Helm 2009), but the EU is still in a learning process. Phase 3 will be implemented in 2013, further broadening the scheme and tightening its operation, and will run to 2020. The carbon price was below $10 in 2012 and this failed to send the necessary signals to carbon-intensive industries – witness the expansion of coal-fired power generation based on cheap coal imports from the US at the expense of more expensive natural gas. Thus, there is a growing view that more radical measures, such as the withdrawal of allowances, are required in Phase 3 to get the ETS back on track. An alternative would be to introduce a tax on carbon, but this would have to be global in coverage to avoid carbon-intensive industries moving to avoid taxes on their emissions (Helm 2012: 175–94). In the meantime, if nothing else, the ETS is proving to be a very useful learning exercise for those who are seeking to implement their own emissions trading systems or considering a carbon tax.

Collectively, the EU-15 are on target to meet their Kyoto Protocol Target; but the member-states have set themselves some very demanding targets to achieve by 2020 – a 20 percent reduction in GHG emissions, a 20 percent reduction in energy demand, and 20 percent of total energy coming from renewable sources. Understandably, progress is variable across the three targets and across the member-states. Further measures are still required in most states to meet the demand reduction target and in some to meet the renewable energy target. Because of the global economic crisis, it is fair to say that the EU's Kyoto Target will be met as much by misfortune as design. However, it is also clear that the achievement of the 2020 targets and beyond is going to require much more fundamental changes in economy and society – the so-called low-carbon transition, coupled to the elusive "Green Economy." Unfortunately, in the current economic circumstances, it will be even more difficult to strike a balance between the three "E's" as economic recovery will understandably dominate the political agenda for some time to come.

However, the new mantra of the "green recovery" declares that it is possible to deliver both economic growth and continued progress toward the 2020 targets. Only time will tell.

Conclusions: A Transatlantic Divide

The high-energy economies of the developed world are at the center of the global energy dilemma for the simple reason that their absolute levels of energy consumption and carbon emissions are far greater than each of the other three regions. They are also responsible for the majority of the historic emissions that are currently resident in the atmosphere. This means there is a strong moral imperative for them to take significant action to reduce their carbon emissions. This is recognized by their status as Annex-1 countries in the Kyoto Protocol, and by the acceptance of the principle of "common but differentiated responsibilities and respective capabilities" that is enshrined in the UNFCCC. There is also recognition through various statements by the G8 and at recent Climate Summits that the wealthy economies of the OECD should help to finance energy access and climate-change mitigation measures in the developing world. Unfortunately, the reality demonstrates a distinct lack of solidarity amongst the world's richest economies. As this chapter has demonstrated, there is a substantial difference between the current stance of North America (Canada and the United States) and the European Union, both on energy security and climate change. In 2008, the US and EU (27) combined accounted for just under 40 percent of the cumulative emissions of CO_2 between 1990 and 2008 (CAIT), yet data from UNFCCC shows that between 1990 and 2010 cumulative CO_2 emissions from energy grew by 13.3 percent in the US, while they fell by 5.7 percent in the EU (15). The EU has adopted a strong top-down approach to energy and climate-change issues, with binding targets to be met by 2020 and a longer-term commitment to an 80 percent reduction of emissions by 2050. While there is some resistance to this approach by member-states, particularly in relation to its costs in the current economic climate, there is a common recognition of the need to improve energy intensity further and to reduce the carbon intensity of energy use through the development of low-carbon sources of energy. At the same time, the EU remains committed to the ETS as a mechanism for reducing carbon emissions, but strong political action is urgently required to rescue the ETS from its current crisis. Energy security remains a concern, particularly in relation to Russia, and is being used to justify a European energy strategy and to encourage the creation of a single European energy market. Yet it remains to be seen if all of these initiatives can be achieved without burdening EU citizens and businesses with excessive energy costs that might undermine economic competitiveness. The United States, by comparison, has failed to demonstrate global leadership. Concerns about the cost of climate-change mitigation meant that it did not ratify the Kyoto Protocol, and the Obama administration has been unable to deliver on its first-term election pledge to set emissions targets and develop a carbon trading system. Instead, energy security in the guise of "Energy Independence" now dominates the political landscape as the development of unconventional fossil fuels is reducing US energy-import dependence. While the low cost of shale gas is reducing coal consumption in the power-generation sector, it remains unclear what the cumulative benefits are in terms of emissions reduction. There cannot fail to be similar doubts about the negative environmental consequences of the expansion of oil sands production. One positive aspect is that the lack of action at a federal level is partially compensated for by the action of individual states and cities. However, this bottom-up approach cannot deliver the scale of change needed to reduce US emissions significantly any time soon. A different problem confronts the energy-exporting economies of the OECD – principally Australia, Canada, and Norway – where their economic prosperity is tied to the export of fossil fuels. For example, how does Norway reconcile the difference between its domestic energy mix that is dominated by low-carbon hydroelectric power with its reliance on the export of oil and gas? Likewise, Canada has now withdrawn from the Kyoto Protocol as it has recognized that its energy-intensive domestic economy and reliance on energy exports were making it prohibitively expensive to achieve its reduction targets. Equally, Australia may have adopted a carbon tax, but it remains the highest per capita carbon emitter in the OECD and its current economic prosperity is tied in large part to the export of fossil fuels to China. In a very different context, the challenges in Japan after the Great East Japan earthquake in March 2011 are actually forcing it on to a more carbon-intensive energy pathway, as fossil fuels have to compensate for the loss of nuclear power-generating capacity. It remains to be seen if this will be a long-term trend. When one assesses the current position of the high-energy societies in relation to the three energy challenges identified at the end of chapter 1, the progress is mixed at best. Only the EU is demonstrating leadership and commitment, and without the US matching that commitment it is difficult to be optimistic about the prospects for dramatic emissions reductions from the developed world, which means that the emissions headroom is not being created to allow for economic development in the rest of the world without substantial increases in carbon emissions.

CHAPTER FOUR

Legacies and Liberalization
Energy Dilemmas in the Post-Socialist States

Introduction

Following a period of political and economic turmoil that culminated in the collapse of the Berlin Wall in November 1989, followed by the disintegration of the Soviet Union in December 1991, a group of newly independent states emerged and embarked on a difficult transition away from the Soviet centrally planned economy, single-party rule, and isolation from the global economy. For many, that transition is more or less complete, but for some there is still a distance to be traveled before they can be considered to be democracies with full-functioning market economies, which is what the West assumes everyone aspires to be. In this analysis, they are treated as a separate group because they share a common set of energy dilemmas that have their origins in the nature of the centrally planned economy. Thus, they share common legacies that have left an indelible mark upon their energy landscapes and that pose particular challenges to the development of more secure and sustainable energy systems. That said, there is considerable difference in the "transformation trajectories" of the 27-plus countries that today comprise the so-called "post-socialist states" or "transition economies" (Bradshaw 2001; Smith and Timár 2010).

Defining this grouping of countries and arriving at an acceptable nomenclature to describe its various sub-regions is a complex task fraught with political difficulties. A useful starting point is to identify the countries that are clients of the European Bank for Reconstruction and Development (EBRD), which was created to support the development of markets and democracies in the region. Table 4.1 lists the countries currently served by the EBRD that are considered in this chapter, organized into the regional groupings used by the bank. Turkey, which is the EBRD's newest country of operation, is not present in this table as it is not a post-socialist state (it is considered in the next chapter). Equally, the Czech Republic has been added, even though the EBRD stopped making investments there at the end of 2007. A cursory glance at the table reveals the complexity of the situation. In January 2004, eight of the countries in the Central Europe and Baltic States (CEBS) region joined the European Union, the one exception being Croatia that remains a candidate country and should join in 2013. In 2007, two states from South-Eastern

TABLE 4.1 The regional groupings of the EBRD

Central Europe and the Baltic States	South-eastern Europe	Eastern Europe and the Caucasus	Russia	Central Asia
Croatia	Albania	Armenia		Kazakhstan
Czech Republic	Bosnia and Herzegovina	Azerbaijan		Kyrgyz Republic
Estonia	Bulgaria	Belarus		Mongolia
Hungary	FYR Macedonia	Georgia		Tajikistan
Latvia	Romania	Moldova		Turkmenistan
Lithuania	Montenegro	Ukraine		Uzbekistan
Poland	Serbia			
Slovak Republic				
Slovenia				

Source: EBRD database (<www.ebrd.com>)

Europe (SEE) joined the EU, bringing the total number of "transition economies" in the EU to 10 (the EU-10); Macedonia and Montenegro remain EU candidate countries. Of course, one of the countries not included in the table is East Germany (the German Democratic Republic or GDR), which was one of the most developed East European economies; with German unification, it joined the EU in October 1990. As is clear from discussions in the previous chapter, EU membership brings with it a commitment to strong action on energy security and climate change. A further complication is that some of the states that have emerged out of the former Yugoslavia have only recently come into being – Montenegro split from Serbia in 2006 and Kosovo declared its independence in 2008. The situation with the former Soviet republics is equally complex. The three Baltic States (Estonia, Latvia, and Lithuania) were previously republics in the Soviet Union, but are now independent states and members of the EU. The remaining 12 republics, with the exception of Georgia, created the Commonwealth of Independent States (CIS). Georgia joined the CIS in 2006 and then left in 2009, in the wake of the conflict with Russia over South Ossetia. In 2006, Turkmenistan left the permanent membership to become an associate member. The CIS is a much looser organization than the EU, though some of its members (Russia, Belarus, and Kazakhstan) have created a more formal customs union. The other country included in the EBRD's Central Asia is Mongolia. Though never part of the Soviet Union, Mongolia had very close ties and now faces many of the same problems as the post-Soviet states of Central Asia.

One of the consequences of the complex history and geography of the region is that it is difficult to get comprehensive and comparable information on the energy, economic, and environmental situation, and there is very little time-series data that examines change through the Soviet and post-socialist period. Not surprisingly, there is a lot more data on the states that are members of the EU and/or the OECD, or that are major energy exporters. This chapter pieces together the evidence to consider the characteristics and legacies of the centrally planned economy in terms of the relationship between energy, economy, and environment. First, it explains the impact of the collapse of the Soviet system and the "transition to the market" upon the region. Second, it considers the impact of economic transition on the relationship between energy, economy, and environment. Third, it examines the case of Russia in more detail, as it is the largest economy in the group and the world's leading exporter of oil and gas. The chapter concludes by assessing the relevance of their post-socialist past in determining the energy futures of this group of countries.

The Characteristics and Legacies of the Soviet Planned Economy

For more than 40 years, the states of what, until 1989, was known as "Eastern Europe" were part of the Soviet bloc and they followed a common development path together with the 15 Union Republics of the Soviet Union. Some of the most important characteristics included: state ownership of economic activity, the use of central planning to determine the strategic direction of economic development and to implement national plans, the priority of industrial output over consumer goods, single-party rule by the Communist Party, and incorporation into the international socialist division of labor through membership of the Council for Mutual Economic Assistance (CMEA or Comecon). Not surprisingly, the nature of the "centrally planned economy" (CPE, the shorthand that we will use to describe the system hereafter) had a significant impact on the relationship between energy and economy, and also had significant consequences for the natural environment (Hoffman and Dienes 1985).

Research on the energy systems in the Soviet Union and Eastern Europe identifies a number of special characteristics (Gray 1995). The first concerns very high levels of energy intensity. Though estimates vary, it is agreed that the CPE was very inefficient when it came to the amount of energy consumed per unit of economic output produced. Gray (1995: 1) suggests that the level of energy intensity in the CPE was 4–8 times higher than that of the OECD countries, and that in large part this was because the share of heavy industry was much higher and far less efficient than that in the OECD (see also Salay et al. 1993: 188–91). Analysis by the EBRD (2001: 75) observed that during the 1970s the CPE economies were relatively isolated from the impacts of the energy crisis that promoted de-industrialization in the OECD and actually continued to industrialize with "scant attention given to energy and resource efficiency." According to that same EBRD Report (2001: 91), in 1998 the CEBS used four times the energy per unit of output as Western Europe, SEE nine times as much, and the CIS states 13 times as much. As we shall see below, the collapse of the CPEs had a dramatic impact on energy consumption in the region, but it is projected that even by 2030 levels of energy intensity will still be three times that of the EU and in Russia five times that level (World Bank 2010c: 9). By examining the other essential characteristics of the CPE, the reasons for this high level of energy intensity become apparent.

The second characteristic was the distorted nature of energy prices. Given the current attention being paid to energy subsidies, the "market price" for energy is a fairly elusive notion and it is not unusual for energy prices to be regulated in one way or another. The CPE did not use prices and the market as a means of allocating resources; instead, a materials-balance approach was employed together with physical plans. Enterprises were set physical production targets that paid no attention to energy costs and efficiency; in fact, the ideological bias of the system favored labor as the source of value and natural resources, and the environment had no intrinsic value. Prices were used in the system, but they were based on averages, rather than marginal costs, and physical plan fulfilment was the key success indicator. The net result was that energy costs were much lower than in market economies and there was little or no incentive to promote increased energy efficiency; in fact quite the opposite, as enterprises sought to maximize the energy quota allocated to them (Salay et al. 1993: 190). Buzar (2007: 1) notes that: "Before 1990, tariffs were set at below cost-recovery levels and there were extensive cross-subsidies from industry to the residential sector." Hughes (1991: 77) concludes that "energy prices are among the most distorted prices in centrally-planned economies." Kramer (1991: 58) maintains that "Excessive consumption is inextricably related to the Stalinist model of economic development and organisation."

Prior to the 1970s, the East European members of CMEA were relatively self-sufficient on the basis of domestic coal production. Much of the coal mined was of low quality and the industry itself was inefficient by international standards; this reliance on low-quality domestic coal created a "Black Triangle" between Poland, Czechoslovakia, and East Germany, where 80 million tons of lignite were burned annually, resulting in levels of carbon emissions per unit of output that were among the highest in the world (Ürge-Vorsatz et al. 2006: 2280). By the 1970s, domestic energy production in Eastern Europe could no longer keep up with the growing demand, and imports of oil, and later gas, from the Soviet Union became increasingly important. When it came to trade within CMEA, energy flows contributed to a market-clearing system, whereby Soviet exports of oil and gas generated credits that covered the import of industrial and consumer goods from Eastern Europe.

Prior to 1976, the energy prices in intra-CMEA trade were fixed at the beginning of each Five-Year Plan, which worked while international prices were stable. However, after 1976, due to both the rapid increase in world prices and the growing cost of Soviet oil and gas production, the so-called Bucharest formula was introduced based on a moving five-year average of world market prices. Although this increased the cost of Soviet oil and gas imports, they still remained considerably below the world price and the volume of energy imports from the Soviet Union continued to rise. During the 1960s and 1970s, it was relatively easy for the Soviet Union to meet its own energy needs and also expand exports. However, during the 1980s, world price volatility, rising energy costs in the Soviet Union, and domestic economic stagnation placed stress on the CMEA price mechanism. Finally, when the CMEA trading system collapsed at the end of the 1980s and the Soviet Union insisted on payment at world price levels with convertible currency, an energy shock on the newly independent countries in Eastern Europe was imposed.

Following from the discussion of intra-CMEA trade, a third characteristic was the dominance of the Soviet Union as a supplier of subsidized oil and gas exports to Eastern Europe. Within the Soviet Union itself, this situation was paralleled by the dominance of the Russian Federation as a supplier of energy resources to the other Union Republics. By 1982, the Soviet Union supplied the six CMEA countries with over 80 percent of the oil and 99 percent of their gas needs. Hoffman and Dienes (1985: 11) observe that the industrial modernization of Eastern Europe greatly increased their "energy materials dependency on the Soviet Union." They also noted that "the Eastern European CMEA countries had shifted from being an economic asset to being an economic burden to the Soviet Union."

One of the reasons for the growing cost to the Soviet Union was the fact that its energy industry was experiencing a shift eastwards (Dienes and Shabad 1979). This was increasing the cost of development as production moved into regions in West Siberia that lacked industrial infrastructure. It also required the construction of costly oil and gas pipeline networks, and an increase in railway traffic to move coal westwards from northern Kazakhstan and southern Siberia. Thus, one way or another, the Soviet economy did experience its own energy crisis as more and more had to be invested to supply both domestic and exports markets with energy resources (Gustafson 1989). By 1986, energy's share of capital investment in the Soviet Union had reached 24.3 percent, when the plan stipulated that it should have stabilized at 20–22 percent (Locatelli 1990: 135). By the late 1980s, energy was accounting for more than 40 percent of industrial investment, which was having a detrimental effect on efforts to restructure and modernize the Soviet economy. The Soviet Union tried to share the burden of its growing energy by involving its CMEA partners in joint development schemes. This policy started with the "Druzhba" (Friendship) pipeline that connected fields in the Urals region of Russia with Eastern Europe, and was followed by numerous projects to build and extend pipelines and electricity transmission systems. As Bouzarovski (2009: 454) observes: "Energy transmission infrastructures were constructed in such a way so as to allow centripetal links between the Soviet Union and the Comecon states, rather than lateral connections between the latter." The expansion of nuclear power was another way in which the Soviet Union sought to build a technological dependency, while also increasing domestic energy production in Eastern Europe, and some 300 megawatts of nuclear capacity was installed in six countries, including Lithuania where in 2002 nuclear power produced 82.7 percent of total electricity generation, Bulgaria (51.5 percent), Slovakia (55.5 percent), and Hungary (39.7 percent) (Ürge-Vorsatz et al. 2006). After the Chernobyl disaster in Ukraine, in 1984, the world was alerted to the design problems associated with many of the older Soviet-built reactors. As a condition of accession to the EU, eight Soviet-designed nuclear reactors were closed in Bulgaria, Slovakia, and Lithuania.

During the 1980s, the pipeline systems were extended into Western Europe, as the Soviet Union became a major exporter of natural gas. The expansion of gas production in West Siberia and the associated transcontinental gas pipeline network were financed in part by gas-for-pipe deals with continental Western Europe – primarily Germany, France, and Italy. Under these agreements, credits were supplied to the Soviet Union to purchase the large-diameter pipe, compressor stations, and other equipment needed to build the pipelines. These credits were then paid off by subsequent deliveries of natural gas. This trade, and the expansion of oil exports, became a vital source of convertible currency for the Soviet Union, which it used to purchase imports of grain and Western technology to prop up its failing economy. In this context, by the 1980s, the subsidized export of oil and gas to its CMEA partners in Eastern Europe had become both an intervening opportunity and an opportunity cost to Moscow.

In summing up the negative energy legacies of the CPE, Ürge-Vorsatz et al. (2006: 2281) identified three issues: the system did not reward efficiency, energy prices were highly subsidized, and natural resources were undervalued. As a result, they observe that "there was no market mechanism to signal resource scarcity, market shortages or environmental damage associated with the use of a resource." Of course, the latter is also true of energy prices in market economies. However, unlike most commentators on the energy legacies of the CPE, Ürge-Vorsatz et al. (2006: 2284) also identified some positive legacies. First, was the high share of public transport, particularly in urban areas (and one might add the low levels of automobile ownership due to the high cost and scarcity of private cars). As a result, the share of trips made by public transport was much higher than in the OECD countries. Second, was the relatively compact settlement structure that also allowed for the use of district heating and combined heat and power (CHP). Although this was most prevalent in Russia, it is also important in some of the EU-10 countries. Third, was the dominance of multi-family housing, the landscape of endless tower blocks that is associated with the "socialist city." This benefit was partially offset by the fact that the building quality was generally poor, the heating systems rudimentary, and the thermal efficiency very low. Fourth, and finally, was the low level of individual consumerism enforced by the shortage economy, which also promoted reuse and recycling. As we shall see below, most of these "positive legacies" have been eroded by the transition to the market economy, and many of the energy problems associated with high-energy market economies are now increasingly prevalent in the post-socialist world.

This analysis of the energy landscape of the CPEs is of more than passing historical interest; it provides the essential backdrop for understanding the impact of economic transition and also the challenges posed by the eastern expansion of the EU. Many of the negative legacies discussed above continue to shape the relationship between energy, economy, and environment, and most of the positive legacies are fast disappearing. The energy dilemmas that face the post-socialist world today are a product of both their past as CPEs and also the different transformation trajectories that have been taken over the last 20 years. The next section charts the impact of "transition" and pays particular attention to the issues of energy security, energy intensity, economic structure, and GHG emissions.

Post-Socialist Transition, Recession, and Recovery

The fall of the Berlin Wall and the subsequent collapse of the Soviet Union, between late 1989 and the end of 1991, brought an abrupt end to the Soviet system. Unfortunately, there was no blueprint to manage what happened next. The process of transition away from the CPE was experienced very differently by the states of Eastern Europe and the Baltic Republics. For them, it was a "return to Europe" with the Soviet period being seen as an aberration that was best quickly forgotten. They also had a clear final destination for the transition process, full membership of the EU. With that came a set of tests in the accession process, the so-called "Copenhagen Criteria." In the case of East Germany, the process of unification dealt with EU accession. Tragically, the state of Yugoslavia, which had not been part of the Soviet bloc, disintegrated into warring factions, resulting in considerable loss of life and economic disruption. For the remaining 13 post-Soviet Republics it was a different matter as they were a product of the Soviet period. However, in every case, the new post-socialist states had to orchestrate a "triple transition" of polity, economy, and civil society, from communist state to democracy, from planned economy to market economy, and from autocracy to civil society. In many cases, independence also meant the establishment of a new national identity, often in the face of conflict. Finally, the post-socialist states had to find their own place in an increasingly globalized economic system.

The Western governments and international financial institutions quickly imposed a transition orthodoxy (also known as the Washington Consensus) that advocated rapid reform via the so-called four pillars of transition: privatization, liberalization, stabilization, and internationalization. With the benefit of hindsight, we now recognize that the problem was that the post-socialist states lacked the institutional structures needed to manage the transformation process. I favor the term "transformation" over "transition" as much of the old system remained in place, while new institutions and ownership structures developed, and even today there are still remnants of the socialist past that are clearly visible. Furthermore, not all post-socialist states fully embraced the transition orthodoxy and some favored "shock therapy" over "gradualism." Whatever the strategy adopted by individual states, all suffered deep economic recession and falling living standards as the old system fell apart without a new self-sustaining system in place.

Energy, Environment, and Transitional Recession

The rapid fall in economic output triggered by transitional recession brought with it a dramatic reduction in energy demand and windfall benefits for the environment. Figure 4.1 illustrates the key trends from 1990 to 2007. The data are from the CAIT database and include all 27 transition economies. The data on GDP per capita illustrate the depth of the recession experienced in the early 1990s, with income falling by more than 30 percent; in many cases the fall in industrial output was even greater. As a result, the carbon intensity of the economy fell dramatically as energy demand and industrial output fell (this is discussed in more detail later). Much of that industrial output disappeared forever; as a consequence when the economies rebounded from recession and started to grow, the carbon intensity of the economies continued to fall. This was the result of economic restructuring, whereby it was the manufacturing and services sectors that led the recovery and the overall share of industry in national output fell. In many instances, this also resulted in a dramatic improvement in air quality and public health. However, the graph also shows that as income per capita recovered, so carbon emissions per capita started to increase. This is because improving living standards have resulted in increased levels of consumer goods consumption and car ownership, which has increased commercial and household demand for energy services.

In 2001, the EBRD (2001: 91) reported that across the transition economies total primary energy consumption had fallen from 1,925 mtoe in 1989 to 1,250 mtoe in 1999, a 35 percent fall in energy consumption. Of that fall, 86 percent was due to falling output and only 14 percent to efficiency gains. However, there were considerable cross-country variations in the resulting levels of energy intensity that are discussed below. As a result of the fall in energy consumption, the post-socialist states are the only group of countries

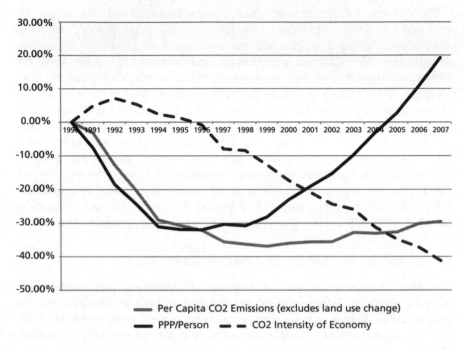

Source: CAIT.

Figure 4.1 Trends in GDP per capita, CO_2 emissions per capita, and CO_2 intensity of the economy in the transition economies, 1990–2007

to experience a decline in CO_2 emissions since 1990. The World Bank (2010c: 74) reports that after the recession of the 1990s emissions declined by 38.7 percent, that is, from 5.2 billion metric tons in 1988 to 3.3 billion in 2005, representing a fall equal to 17 percent of global emissions. Thus, the collapse of the CPE has done far more to reduce carbon emissions to date than the Kyoto Protocol, or put another way, had the Soviet system not collapsed GHG emissions would be significantly higher than they are today. As table 4.2 details, the actual levels of GHG emission reductions achieved are much more substantial than the Kyoto targets agreed by the post-socialist states. The data are for 2008 and capture both the impact of the transition recession and the subsequent recovery. Since then global economic crisis has further reduced the level of emissions as it has depressed the level of economic activity across the region. The question that remains concerns what will happen when moving forward.

Research on the transformation trajectories of the post-socialist states identifies a number of common patterns that, one way or another, relate to the pace and penetration of market reforms. Put simply, the more quickly and

TABLE 4.2 Post-socialist states' Kyoto targets versus actual emissions in 2008

	Actual reduction 1990–2008	Reduction target by 2012	Difference in 2008
Slovenia	5.2	−8	+13.2
Croatia	−0.2	−5	+4.8
EU-15	−11.3	−8	−3.3
Czech Rep	−27.5	−8	−19.5
Poland	−29.9	−6	−23.9
Russia	−32.9	0	−32.9
Slovakia	−33.9	−8	−25.9
Hungary	−36.1	−6	−30.1
Bulgaria	−41.9	−8	−33.9
Romania	−46.9	−8	−38.9
Estonia	−50.4	−8	−42.4
Lithuania	−51.1	−8	−43.1
Ukraine	−53.9	0	−53.9
Latvia	−55.6	−8	−47.6

Source: UNFCCC.

more purposefully market reforms were introduced the more rapidly an economy recovered from recession and returned to growth. Figure 4.2 charts average growth rates based on a sample of countries to show the difference in the timing and depth of recession and recovery in CEBS and the CIS. The CEBS countries experienced a shallower recession earlier on and recovered earlier; by contrast, the CIS suffered a later and deeper recession and the recovery of the CIS countries was damaged by the Russian financial crisis in 1998. Thereafter, both groups experienced a boom that was brought to an abrupt end by the global economic crisis in 2008 (Smith and Swain 2010). As a consequence, by 2006 most of the post-socialist states had regained or surpassed their 1990 levels of GDP. In this analysis we are particularly interested in the impact that recession and recovery had on the various elements of the Kaya Identity. In all cases, population growth has not been a factor in driving energy consumption and carbon emissions; in fact most countries in the region have very low rates of population growth, again a consequence of the transition period. Rather, it is the other three elements that are significant: the growth of economic output (and levels of consumption), energy intensity, and the carbon intensity of energy use.

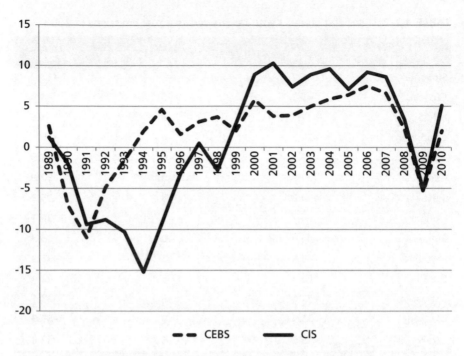

Source: EBRD database (<www.ebrd.com>)

Figure 4.2 Annual GDP growth rates in CEBS and the CIS, 1989–2010

The Kaya Consequences of Economic Recovery

This analysis of the changing Kaya characteristics is based on a sample of countries across the various groups, the aim being to chart the different dynamics across the region. The pattern of economic growth has already been discussed and we can identify three stages since 1990: the transitional recession during the 1990s that resulted from the collapse of the CPE, a period of recovery and sustained economic growth from the late 1990s through to 2008, and, finally, the impact of the global economic crisis, followed by a rebound to positive growth in 2009. However, it is uncertain what impact the Eurozone crisis will have on the region and it seems safe to assume that we will not see a return to the growth rates of the last decade any time soon. Figure 4.3 charts the changing energy intensity of four transition economies from 1990 to 2007. The measure used is the amount of GDP produced per unit of energy consumed; thus, an increasing trend means that the amount of wealth per unit of energy consumed is increasing. All of the countries demonstrate an improving trend during this period; however, Russia and Ukraine show a rather different pattern during the period of the transitional recession, as the level of energy consumption did not fall as rapidly as the

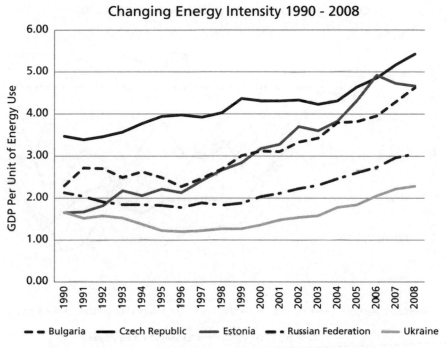

Changing Energy Intensity 1990 - 2008

- ▬ ▬ Bulgaria   ▬▬ Czech Republic   ▬▬ Estonia   ▬ • Russian Federation   ▬▬ Ukraine

GDP per unit of energy use (constant 2005 PPP $ per kg of oil equivalent)

Source: World Bank Development Indicators Database (<http://data.worldbank.org/indicator>)

Figure 4.3 Changing energy intensity of selected transition economies, 1990–2008

level of economic output. This is because the absence of hard budget constraints meant that many industrial enterprises remained operational even though their output fell dramatically. In the CEBS, the more stringent application of economic reforms related to future EU accession forced many industrial enterprises into bankruptcy. In the period of sustained economic growth that followed, growing levels of GDP, rather than further substantial falls in energy use, accounted for the improvements in energy intensity, and the changing carbon intensity of energy use further supports this (figure 4.4). As these economies experienced economic recovery, so the levels of carbon intensity leveled off and then more recently began to experience an upward trend. Data on total reduction in GHG between 1990 and 2008 for the EU-10 countries show a clear contrast in rates of decline in the 1990s, compared to the last decade. For example, in Poland total GHG emissions fell by 13 percent in the period 1990–2008, but only by 2 percent between 2000 and 2008. In

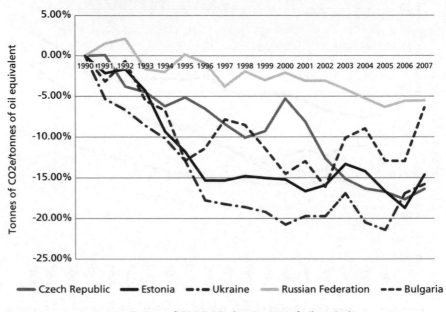

Changing Carbon Intensity of Energy Use: 1990 - 2007

━━ Czech Republic ━━ Estonia ━•━ Ukraine ━━ Russian Federation ━━━ Bulgaria

Tonnes of CO2 Equivalent/tonnes of oil equivalent

Source: CAIT.

Figure 4.4 Changing carbon intensity of energy use in selected transition economies, 1990–2007

the other cases, while emissions fell over the 1990–2008 period, they actually increased in the post-2000 period. For example, Lithuania saw a 52 percent decline in emissions between 1990 and 2008, but between 2000 and 2008 emissions actually increased by 25 percent (European Environment Agency 2012: 30). Thus, in CEBS, economic recovery brought with it increased GHG emissions. Throughout the period, Russia's carbon intensity remained high, reflecting both the energy inefficiency of its economy and the fact that its energy and resource-intensive sectors remain the engine of economic growth. In the growth phase, improvements in living standards, and in particular increasing car ownership, drove increased demand for energy, especially for transportation fuels. Buchan (2010: 10) notes a more marked shift from public to private transport, from rail to road, and from bus to car in the new EU member-states compared to the EU-15. Data from the European Environmental Agency show that for CEBS car ownership per 1,000 inhabitants increased from 219 in 1995 to 369 in 2009, an increase of 69 percent, compared to an increase of 23.8 percent to 486 in the EU-15. Thus, while a significant gap still remains between CEBS and the EU-15, one of the positive legacies of the CPE is fast disappearing, while demand for oil products is increasing. In general, we can conclude that with economic recovery the transition economies of CEBS began to show similar energy-demand structures to the developed OECD economies, but they still remain far less efficient in their energy use; in large part this is because of the inherited building stock and energy infrastructure.

The majority of the post-socialist states showed a common pattern of significant de-industrialization during the 1990s as output fell, then in the decade of growth that followed the service sector grew far more rapidly, thus further reducing the share of industry in the economy. The net result is that we see a leveling off in CO_2 emissions from energy, and in some cases even an upward trend by 2007, but as is clear from table 4.2 the total level of GHG emission was in most cases still significantly below 1990 levels and substantially below relevant Kyoto targets.

In their analysis of the energy intensity of transition economies, Cornillie and Fankhauser (2004) decompose the various elements that explain falling rates of energy consumption relative to output across the region between 1992 and 1998. They distinguished four factors as the key drivers: the energy intensity of industry, transport, and the rest of the economy, and the effect of structural change. They identified three distinctive patterns of energy-intensity change. First, in some countries the energy intensity of industry declined, while the residual remained stable; Hungary, Latvia, and Slovenia were included in this group. Second, there was a group of countries where the energy intensity of industry remained constant, but the rest of the economy improved; this included Poland, Romania, and the Slovak Republic. Third, for most of the countries in the CIS, the energy intensity of industry and the rest of the economy went up, in large part due to widespread non-payment for energy that provided little incentive to conserve. This is apparent in figure 4.4, in the case of Russia and the Ukraine. Their final conclusion was that "Overall, there appears to be a strong link between improvements in energy intensity and progress in transition" (note that both authors worked for the EBRD). They pointed out that this was no surprise because "transition is chiefly about creating structures and incentives for the efficient use of resources, and energy is a crucial resource in transition" (Cornillie and Fankhauser 2004: 294). Although it is difficult to quantify, the extent to which economic reform brought about a change in energy prices and imposed hard budget constraints on consumers seems to be the key factor explaining the difference in the changing patterns of energy consumption across the region.

Reforming the Energy Sector

Buzar (2007: 4) provides a succinct description of the intention of energy reform in relation to economic transition:

> Most former socialist countries pledged to adopt neoliberal energy legislation in the early 1990s, requiring the vertical and horizontal unbundling of formerly state owned integrated energy monopolies, the liberalisation of energy markets and prices and the establishment of independent regulatory bodies.

In their analysis Ürge-Vorsatz et al. (2006: 2286) produced a summary of the policy measures required to reduce the high-energy intensities and unsustainable energy practices of the post-socialist states, and this is reproduced in table 4.3. In broad terms, table 4.3 suggests that a transition to a market economy, where prices reflect the true cost of production and delivery and the energy system is largely in private hands, will impose discipline upon energy producers and consumers, thus promoting greater efficiency. The inclusion of EU legislation presumably ensures there is the degree of regulation needed to reduce the potential negative environmental impacts of the market. This was the policy prescription of the European Commission and the EBRD. Not surprisingly, the post-socialist states responded to it with varying degrees of enthusiasm. Those countries seeking accession to the EU had no choice in the matter, as the process required that they demonstrate they had created a "fully-functioning market economy" and they also agree

TABLE 4.3 Policy response to reduce high-energy intensity and unsustainable energy uses in the post-socialist states of the EU

Negative legacies of centrally planned economy	Policy response
No competition, no penalty for inefficiency	Transition to a market economy and privatization
Unrealistic resource evaluation	Introduction of market prices
Subsidized energy prices	Remove subsidies and liberalize energy prices
Flat rates (mainly for district heating)	Consumption-based billing and introduction of metering
Dominance of heavy industry	Transition to a market economy with associated restructuring
Large-scale economies and over-sized enterprises	Transition to a market economy and privatization
Lack of expertise and awareness	Improved data collection and capacity building
Lack of pollution control	Harmonizing environmental legislation with EU, improvement of enforcement and privatization.

Source: Adapted from Ürge-Vorsatz, D., Miladinova, G., and Piazs, L. (2006), Energy in transition: from the Iron Curtain to the European Union. *Energy Policy* 34: 2286.

to be bound by EU legislation. However, the remaining states of the CIS were under no such obligations and many have resisted both the privatization and liberalization of their energy sectors.

Von Hirschhausen and Waelde (2001) characterized the options open to the post-socialist states in relation to energy-sector reform as being between an "Anglo-Saxon" model that favored privatization and liberalization, which was based on the UK/US experience and was the benchmark for the opening up of EU energy markets, and a "French" model that relied on large integrated monopolies, operating with a degree of state ownership and/or planning and regulation. On the face of it, one might have assumed that the post-socialist states of CEBS would go for the French model as it implied a degree of continuity; however, the desire to join the EU meant that the "Anglo-Saxon" model was the preferred option. Scanning across all the transition economies, they identified what they called three "stylized outcomes of systemic transformation" in relation to energy policy. First, in CEBS, the "societal consensus is an outright rejection of the socialist system and binding commitment to a market economy (the Anglo-Saxon model)." Second, they identified a group of countries that they called "post-Soviet mixed economy," which was "a blend of incoherently functioning elements of a market economy and straightforward central planning" (Von Hirschhausen and Waelde 2001: 103). This group included Russia and Ukraine, and to a lesser extent Belarus. Third, there was a group of countries they called "the Caspian state economy," which "had not even considered introducing market-oriented institutions, but had opted to use its newly-gained independence to transform Soviet socialism into an autocratic, clan based regime based upon a strong state involvement in the economy." Although this analysis was conducted a decade ago, the three models remain and the differences between them have become even more marked. The majority of CEBS are now members of the EU and are grappling with the consequences of its energy and climate-change policies. If anything has changed, it is that the boundary between the second and third categories has become more blurred. In Russia, as is discussed below, under President Putin, the state reasserted its control over the energy sector and the economic crisis has since slowed the pace of liberalization. In the Caspian region, issues such as climate change have little traction and the emphasis is upon developing the region's hydrocarbon potential to sustain autocratic regimes and finance economic development.

The "Great Game" in the Caspian

The Caspian region, comprised of the three trans-Caucasian states – Georgia, Armenia, and Azerbaijan – and the four Central Asian states of Kazakhstan, Turkmenistan, Uzbekistan, and Kyrgyzstan, plus Russia (and Iran to the south), is the subject of considerable geopolitical intrigue when it comes to energy security. As noted above, in the main, these states have preserved strong state control over their economies and autocratic, often clan-based, political regimes control their energy sectors. The notion of the "Great Game" is often evoked to reflect the conflicting interests of the West represented by the EU and US competing against the influence of Russia and of China (Jaffe and Manning 1998; Bahgat 2005; Klare 2008: 113–45). Initially, Russia held the trump cards as the transportation infrastructure made the Caspian states dependent upon it to gain access to export markets. However, since 1991, the major reserve holders in the region – Azerbaijan, Kazakhstan, Turkmenistan, and Uzbekistan – have sought to increase their options by encouraging foreign investment and by diversifying their routes to market. For the most part, Russia's oil and gas companies have lacked the finance to acquire substantial assets in the region and have relied on Moscow's heavy-handed military – witness the conflict with Georgia in 2008 – and diplomatic actions to maintain a degree of control over the flow of oil and gas out of the region (Olcott 2009). For Gazprom – the Russian state-controlled gas company – access to Central Asian gas has been essential to meeting its export obligations and in the past it has had to compromise on price to ensure security of supply. However, the IEA (2011a: 337) maintains that Russia now has a reduced need for Central Asian gas and that access to China for Central Asian producers has reduced its leverage in the region.

In the early 1990s, there was much hype about the hydrocarbon potential of the Caspian region, said to rival that of the Middle East. In 1994, Azerbaijan signed a \$7 billion contract with a Western consortium – with the political support of the US and the EU – to develop offshore oil and gas production. The subsequent construction of the Baku-Tbilisi-Ceyhan (BTC) oil pipeline, which now transports 1 million barrels of oil a day, and the Baku-Tbilisi-Erzurum gas pipeline (BTE) has provided access to new markets and brought an economic boom to Azerbaijan. Kazakhstan also uses the BTC to access world markets as oil is transported across the Caspian Sea by barge. However, the future for Azerbaijan, and the Caspian region more generally, remains uncertain, as the hydrocarbon reserve base has not proved to be as big as first thought and additional pipeline capacity is also needed, which could include the Nabucco gas pipeline discussed in the previous chapter. In Kazakhstan, the Caspian Pipeline Consortium (CPC) oil pipeline commissioned in 2001 has been essential to the development of new production from the Tengiz field, but the fact that it transits through Russia to the port of Novorossiysk places it firmly under Russian control. The CPC plans to expand the capacity of the pipeline, but this has been delayed due to technical difficulties. Since the mid-1990s, Kazakh oil production has increased significantly from 20.6 million tons in 1995 to 78 million tons in 2009 (Vatansever 2010: 18). However, the pace of growth is likely to slow, in particular because of problems at the giant Kashagan field, where foreign oil companies are struggling with challenging environmental conditions and state intervention to develop new production.

While Western consortia have struggled in Central Asia, this is not the case with the oil and gas projects that have been built to China (Xuetang 2006). The Kazakhstan–China oil pipeline now delivers 4 percent of China's oil imports. At the end of 2009, a gas pipeline connected Turkmenistan to China via Uzbekistan and Kazakhstan – about half the gas comes from Uzbekistan and the rest from the other two states. As a result, China has fast emerged as a serious source of competition to both Russian and US influence in the region. China's access to Central Asian oil and gas has also improved its bargaining position in relation to access to Russia's oil and gas resources in Siberia and the Far East. Although there is a huge amount written about the geopolitics of Caspian energy, the principal concern of that work is with the prospects for the delivery of additional supplies of oil and gas to world markets. Whilst the geopolitics of oil and gas developments in the Caspian region are fascinating, it is tangential to our current examination of the interplay between post-socialist economic transition, energy security, and climate-change policy. From an economic standpoint, the post-socialist states of the Caspian region have far more in common with the developing world (the subject of chapter 6). That said, developments in the region are critical to the EU's strategy of developing a southern corridor to reduce reliance on Russian gas; and, as we shall see in the next chapter, the increased use of gas in China has significant implications in relation to climate change.

Continued Dependence upon Russia

A critical and enduring legacy of the CPE, discussed earlier, is the continued dependence on Russian energy exports, and in the case of the Caspian region one might add export infrastructure and market access. When the dust finally settled after the collapse of the Soviet Union the dependencies remained and little has changed to reduce them. Russia has cut off oil supplies to its post-socialist neighbors, both to protect its commercial interests and for geopolitical purpose (Hedenskog and Larsson 2007; Lough 2011). Fortunately, it has been possible to find alternative sources of supply, such as Norway in the case of the Baltic States. However, in the case of gas, dependency is inflexible and physically embedded in the pipelines that carry gas to market. In addition, many of the Central European states also provide transit to markets in Western Europe. The two gas disputes between Russia and Ukraine in 2006 and 2009 had the most significant effect on Central and Southern Europe, but also resulted in reduced deliveries to consumers in Western Europe. Two figures matter when assessing the level of dependence on Russian gas: the share of gas in total primary energy consumption and the share of Russian gas imports in the total amount of gas consumed in a given country. Table 4.4 presents this information for the key countries, including Belarus and Ukraine.

TABLE 4.4 Central Europe and Baltics States' dependence on Russian natural gas imports, 2010

	% Share of Russian gas in total gas imports	% Share of Gas in primary energy consumption	% Gas supply reduction in January 2009
Belarus	100	72.3	n/a
Bulgaria	100	12.8	−100
Croatia	88.0	n.d.	n/a
Czech Republic	73.1	20.3	−71
Estonia	100	10.0*	n/a
Hungary	86.6	41.9	−45
Latvia	100	28.4*	n/a
Lithuania	100	45.9	n/a
Poland	89.5	16.1	−33
Romania	100	34.8	n/a
Slovakia	100	31.5	−97
Ukraine	100	39.8	n/a

*Eurostat data for 2009.

Source: BP (2011), *Statistical Review of World Energy 2011*. London: BP, pp. 24 and 41; and Schmidt-Felzmann, A. (2011), EU member-states' energy relations with Russia: conflicting approaches to securing natural gas supplies. *Geopolitics* 16, 577.

In all instances the level of dependence on Russian gas is very high and in eight cases absolute, but what really matters is the degree of reliance on that gas (Noël 2008). In many instances domestic sources of energy, such as coal, nuclear power, or domestic gas production, and access to alternative suppliers reduce the actual level of dependence on Russia. Two sets of states seem particularly vulnerable, the two Baltic states of Latvia and Lithuania, and the Central European states of Czech Republic, Hungary, and Slovakia. The latter group all serve as transit states and were all affected by the 2009 crisis.

Understandably, the EU-10 have been particularly outspoken about the geopolitical manipulation of energy exports by Russia and about the actions of Gazprom in their domestic markets. No doubt, they hoped that by joining the EU they would benefit from consolidated action in dealing with Moscow; however, until recently, Brussels has seemed more concerned with the liberalization agenda and climate change. The 2009 Russia–Ukraine gas crisis served as a wake-up call, and has prompted new legislation on gas security and more concrete investment in interconnectors to improve gas security in Central Europe. More generally, the issue of Russia–EU energy relations remains particularly problematic as it reveals the tensions between unilateral initiatives to guarantee security of supply, which in some cases means appeasing Russia's interests, and more coordinated action at the EU level (Miller 2008; Schmidt-Felzmann 2011). In reality, it reflects the failure of the EU to act collectively and to demonstrate the "spirit of solidarity" that is supposed to underpin the EU's energy strategy (see previous chapter). More generally, the EU is caught between a need to address energy security imperatives driven largely by Russian actions and the low-carbon energy and climate policy imperative emanating from Brussels. Thus, there remains a clear East–West divide in the EU in terms of what should be the priority: energy security or climate change. It may be that a combination of the diversification of gas imports and the ongoing anti-trust case against Gazprom will herald a period of greater solidarity and cooperation between EU member-states in relation to gas security.

Legacies and Differentiation

The Kaya characteristics of the post-socialist states are presented in table 4.5, and figure 4.4 charts the relationship between energy consumption and GDP per capita. In the other chapters, this information represents the starting point in the analysis; here, it represents the end point. That is because the current characteristics are the result of two decades of transition away from the CPE. One thing that is clear from table 4.5 is the degree of variation and difference that now exists among the post-socialist states, both in terms of their levels of economic development and the energy and carbon intensities of their economies. This is also reflected in figure 4.5, where in the bottom left-hand corner we have a group of economies that are relatively undeveloped and consequently have low levels of energy consumption. In the middle ground we have two groups of countries, one made up of CIS states, where the levels of energy consumption are higher than one would expect given their level of economic development, and one made up of EU member-states, where the opposite is true. The outliers of Turkmenistan, Kazakhstan, and the Russian Federation are all major energy producers and exporters. Estonia's position relates to its reliance upon oil shale, whose production is both energy and carbon intensive. The current economic situation makes the future difficult to predict. There is hope that economic growth will return to the region and all the signs are that this would bring with it increased demands for energy, which means energy security would remain a priority for the CEBS. However, even after two decades of market reform, there still remain substantial energy efficiency gains to be had, particularly in the built environment (Froggatt and Canzi 2004). But realizing that potential will require substantial capital investment, as will the development of new energy infrastructure, much of which will have to be low carbon to meet the EU's targets.

TABLE 4.5 Kaya characteristics of the post-socialist states

	CO_2 per capita 2007	Population (,000s) 2010	GNI per capita 2009	Energy intensity 2008	Carbon intensity of energy use
Albania	1.4	3,169	8,840	10.98	1.99
Armenia	1.6	3,090	5,450	5.76	1.81
Azerbaijan	3.7	8,883	9,220	5.26	2.39
Belarus	6.9	9,645	14,020	4.01	2.3
Bosnia & Herzegovina	7.7	3,760	8,970	4.71	3.33
Bulgaria	6.8	7,562	13,210	4.62	2.53
Croatia	5.6	4,430	18,710	8.47	2.56
Czech Republic	12.1	10,535	23,620	5.42	2.72
Estonia	15.2	1,340	19,500	4.66	3.27
Georgia	1.4	4,453	4,960	6.63	1.6
Hungary	5.6	10,005	19,280	6.83	2.08
Kazakhstan	14.7	16,316	10,610	2.31	2.91
Kosovo	Na	1,815	na	na	na
Kyrgyz Republic	1.2	5,365	2,180	3.77	2.18
Latvia	3.4	2,243	16,360	7.88	1.82
Lithuania	4.5	3,319	17,880	6.43	1.62
Macedonia, FYR	5.5	2,060	10,830	5.79	3.15
Moldova	1.3	3,562,	3,340	3.14	2.37
Mongolia	4.0	2,701	na	2.75	3.69
Montenegro	Na	626	12,710	na	na
Poland	8.3	38,178	19,020	6.4	3.22
Romania	4.4	21,450	14,050	6.44	2.49
Russia	10.8	141,750	19,190	3.05	2.42
Serbia	Na	7,289	na	4.69	na
Slovak Republic	6.8	5,430	23,140	6.06	2.17
Slovenia	7.5	2,065	26,970	7.11	2.26
Tajikistan	1.1	7,075	2,060	4.83	1.81
Turkmenistan	9.2	5,177	7,160	1.65	2.53
Ukraine	6.8	45,760	6,580	2.28	2.34
Uzbekistan	4.3	28,160	3,090		2.38

See table 3.1 for an explanation of the indicators.

Source: World Bank Development Indicators Database and CAIT

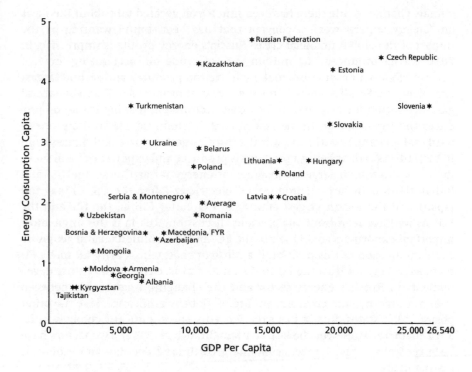

Source: CAIT.

Figure 4.5 The relationship between energy consumption and GDP per capita in the post-socialist states (2007)

In the CIS, the situation is very different; these states remain energy profligate, although their absolute levels of energy consumption are low, and have made limited progress in implementing measures that would drive increased energy efficiency. Equally, the energy-rich states of the region show limited interest in economic diversification and are likely to remain energy intensive for some time to come. Russia is both a major consumer of fossil fuels (and a major emitter of GHGs) and one of the world's leading exporters; thus, the remainder of this chapter examines the particular challenges that face Russia in terms of energy security, economic globalization, and climate change.

Russian Energy at the Crossroads

Our purpose here is not to provide an exhaustive analysis of Russia's energy sector; rather, it is to focus on the changing energy intensity of the economy, trends in oil and gas production, consumption and export, and attitudes to climate change. While there has been much exaggerated talk about Russia as an "energy superpower," a concept that has been found wanting by the impact of the global financial crisis, Russia's energy profile is impressive. In 2010, Russia produced 502 million tons of crude oil, accounting for 12.6 percent of global production, making it the top producer and second largest exporter (after Saudi Arabia). In the same year, it produced 637 bcm of natural gas, accounting for 19.4 percent of world production, making it the top producer and top exporter. In the case of coal, it produced 248 million tons of hard coal, placing it sixth, and was the third largest exporter (all figures from IEA 2011d). As well as being a prodigious producer and exporter of fossil fuels, Russia is the fourth largest consumer of energy (after China, the US, and India), the fourth largest producer of electricity (after the US, China, and Japan), and the fourth largest emitter of CO_2 (after China, the US, and the EU). As we have seen from our previous discussion, Russia is the single most important exporter of fossil fuels to the EU, and its commercial and geopolitical manipulation of this position is a cause of energy insecurity for many EU member-states, not least the EU-10. Given its status, current and future developments in Russia's energy sector and the changing relationship between energy, economy, and environment are of global significance. Like the other post-socialist states, Russia has experienced some significant changes in its Kaya characteristics over the last 20 years (Bradshaw 2012). Two factors have been central to this change: economic growth (and decline) and economic restructuring.

Economic Restructuring and Energy Intensity

During the 1990s, Russia experienced a significant decline in the level of economic activity, energy consumption, and both energy and carbon intensity (see figure 4.6 and table 4.6). Our earlier discussion of the impact of transitional recession upon energy intensity pointed out that in the case of Russia energy intensity actually increased during the first part of the 1990s and peaked in 1996, as economic output fell at a much faster rate than energy consumption. From the late 1990s onwards, the economy then grew more rapidly than energy consumption and intensity started to fall again. But, as is clear from figure 4.4, Russia has not closed the gap with CEBS, let alone the OECD countries, when it comes to the amount of energy consumed per unit of output. A recent OECD (2011b: 138) study suggests three reasons why Russia is so energy intensive: first, it suffers from a harsh climate; second, it has an industrial structure that is biased toward energy-intensive sectors – fossil fuels, petrochemical, metals, and forestry all remain important to the economy; and, third, it suffers from an aged and inefficient capital stock. To this list we can add the wasteful practices of its energy sector and the partial liberalization of energy prices, both of which are discussed in more detail below. The substantial fall in primary energy demand identified in table 4.6

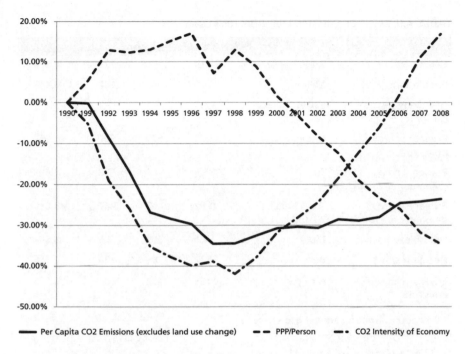

Source: CAIT.

Figure 4.6 Trends in GDP per capita, CO_2 emissions per capita, and CO_2 intensity of the economy in Russia, 1990–2008

is in large part due to the de-industrialization of the economy, which together with the growth of the service economy has resulted in a significant restructuring of the economy. The same OECD (2011b: 137) study reports that structural change (shifts between sectors) accounted for two thirds of the reduction in the energy intensity of GDP between 2000 and 2009 and the figure would be even higher for the 1990s. Improvements in technology only accounted for a reduction of 10 percent, which is in line with the OECD countries. Thus, we can conclude that Russia's improving energy intensity and falling emissions are overwhelmingly due to de-industrialization and economic restructuring, rather than economy-wide improvements in efficiency (more on this issue below).

The End of Easy Russian Oil

In the Soviet Union, the country's oil and gas wealth was exploited by the state and was used to meet its economic and geopolitical needs with scant attention being paid to the costs of development and its environmental

TABLE 4.6 Key energy-related indicators for Russia

	Unit	1991	2000	2010	2000–2010*
GDP (PPP)	$ 210 billion	1973	1395	2223	4.8%
Population	Million	148	147	142	−0.4%
GDP (PPP) per capita	$2010 thousand	13.3	9.5	15.7	5.1%
Primary energy demand	Mtoe	872	620	687	1.0%
Primary energy demand per capita	Toe	5.9	4.2	4.8	1.4%
Primary energy demand per GDP	Toe/$1000 2010**	0.67	0.67	0.47	−3.6%
Net oil export	Mb/d	4.4	3.9	7.5	8.5%
Net gas export	Bcm	177	185	190	0.3%
Energy-related CO_2 emissions	Mt	2168	1492	1604	0.7%

*Compound average annual growth rate.
**Market exchange rate.

Source: IEA (2011), *World Energy Outlook 2011*. Paris: IEA, p. 246.

impact. As discussed earlier, exports of oil and gas were an essential part of the Soviet Union's relationship with Eastern Europe and a crucial source of hard currency earnings from exports to the West. When the Soviet Union collapsed Russia's oil and gas industries followed very different paths. The oil industry was broken up into smaller vertically integrated companies, many of which were privatized (Gustafson 2012). The gas industry, by comparison, remained consolidated in a single company – Gazprom – with substantial state ownership and control.

In the first half of the 1990s, the collapse of the Soviet economic system hit the oil industry hard and it was ill equipped to deal with the changes that followed (see Grace 2005: 65–84). The net result was plummeting production, which bottomed out in 1994–5 (see figure 4.7). Thereafter, further privatization – including the infamous loans for shares deal – and the emergence of large "private" oil companies, such as Yukos and Lukoil, helped to revive production. The financial crisis of 1998 and the rouble devaluation that followed made exports profitable and stimulated growth, just at a time when the world oil price started to pick up, which breathed new life into the industry. Investment picked up, new wells came into production, and enhanced recovery techniques and better management, often with the assistance of foreign oilfield service companies, bolstered production in existing fields.

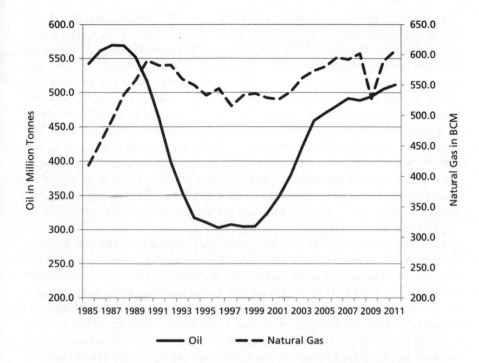

Source: BP (2012b), *BP Statistical Review of World Energy June 2012*. London: BP, pp. 8 and 22.

Figure 4.7 Dynamics of Russian oil and gas production, 1985–2011

Russia provided the incremental production needed to meet the surge in global oil demand created by the growth of the emerging economies. The improved fortunes of the oil industry and the oligarchs that were profiting from it soon attracted the attention of new Russian President Vladimir Putin. As the world price continued to increase and Russian production rebounded, so the Russian state sought to reassert control over the industry and taxed its profit to finance domestic consumption. The destruction of the private oil company Yukos, the imprisonment of its senior executives, and sale of its assets to the state companies Rosneft and Gazprom, together with actions against the international oil companies involved in the Sakhalin-2 project in the Russian Far East, heralded a new phase of state control over the oil industry (Bradshaw 2009b; Goldman 2008). The acquisition of the private company TNK-BP by the state-controlled Rosneft in late 2012 further consolidated the Kremlin's control. Rosneft alone is now responsible for more than 40 percent of Russia's oil production. All of this has been happening at a time when it has become clear that to sustain current levels of production substantial investment is needed to develop new fields and that these are likely to be in the more remote regions of East Siberia and also offshore in the Caspian Sea, the Arctic, and the Sea of Okhotsk. As a result, there has been a change in attitude toward foreign investment in the offshore oil and gas industry, and tax incentives are being introduced to encourage frontier exploration and development, the most obvious examples of this being the agreement between ExxonMobil and Rosneft to explore the Kara Sea in 2011, and BP's purchase of a significant share of Rosneft as part of the TNK-BP deal in late 2012. The end of easy oil in Russia also means that future production is unlikely to rise above the current levels. This means that Russia has no capacity to expand production to meet incremental demand and is likely faced with a production plateau, followed by a decline as longstanding fields fall out of production. The rate of that decline will depend on the success of future frontier exploration and development.

The repercussions of the global financial crisis have also complicated matters as the Russian state is even more reliant on sustained oil and gas tax revenues to finance the federal budget and the modernization of the economy; thus, the fortunes of the sector are crucial to national economic performance. It is difficult to work out just how dependent Russia is on its oil and gas industry as much of the value is ascribed to trading companies that are allocated to the service sector of the economy. The IEA (2011a: 330) estimates that oil and gas accounts for two thirds of Russian exports, and that oil and gas revenues provide about half of the federal budget. They also estimate that the oil (excluding refining) and gas sectors produced 17 percent of GDP in 2007, 24 percent in 2008, and 21 percent in 2010. Thus, Russia finds itself in a catch-22 position; it wishes to modernize its economy and diversify away from its dependence on the energy sector, but to do that it needs to invest significant amounts to sustain the oil and gas industry to earn the revenues to finance modernization (Baev 2010: 893).

Gazprom Seeks Security of Demand

The situation in the gas industry is very different, as it has remained consolidated within the state-controlled company Gazprom, which is responsible for the vast majority of domestic production, owns the entire pipeline infrastructure, and has monopoly control over exports of gas. The IEA (2011a: 303) estimates that Russia has total recoverable resources of close to 130 tcm (13 percent of global reserves), of which 21 tcm have been produced. Gazprom has no shortage of reserves; rather, it now faces the problem of balancing the need to invest in new projects with anticipated future demand, which is increasingly difficult to determine. The Russian gas balance, or gas matrix as Stern (2009) calls it, is comprised of a number of key interactions, all of which are in a state of flux. On the supply side, Gazprom has traditionally supplemented domestic gas production with imports from Central Asia to meet its market obligations and, as explained below, non-Gazprom production is now of growing significance. According to Stern (2009: 4), in 2008, Gazprom production was 550 bcm, non-Gazprom production 114, and Central Asian imports 61 bcm. In 2008, those market obligations include the domestic market (353 bcm), plus exports to other CIS countries (92 bcm), as well as exports to Europe (159 bcm). The problem with the domestic market has been the low price paid for gas. As figure 4.6 shows, gas production proved far more resilient during the 1990s than oil production. Natural gas accounted for 43 percent of Russia's primary energy supply in 1991, and by 2009 that share had increased to 54 percent; however, the 2009 Energy Strategy aims to reduce that share to 46–47 percent by 2030 (IEA 2011a: 265). Domestic prices have at times been below the cost of production and have always been lower than the price charged to customers in the CIS, and considerably below the price paid by European customers. The dominance of gas in power generation, much of which is part of a CHP system – which covers 70–80 percent of the housing stock – made it very difficult to raise prices or cut off supply in the face of non-payment; in fact it is acknowledged that Gazprom did not make a profit from domestic gas sales until 2009. Thus, over the past two decades, Gazprom has provided a substantial energy subsidy to Russian industry and gas consumers. The Russian government, which regulates the domestic price, made a commitment in 2006 to change this situation and aimed to achieve a "European netback price," that is, the cost charged to European customers minus the transportation costs, by 2011. However, that has not been achieved and price convergence has been complicated by the impact of the global financial crisis that has impacted on global gas prices and also on the ability of Russian consumers to pay higher prices (Henderson 2011). The issue of the prices paid by CIS importers has been the subject of geopolitical manipulation as Russia has rewarded countries and governments that are loyal to Moscow with lower prices, while allegedly punishing those who transgress (see Pirani 2009). As we know from earlier discussions, relations with Ukraine have been particularly sensitive. As Gazprom enjoys a monopoly over gas exports, the price it obtains goes straight to its bottom line and it has an interest in maximizing export earnings. This means that security of export demand is a key issue for Russia and for Gazprom when it plans its investments. In the recent past, exports to the EU have accounted for as much as 75 percent of Gazprom's income, while only accounting for 25 percent of the volume of gas produced. This was because it was losing money on the domestic market, which accounts for the bulk of its production. However, as domestic prices increase, then the domestic market becomes a major asset on the company's balance sheet. This is important as Gazprom is losing market share in Europe; in fact over the last decade its share of the EU market has fallen from almost 50 percent in 2000 to 28 percent in 2009, and 34 percent in 2010 (IEA 2011a: 343). The reasons for this have been discussed earlier; the bottom line is that the EU does not represent a growth prospect for the future and the IEA's New Policies Scenario projects Russia's share of EU gas imports to be 35 percent in 2020, or 27 percent of EU gas production. As a consequence, Gazprom is now looking to develop new export routes to North-East Asia. Russian exports to the region started in 2009 when production began at the Sakhalin-2 LNG plant. Gazprom acquired a controlling share of the Sakhalin-2 project in 2007, as a result of a concerted campaign against its foreign shareholders (Bradshaw 2007). Gazprom's Asian ambitions are formalized in its so-called "Eastern program" that foresees a network of pipelines delivering gas from Siberia and the Far East via pipeline to China, and via LNG from plants at Vladivostok and on Sakhalin. Gazprom has grand plans to export over 60 bcm of gas to China by the end of the decade, but agreement has yet to be reached (Paik 2012). In its 2009 *Energy Strategy*, the Russian government (2010: 23) maintains that gas exports will reach 19–20 percent of total exports by 2030, while the IEA (2011a: 343) New Policies Scenario sees them at 35 percent by 2035, when they would represent 15 percent of total Chinese gas consumption. Thus, Gazprom aims to counteract stagnant demand in Europe by expanding exports to Asia, but will it have sufficient gas to meet both its domestic and export obligations? Again, this is not a straightforward question.

Much like the oil industry, Gazprom has to invest considerable sums in developing new fields to compensate for the decline from its Soviet-era mega projects. This has meant moving further north on the Yamal Peninsula in Siberia to develop the Zapolyarnoe field in the early 2000s, and most recently starting production at the Bovanenkovo field in 2012. At the same time, Gazprom – together with Total and Statoil – had planned to develop the Shtokman project in the Barents Sea, but the project has been suspended indefinitely due to rising costs and a lack of market opportunities. These developments require substantial investment in new infrastructure and, in the case of Shtokman, new technological solutions for deep-water offshore production in Arctic conditions. At the same time, Russia's overall level of gas production is now being bolstered by gas being supplied by the oil companies and by the emergence of new private gas companies, most notably Novatek that is seeking to develop an LNG project on the Yamal Peninsula. According to Henderson (2010), there are about 80 gas-producing companies in Russia; Gazprom accounts for 80 percent of production, and Novatek 10 percent, with the rest being divided between foreign companies and small local independents. One of the consequences of Gazprom's ownership of the Russian gas pipeline system was that it denied the oil companies and independent producers access to its networks. Consequently, they had no alternative but to flare off associated gas, and the oil companies had no incentive to develop the gas associated with their oil projects. The net result was a waste of a valuable resource and the emission of substantial amounts of the GHG methane into the atmosphere. The Russian government has now forced Gazprom to allow third-party access, and financial incentives are being provided to reduce the amount of flaring (Kulagin 2008: 5–6). There is no precise measure of the level of gas flaring in Russia, but the IEA (2011a: 311) reports that since 2002 the output of associated gas has grown at a faster rate than the growth of oil production. On the basis of satellite estimates, the World Bank-led Global Gas Flaring Reduction Partnership (GGFPR) estimates that 35 bcm was flared in Russia in 2010, out of a global total of 134 bcm. The OECD (2011b: 139) reports a figure of 40 bcm of natural gas being flared in 2008, which is about 25 percent of the amount of gas exported to Western Europe. On average, the utilization rate (the amount of gas produced and not flared) is about 75 percent – though the state companies Rosneft and GazpromNeft flare off more than half of their gas produced. If the level of utilization was increased to 95 percent, the IEA (2011a: 312) estimate that another 20 bcm per year of gas could be produced. Thus, by allowing the oil companies to make better use of their associated gas and by allowing them and private gas companies to develop gas fields, a substantial new source of gas production is emerging from non-Gazprom producers. Gazprom still maintains a monopoly over exports and it may serve their purposes to surrender a share on the less profitable domestic market, allowing it to focus on the more lucrative, but increasingly competitive, export market. In short, the key issue for Gazprom and for Russia in moving forward is maintaining an exportable gas surplus and securing export markets, which appears to mean moving into LNG and building new pipelines to Asian markets.

Domestic Demand and Energy Efficiency

In the case of both oil and gas, the amount of resource available for export is the residual of production minus domestic demand. Of course, it is more complicated than that, but the key point is that to increase its energy exports, which are central to its economic well-being, Russia must either increase production or substantially reduce domestic consumption to increase the amount available for export. As we have seen, in the future increasing oil and gas production is going to be a much more expensive proposition. In the past, falling domestic demand in Russia has been associated with economic crisis, but there is an alternative scenario, namely, that the economy can continue to grow and consume less energy by becoming more energy efficient. Russia has all the inherited energy inefficiencies of the post-socialist states in abundance. According to a study conducted by the World Bank with the Russian Center for Energy Efficiency (World Bank 2008b), Russia could save up to 45 percent of its total primary energy consumption if it implemented economy-wide energy efficiency measures. The Russian government's 2009 *Energy Strategy* suggests that through organizational and technological savings the total volume of domestic energy consumption could fall by 40 percent. President Medvedev has set improvements in energy efficiency as a strategic priority, and set the target to reduce energy intensity by 40 percent in 2020 (relative to 2007). This was subsequently enshrined in legislation introduced in 2009 (Kononenko 2010: 4). Realizing these efficiency savings will not come cheap: a study by UNDP Russia (2010: 92) has calculated that to improve Russia's energy efficiency by 45 percent compared to 2005 would cost $324–57 billion. But they also point out that by exporting all of the oil and gas saved by these efficiency improvements, Russia could earn an additional $80–90 billion a year and could also keep GHG emissions well below the 1990 level, even with strong economic growth. One of the main reasons why energy consumption remains high is that prices are often subsidized, providing little incentive to conserve energy. The IEA (2010: 601) has calculated that in 2009 the total cost of natural gas subsidies in Russia was $34 billion, the equivalent of $238 per person or 2.7 percent of GDP. As Kulagin (2008: 3) points out, the gas-intensive nature of Russia's GDP is a major problem as the efficiency of gas power units in Russia is 33 percent, while in Europe the figure is 55 percent. In their assessment of the Russian energy sector, the IEA (2011a) identify numerous ways in which substantial energy efficiency savings could be made. Much of the existing infrastructure dates back to the Soviet era and is now in need of replacement; for example, according to the Russian Ministry of Energy, 80 percent of Russian boilers are over 30 years old. Russian industry accounts for nearly 30 percent of total primary energy consumption and is biased toward the more energy-intensive sectors, but by international comparison Russian industry is still energy inefficient. Thus, investment in new plants and equipment could deliver significant energy savings, an investment that would pay off more quickly if energy subsidies were removed. Mention has already been made of the widespread use of district heating and CHP plants; again, much of this infrastructure is old and inefficient and in need of replacement, but the sector has been starved of investment. The building sector, which accounts for 35 percent of total Russian energy consumption, is also a major source of energy waste, but again this needs substantial investment. The IEA (2011a: 279) reports on a World Bank project in Cherepovets in the late 1990s that retrofitted 650 buildings and reduced heat demand by 45 percent. The message is clear: there are very significant energy-efficiency savings to be made, but in the short term they need substantial investments that could then reap substantial long-term benefits. The challenge, as elsewhere, is to create a virtuous circle that encourages those investments; as ever, and in common with governments elsewhere, the Russian government is setting ambitious targets and saying all the right things but is not making the financial commitments needed to make a difference. Instead, it seems more inclined to provide subsidies and tax breaks to support new oil and gas production.

The IEA (2011a: 245) maintains that if Russia managed to raise energy efficiency in each sector of its economy to levels comparable to the OECD countries it could save more than 200 mtoe of primary energy a year, which is 30 percent of current demand. Such an aspiration clearly sits well with the

Russian government's modernization agenda and it could also maintain an exportable surplus of oil and gas without having to commit ever-larger amounts of investment in frontier oil and gas projects. The IEA (2011a: 259) suggests that through increased efficiency, a reduction in flaring, and demand reduction Russia could realize savings of almost 180 bcm of gas, which is equivalent to the three largest fields that will be developed on the Yamal Peninsula and also close to Russia's net exports of natural gas in 2010. Furthermore, investment in infrastructure renewal, building renovation, and new more efficient capital equipment would also provide more employment and generate a positive economic multiplier, thus delivering the so-called green recovery that would diversify the economy and promote more sustainable economic growth; it would also deliver sustained reductions in carbon emissions.

Russia Remains a Kyoto Skeptic

There is more than a little irony in the fact that it was ratification by the Russian Parliament in February 2004 that enabled the Kyoto Protocol to come into force in February 2005. This was not the result of a greening of the Russian government, but had more to do with entry into the World Trade Organisation (WTO) that Russia finally joined in December 2011 after 18 years of negotiation. Russia's significance lay not so much in its own Kyoto target, which is a zero percent change in emissions, but rather the fact that in 1990 it accounted for 16.4 percent of global emissions and, after the US refused to ratify the Protocol, Russia's ratification was necessary to cross the 55 percent of emission threshold that would bring the agreement into force. In Russia itself there was little enthusiasm for the agreement; in fact many thought that it might act as a break on future economic growth. For all the reasons explained above, it is no surprise that Russia's transitional recession brought with it a substantial reduction in GHG emissions. However, the situation changed after 1998 when the decline in emissions leveled off and then started to increase, though it is estimated that the global economic crisis has resulted in a 7–8 percent decline in emissions in 2008–9 (Safonov and Lugovoy 2010: 15). As figure 4.6 illustrates, by 2008 Russia's carbon emissions were 32.9 percent below 1990 levels, suggesting significant headroom in terms of future emissions growth. Not surprisingly, Russia wants to bank this reduction against any future global agreement and it also wants greater recognition for the ecosystem services that its forests provide, while being wary of signing up to further reduction targets post-2012. That said, the Russian government now accepts that anthropogenic climate change is real and that its overall impacts on Russia will be negative.

In 2009, President Medvedev stated that "climate change is real, that global warming threatens Russia's future, that Russia has a responsibility to address it both domestically and in international forums, that doing so can be economically beneficial" (quoted in Charap 2010: 11). This came after President Putin famously claimed that climate change would be good for Russia. In the run up to the Copenhagen Summit, in June 2009, President Medvedev stated that Russia's post-Kyoto target would be 10–15 percent below 1990 levels, which would actually be an effective 30–35 increase over 2007 levels! Ahead of the Copenhagen Summit, he indicated that Russia might accept a deeper target of 22–25 percent, and Russia now seems committed to a 25 percent reduction on 1990 levels by 2020. Russia does not have an explicit climate-change policy, though it does have a climate-change doctrine, and reductions or increases in GHG emissions seem to be the result of other policies relating to improvements in the overall energy efficiency of the economy (discussed above). Analysis by Novikova et al. (2009) suggests that Russia could easily achieve a 30 percent reduction by 2020 without compromising economic growth. Furthermore, Russia did sign the Copenhagen Accord and agreed to pay into the Green Climate fund. Thus, it seems strange that Russia has become increasingly skeptical about a post-Kyoto agreement. At the Cancun Summit, in December 2010, Russia announced that it would not sign up to a post-Kyoto agreement that would tie it to specific emission targets. As noted above, Russia has reservations about how such targets would be set and has not benefited as much from selling its surplus emissions (though Gazprom is involved in carbon trading) or from the Joint Initiative Programme aimed at assisting transition economies. Most recently, at the Durban Summit in December 2011, Russia, together with Canada and Japan, backed out of a second commitment period for the Kyoto Protocol. Russia's chief negotiator at the talks, Alexander Bedritsky, stated: "the Kyoto Protocol in its current form – i.e. without the participation of key emitters – neither resolves the problems of global warming, nor ensures meeting the global two-degree target, nor provides environmental integrity. For this reason, Russia is not committing to quantitative obligations in the second period of the Kyoto Protocol" (Bellona 2011). This position echoes the reasoning behind the refusal of the US to ratify the Protocol and points to its major weakness – the fact that it does not include some of the fastest-growing emitters, such as China and India, who are the subject of the next chapter.

Russia at the Crossroad of the Energy Dilemmas Nexus

As Russia struggles to recover from the global economic crisis it faces some major challenges in terms of the relationship between its energy sector, economic modernization, and climate change. Russia's *Energy Strategy* commits to a substantial reduction in the energy intensity of the economy; much of this is to be achieved by improvements in energy efficiency and demand reduction. The net result should be a substantial decline in domestic demand for fossil fuels that should make it easier to maintain the exportable surplus needed to generate the income required to finance modernization. At the same time, the reduction in energy intensity will bring with it continued reductions in GHG emissions. To create this virtuous circle requires a leap of faith that the medium- to long-term benefits will be realized, and a strong government commitment to the efficiency and modernization agenda. As the experience of CEBS demonstrates, the removal of energy subsidies and the complete liberalization of energy prices is a critical component of this new direction as it will force consumers to invest in efficiency to reduce energy demand. The danger is that the Russian government will forsake this cleaner leaner approach to economic growth for the muddling through associated with business as usual. This will then commit Russia to higher than necessary investments in new fossil-fuel production that will also hamper the wider modernization of the economy. It will also mean that Russia will continue to perceive a global climate-change agreement as a threat to its economic prosperity, rather than an additional drive for modernization and a more sustainable model of economic development.

Conclusion: Does Post-Socialism Still Matter?

The post-socialist states were identified as a distinct group because they share a common legacy in terms of the imprint of the centrally planned economy. For Russia and the other post-Soviet States (excluding the three Baltic States), this was a period that lasted almost 70 years, for the Baltic States just over 50 years, and, for the rest of East-Central Europe, 44 years from the end of World War II to the collapse of the Berlin Wall in 1989. In retrospect, these different histories are important to understanding the development of the region since 1991 when the Soviet Union collapsed. For the Baltic States and East-Central Europe, this was a return to Europe and a desire to join the European Union seemed a natural aspiration. For Russia and the remaining post-Soviet Republics, the challenge was to establish an independent identity in the global political and economic system. The transitional recession that swept across the region in the early 1990s created considerable hardship, but brought with it an environmental windfall as energy-wasteful, polluting heavy industry collapsed across the region. For the Baltic States and East-Central Europe, the desire to join the EU provided a roadmap for their transition to market economies, and they also committed themselves to the Kyoto Protocol. However, as these economies climbed out of recession and started to enjoy economic growth, they soon found themselves having to pay greater attention to their energy and the climate-change commitments of the EU. Prior to the global economic crisis, there were signs that increasing levels of consumption were placing these economies on the same path as the high-energy societies of the EU-15. At the same time, tensions have appeared as a result of their dependence on imports from Russia and the failure of the EU to build a robust relationship with Moscow. Poland, for example, with its high reliance on domestic coal, sees the EU's climate-change policies as undermining its energy security by forcing it into greater reliance on imported Russian gas. They hope that domestic shale gas production will help to alleviate the situation, but that seems some way off in the future. Thus, the particular energy dilemmas of the East-Central European members of the EU pose a challenge to the EU energy and climate strategies.

The post-Soviet Republics can be best divided into those that are energy-rich exporters – Azerbaijan, Kazakhstan, Russia, and Uzbekistan – and those that are not. The energy-poor states of the Caucasus and Central Asia – Armenia, Georgia, Kyrgyzstan, and Tadzhikistan – have joined the ranks of the World Bank's middle-income economies and face problems common with the developing world. The two Slavic states of Belarus and Ukraine, plus Moldova, face particular problems in terms of their location between the EU and Russia. All three are important transit states, but the EU is ambivalent about extending membership to them beyond the creation of the Eastern Partnership, and Russia is adamant that it will improve its gas-transit security by circumventing them. Russia itself occupies a special position as the most significant economy amongst the post-socialist states and a would-be emerging economy through the notion of the BRICS (discussed in the next chapter). Russia also carries the deepest imprint of the centrally planned economy and remains an energy-intensive economy reliant on the export of oil and gas, alongside other natural resources and energy-intensive goods. Russia vies with Saudi Arabia as the largest exporter of oil and is the largest producer and exporter of natural gas. At the same time, it is a major emitter of GHGs, yet its forests provide an ecosystem service on a global scale. It remains skeptical about the Kyoto process, as it does not wish to compromise its future economic growth, which is likely to remain carbon intensive.

Perhaps the most important issue for this group of countries is not where they have come from, but where they are going. As time passes, their status as post-socialist states becomes less and less relevant. For those who are members of the EU, their future energy and climate trajectories will be determined within the framework of EU strategy. The key challenge will be to recover from recession and sustain improvements in living standards without aggravating energy security concerns and increasing carbon emissions. The energy-exporting states will remain integrated into the global economy through their role as suppliers of oil and gas; they continue to be courted by energy-importing states, and they are already suffering from the political and economic pathologies often associated with being resource rich. The resource-poor states of the region – particularly in the Caucasus and Central Asia – have become part of the global periphery and are only loosely integrated into the global economy. As ever, it is Russia that presents the greatest degree of uncertainty. As discussed above, Russia stands at the crossroads, it could follow a path of diversification and modernization that would promote energy efficiency and conservation, while also reducing the energy and carbon intensity of the economy and preserving an exportable surplus of oil and gas without the need for expensive frontier oil and gas development. Unfortunately, all the signs are that under President Putin it will be business as usual and Russia will continue along an energy- and carbon-intensive path of development that will not only fail to meet the material needs of its population, but will also compromise its status as a major oil and gas exporter. This means that it will also remain hostile to a future global agreement on climate change.

In the context of the current analysis, post-socialism mattered because of the desire to understand the changed relationship between energy security, economic development, and climate change over the more than 20 years since the collapse of the Soviet Union; however, it does not matter when looking forward over the next 20 years. During that time, each of the post-socialist states will find its position amongst the ranks of the developed, emerging, or developing economies.

CHAPTER FIVE

Fueling Growth
Energy Dilemmas in the Emerging Economies

Introduction

This chapter deals with a group of countries whose rapid economic growth over the past two decades has played a major part in the global shift in energy demand described in chapter 2. Furthermore, these countries will contribute the bulk of the projected future growth in energy demand and GHG emissions. Eight of the countries in the group are part of the G20 whose membership accounts for 90 percent of global GDP, 80 percent of international trade, and 80 percent of fossil fuel CO_2 emission. The acronym BRIC – Brazil, Russia, India, and China – is most commonly used to define the core members of the so-called emerging economies. The notion of the BRICs came from Goldman Sachs (O'Neill 2001) and it has become accepted shorthand for a group of emerging economies that have the potential to become a major force in the global economy. An alternative grouping is BASIC – Brazil, South Africa, India, and China – which has greater traction in terms of climate-change policy as it stands for a group that has adopted a common position in the post-Kyoto climate negotiations (Hallding et al. 2011). For that reason, a project at the Stockholm Environment Institute on "Emerging Economies and Climate Change" also uses the BASIC grouping. The same group of countries has also been the subject of analysis as the so-called "Southern Engines" of growth, which refers to their role as the key drivers of growth in the global South, and the acronym CIBS is used to describe them (Santos-Paulino and Wan 2010). Finally, the IEA (2011a: 19) has used the term "BRICS" to refer to Brazil, Russia, India, China, and South Africa, a group of emerging economies that are changing the regional demand for energy. As they note, in 2009, together these five countries accounted for 33 percent of global energy use and 37 percent of the CO_2 emissions from energy use. According to IEA (2011e: 48–56) data, the BRICS group alone accounted for 40.4 percent of global population, 29.5 percent of global GDP (PPP), and 27.3 percent of total primary energy supply. While the bulk of the analysis in this chapter is devoted to the BASIC group (for reasons discussed later the CIBS acronym is employed), the analytical framework described in chapter 2 employs a wider notion of "emerging economies."

The countries that are classified in this group are listed in table 5.1, which presents their "Kaya Characteristics." As the data make clear, this is a heterogeneous group that includes in it very large emerging economies, both in terms of territory and population, on the one hand (China, India, Indonesia, and the Philippines), and micro- and city-states, on the other hand (Bahrain, Singapore, Qatar, and UEA). Their very high levels of per capita income distinguish the latter, while in the case of the former the per capita levels are low, but the absolute levels are high due to the size of their populations and the structure of their economies. In the case of the small economies, the variation in CO_2 emissions identifies those economies that are more developed – Singapore and Taiwan – and those that are major energy producers: Bahrain, Brunei, Kuwait, Qatar, and UAE. There is far less variation when it comes to energy intensity and the carbon intensity of energy use. Inclusion in this group of countries reflects not only their economic performance and energy dynamics since 1990, but also their potential to become major drivers of energy demand and GHG emissions over the next 20–30 years.

According to data from the CAIT database, this group's share of global emissions has risen from 23.7 percent of the global total in 1990 to 38.6 percent in 2007, and its share of energy use from 22.1 percent in 1990 to 34.5 percent in 2008. One could debate the inclusion of particular countries in this group and the exclusion of others, but, as we shall see below, the reality is that it is really only China and, to a lesser degree, India that are currently driving the global impact of this group. Figure 5.1 charts the relationship between energy consumption and GDP per capita. Because of the degree of variation between the countries and the presence of some extreme outliers, a log scale has been used in relation to energy consumption per capita.

From the chart in figure 5.1, it is possible to identify three groups of countries. In the bottom left-hand corner we have the large less-developed members of the group; their per capita measures are low but because of their size their absolute share of population, economy, and energy is high. The second group in the middle chart is the most significant as it contains the majority of the dynamic economies that are driving growth. But this is a diverse group, with China having lower energy consumption and income per capita measures, while its sheer size makes it the key driver. This group includes two OECD member-states, Turkey and Mexico, and the latter is also involved in a free-trade agreement with the US and Canada – NAFTA. Additionally, the graph highlights the variation that exists within the CIBS group. The final group in the top right-hand corner consists of the high-energy and high-income economies; here Saudi Arabia is the outlier as all the others are small states with high incomes and/or high levels of energy consumption due to their role as energy exporters. This chapter focuses on those members of the emerging economies group that currently exert the greatest pressure on global energy supplies and that are major sources of GHG emissions. The chapter is organized in the following manner. The next section examines the current status

TABLE 5.1 The Kaya characteristics of the emerging economies

	CO_2 per capita 2007	Population (,000s) 2010	GNI Per capita 2009	Energy intensity 2008	Carbon intensity of energy use 2008
Bahrain	29.6	807.1	***33,530	2.7	2.43
Brazil	1.9	194,945.0	10,410	7.39	1.59
Brunei – Darussalam	19.7	407.1	48,760	**5.56	2.15
Chile	4.3	17,134.3	13,260	7.16	2.39
China	5.0	1,338,300.0	6,860	3.58	3.43
Hong Kong	5.8	7,041.3	44,270	19.30	n.d.
India	1.4	1,170,938.0	3,260	5.10	2.37
Indonesia	1.8	232,516.8	4,030	4.22	2.10
Kuwait	32.3	2,863.0	*48,900	**4.81	4.81
Malaysia	7.3	27,914.0	13,650	4.89	2.60
Mexico	4.5	108,523.0	14,200	7.91	2.54
Philippines	0.8	93,616.8	3,070	7.13	1.97
Qatar	55.4	1,508.3	*155,400	4.46	2.50
Saudi Arabia	16.6	25,988.9	23,900	3.33	2.48
Singapore	11.8	5,140.3	49,430	12.54	1.68
South Africa	9.0	49,963.2	10,010	3.48	2.62
Taiwan	12.5	*23,071.2	*32,300	n.d	n.d.
Thailand	4.1	68,139.2	7,650	4.69	2.34
Turkey	4.0	75,705.2	13,480	8.93	2.90
UAE	31.0	4,707.3	*49800	4.16	2.68

*data from CIA World Factbook.
**data for 2007.
***data for 2008.
See table 3.1 for an explanation of the variables.

Source: World Bank Development Indicators Database and CAIT.

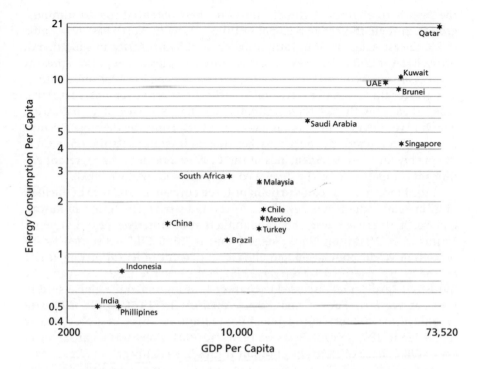

Source: CAIT.

Figure 5.1 The relationship between energy consumption and GDP per capita, 2007

and dynamics of the CIBS group. There then follows a more detailed analysis of energy security challenges that face China and the strategies being adopted to address them. The final section turns to the energy dilemmas facing the group's major energy exporter, namely, Saudi Arabia, which needs to constrain domestic-energy demand growth to maintain its exportable surplus of crude oil. A failure to do so would have dramatic implications for global energy security. The conclusion turns to the Kaya characteristics of the group and the major challenges that they present in terms of energy security and climate-change policy.

Fueling the "Southern Engines of Growth"

Just as this group more generally contains a variety of "types" of economy, so the members of CIBS are quite different from one another. The common denominator of the group is their relative weight and dynamism in both continental and, in the case of India and China, global terms. The concept of the "Southern engines of growth" refers to their potential role to stimulate growth in their respective regional settings: China in North-East Asia, India in South-East Asia, Brazil in Latin America, and South Africa in sub-Saharan Africa (Nayyar 2008). Their exact role is more complex as they also represent major sources of competition from export markets and FDI for one another, and also for the developing economies in their respective regions. At a global scale, their growth has been facilitated by the processes of globalization which have provided substantial amounts of FDI from the developed economies, which are also the major markets for their exports. At the same time, the energy and resource demands of the CIBS economies now represent significant competition for the developed economies (Rowthorn 2006).

As the literature is at pains to point out, the current ascendance of the likes of China and India is not new. Prior to the Industrial Revolution in Europe and North America, it was China and India that dominated world commerce. Estimates by Maddison (2003) suggest that in 1820 CIBS accounted for 57 percent of world population and almost 50 percent of world income (these estimates are also used by Nayyar 2008: 2–3). Over the next 150 years, the Industrial Revolution, discussed in chapter 1, brought about a global shift in favor of Western Europe and North America. In 1973, while CIBS still accounted for 40.5 percent of global population, its share of global income had fallen to 10.8 percent. Between 1973 and 2001, there was a partial recovery in CIBS' share of global income, but things have really gathered pace over the last decade. Table 5.2 provides more recent information on the changing global role of CIBS in terms of the key indicators that drive energy demand and carbon emissions.

The data for table 5.2 are taken from the World Bank's Development Indicators database and use a purchasing parity measure of GDP whereby the exchange rate is based on a basket of goods approach, rather than market rates. According to these data, CIBS' share of global GDP has increased from 14.3 percent in 2000 to just over 20 percent in 2008. The global economic crisis has served to accelerate this trend as the CIBS economies have fared much better than those of the developed world. World Bank data suggest that CIBS share of global GDP increased to 21.7 percent in 2009 and 22.6 percent in 2010. All of the projections suggest that the emerging economies will continue to grow at a faster rate and this is the central tenet of the Goldman Sach's view of the BRICs; in their 2003 analysis, they suggested that China's economy could be larger than the US by 2041, and India's economy larger than Japan's by 2032 (Wilson and Purushothaman 2003: 3). Current trends suggest that these milestones might be reached sooner than initially anticipated. The figures in parentheses show the role of China and make it clear that it is responsible for more than half of the economic growth in CIBS over the past decade. The key question for this chapter is what are the implications of the rapid economic growth of the CIBS for global energy security and climate-change concerns? As the data in table 5.2 make clear, the rate of

TABLE 5.2 The changing global role of CIBS, 2000–2008 (percentage of global total)

	2000	2005	2007	2008	CIBS % change 2000–8
Energy use (KT of oil equivalent)	19.1 (11.2)	23.2 (15.2)	25.1 (16.8)	26.3 (17.8)	69.0 (93.4)
Total CO₂ emissions (KT)	21.4 (13.8)	26.8 (19.5)	29.4 (21.7)	29.9 (21.9)	81.5 (106.5)
Total population	41.1 (20.8)	40.7 (20.2)	40.6 (19.9)	40.5 (19.8)	8.3 (4.9)
GDP, PPP (constant 2005 $)	14.3 (7.0)	17.3 (9.4)	19.2 (10.9)	20.1 (11.6)	89.5 (124.7)

Figures in () are for China only.

Source: World Bank Development Indicators Database.

growth of energy use and CO_2 emissions is even higher than that of GDP, particularly so in the case of China, which suggests a more energy- and carbon-intensive pattern of economic development.

The Kaya Identity tells us that the key issues we should be concerned with are population size and rate of increase, economic output and rate of increase, energy intensity and the carbon intensity of energy use. Table 5.1 provides a snapshot of information relating to these issues, but we should pay most attention to their dynamics, as it is the recent and potential future contribution of CIBS to global energy demand and carbon emissions that are of particular concern. When it comes to population, China and India stand out as global giants, both with a population of over 1 billion people; Brazil and South Africa lag a long way behind with 195 and 50 million respectively. In combination, in 2010 the CIBS group had a population of 2.75 billion people, which is just about 40 percent of the world's population. As table 5.2 shows, the group's share of the global population is actually declining as population growth rates slow relative to the developing world. Figure 5.2 shows the UN population projection (medium variant) for CIBS countries to 2050.

This figure illustrates the relative weight of China and India, which have both experienced rapid rates of population growth; however, China's aggressive population-control measures and the impact of modernization have reduced its fertility rate. The UN's medium-variant projection to 2050 suggests that China's population should peak around the 1.4 billion mark in the middle of the next decade and then fall back to 1.3 billion by 2050. The situation in India is quite different as its population is projected to continue to grow at a rapid rate. As we shall see, India is behind China in terms of its

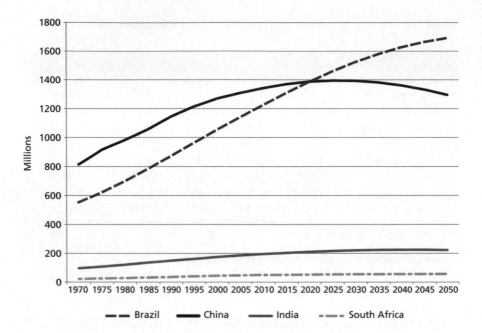

Source: UN Department of Economic and Social Affairs, Population Division, World Population Prospects, the 2010 Revision.

Figure 5.2 Population growth in CIBS, 1970–2050

stage of economic development, and its demographic characteristics are more akin to the developing world. As a result, India's population will pass that of China's in the middle of the next decade and will continue to grow, reaching nearly 1.7 billion by 2050. Both Brazil and South Africa show relatively stable populations with low rates of increase, and in both cases population growth is not a key variable driving energy demand and carbon emissions. In the case of China it is the size of the population, rather than its future growth, that is the key factor as it is the levels per capita of income and consumption that will drive future demand for energy. In the case of India, population growth and income and consumption are all key factors.

Arnal and Förster (2010: 22) point out that the main challenge to CIBS has been to increase employment quickly enough to match the growth of the labor force. According to their analysis: "In the period since 1993, the labour force population aged 15–64 increased on average by 7 million people each year in China, by almost 6 million in India, by around 2 million in Brazil and by 300,000 in South Africa." Fortunately, both India and China have achieved high rates of GDP growth. According to World Bank data (2011c: 195–6), in the period 1990–2000 China recorded an annual average rate of GDP growth of 10.9 percent, a level that it maintained in the 2000–9 period; India's growth in the 1990–2000 period was 5.9 percent and this accelerated to 7.9 percent in the 2000–9 period. By comparison, Brazil and South Africa recorded less impressive rates for growth: for Brazil, 2.7 percent in the 1990–2000 period and 3.6 percent in the 2000–9 period; for South Africa, a rather sluggish 2.1 percent in 1990–2000, when the country was dealing with the collapse of the apartheid system, and a more impressive 4.1 percent in the 2000–9 period. By comparison, the high-income economies recorded growth rates of 2.7 percent in 1999–2000 and 2.0 percent in 2000–9. As a result, the relative weight of CIBS in the global economy has changed significantly, as shown in table 5.2. Data for 2009–10 show that while the CIBS economies were impacted by the global financial crisis that started in 2008, they rebounded quickly, but the sustainability of these high growth rates must be in question given their reliance on the capital investment and purchasing power of the developed economies that are still suffering from stagnation. The IMF's (2012: 2) *World Economic Outlook* projections reflect these concerns, as China's growth rate is forecast at 8.2 percent in 2012 and 8.8 percent in 2013; India's at 7.0 percent and 7.3 percent; Brazil 3.0 percent and 4.0 percent; and South Africa 2.5 percent and 3.4 percent.

It is worth remembering that if an economy grows by 10 percent a year, as China's has for the last two decades, then the compound nature of that growth means that the economy doubles in size in seven years, at 7.0 percent, which is close to what India has achieved, doubling every 10 years, and, at 5 percent, doubling every 14 years (Nayyar 2008: 7). This puts in perspective the relative rates of growth within the CIBS group. The relationship between the rate of population growth and the rate of economic growth is reflected in the measure of GDP per capita. Table 5.3 presents data on the dynamics of per capita income and figure 5.3 shows changes in UNDP's Human Development Index for the CIBS group. It is noteworthy that in 1980 China had a lower level of GDP per capita than India, but it passed India during the 1990s and now has a level that is more than twice that of India.

The relative levels of GDP per capita and the trends in the HDI reflect both the recent fortunes of the individual CIBS countries and their relative levels of economic development. The rapid growth of China is very apparent, as is the relative underdevelopment of India. The higher levels of GDP per capita in Brazil and South Africa reflect their smaller populations and lower levels of population increase relative to their rates of growth. In 1980, both were relatively mature economies with higher levels of GDP per capita and their growth rates have not been that spectacular over the last 30 years. The UNDP defines the HDI as "a composite index measuring average achievement in three basic dimensions of human development – a long and healthy life, knowledge and a decent standard of living." In all four cases there have been improvements in the index over the last 30 years, though, as noted above,

TABLE 5.3 Change in per capita income in the CIBS group, 1980–2010 (GDP per capita, PPP (constant 2005 international $))

	1980	1990	2000	2010	Change 1990–2000	Change 2000–2010
Brazil	7,566.5	7,174.8	7,909.1	10,055.9	10.2	27.1
China	524.0	1,100.7	2,667.5	6,816.3	142.4	155.5
India	895.4	1,243.6	1,769.2	3,213.5	42.3	81.6
South Africa	8,762.6	7,974.7	7,641.0	9,477.1	–4.2	24.0
CIBS average	4,437.1	4,373.4	4,996.7	7,390.7	14.3	47.9
OECD	18,768.5	24,889.0	30,418.4	33,423.7	22.2	9.9
World	5,793.6	6,818.0	7,899.3	9,892.3	15.9	25.2
Ratios						
CIBS to OECD	0.24	0.18	0.16	0.22		
CIBS to World	0.77	0.64	0.63	0.75		

Source: World Bank Development Indicators Database.

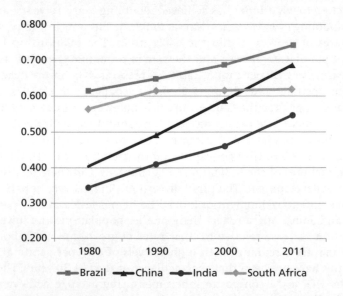

Source: United Nations Development Programme *Human Development Reports.*

Figure 5.3 *Trends in the Human Development Index of CIBS, 1980–2011*

South Africa struggled during the 1990s and more recently has had the challenge of HIV/AIDS to deal with. Interestingly, the trends suggest that the gap between China and India is widening. This view is also supported by data on extreme poverty, which is measured as the percentage of the total population living on less than $1.25 a day (PPP). Data from the World Bank show that, in 1990, in China 60.8 percent of the total population lived in extreme poverty, and in India the level was 53.6 percent. By 2010, the situation had changed dramatically: in China only 15.9 percent were living in extreme poverty and in India the level was still high at 41.6 percent. In fact, China's economic growth has had a global impact on the levels of extreme poverty. Measures like GDP per capita fail to capture the level of inequality between individuals in society and between regions in a national economy. The UNDP provides information on the Income GINI coefficient (where 0 equals absolute equality and 100 equals absolute inequality): the figure reported for Brazil is 53.9, China 41.5, India 36.8, and South Africa 57.8. The lower level for India reflects the fact that the vast majority of the population lives on low incomes in rural areas. These measures serve as a reality check; while the levels of economic growth are impressive, the population pressure is such that the CIBS countries as a group have not closed the gap relative to the most developed economies. That does not mean that the last 30 years have not delivered a dramatic transformation in the economies of CIBS.

Analysis of the changing economic structure of the CIBS economies makes clear the scale of the transformation that has taken place, as well as the different role each of the countries in the group plays in the global economy. The data in table 5.4 provide some sense of the structural change that has been taking place, but it remains the case that agriculture is an important source of employment in the larger CIBS economies. Arnal and Förster (2010: 25) report that while agriculture only accounts for 10 percent of the workforce in Brazil and South Africa, it remains responsible for 40 percent of

TABLE 5.4 Structure of GDP in CIBS, 1995 and 2009 (Percentage of GDP)

	Agriculture		Industry		Manufacturing		Services	
	1995	2009	1995	2009	1995	2009	1995	2009
Brazil	6	6	28	25	19	16	67	69
China	20	10	47	46	34	34	33	43
India	26	18	28	27	18	15	46	55
South Africa	4	3	35	31	21	15	61	66
Middle income	14	10	35	35	23	21	51	55

Source: World Bank (2011c), *2011 Development Indicators,* Washington, DC: World Bank, 198–200.

employment in China and 56 percent in India; furthermore, both China and India are characterized by a large excess of labor in their rural areas and rural poverty remains a major problem. The level of urbanization also reflects these distinctions. In 2008, only 29.5 percent of the population in India lived in urban settlements, and in China the level was 43.1 percent; but in South Africa it was 60.7 percent, and in Brazil 85.6 percent. The four economies also play rather different roles in the global economy. China is by far the largest supplier of labor-intensive manufactured goods; India is significant in this area, but has also experienced rapid growth of its service sector; and both Brazil and South Africa are important suppliers of raw materials and resource-based manufactures. Furthermore, China's export profile shows that it is moving up the value chain and is now exporting more skills-intensive and high-technology products. This is also reflected in the structure of its imports that increasingly comprise components for high-technology products that are assembled in China. India's exports are also skills led, though more in the service economy than manufacturing. Interestingly, both Brazil and South Africa are playing an increasing role in supplying China and India with raw materials (Beeson et al. 2011).

Over the past 20 years, China has experienced a period of rapid economic restructuring driven by export-oriented growth that has brought about a dramatic transformation in its role and standing in the global economy. India has embarked on a similar journey, but it is still lagging somewhat and is following a different route. In 2004, India's service sector accounted for 22 percent of employment, but produced 50 percent of the economy's value added. The problem for India is its vast rural population that is unable to benefit from service-sector growth. This means that India may yet have to turn to labor-intensive manufacturing to promote greater equality of opportunity. Over the same time period, Brazil and South Africa have remained relatively stable in terms of their role in the global economy, although in the case of Brazil there are signs that this is about to change thanks to the expansion of biofuels and offshore oil production. All of these changes have implications for both national and global energy security and climate policy. As is clear from previous analysis, factors such as the rates of population and economic growth, economic structure, and the level of urbanization exert a strong influence on the level of energy intensity in an economy and its change over time.

The dynamics of energy intensity in CIBS reflect the earlier patterns relating to population change and economic growth. Both Brazil and South Africa are relatively static, though Brazil's economy is much more efficient at turning energy into economic output. In this case, South Africa's dependence on its extractive industries explains the lower levels of GDP produced per unit of energy consumed. Both China and India have experienced substantial improvements in the energy intensities of their economies. The specifics of the Chinese case are explained later; in India's case, the significance of the

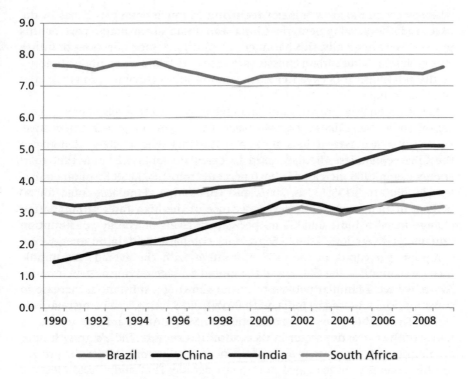

Source: World Bank Developments Indicators Database.

Figure 5.4 Change in energy intensity in CIBS, 1990–2009 (GDP per unit of energy use (constant 2005 PPP $ per kg of oil equivalent)

service sector helps to explain why its energy intensity has stayed above that of China. As table 5.2 shows, overall the rate of growth in energy use between 2000 and 2008 was lower than the rate of growth of GDP, which signifies an improving trend in terms of the amount of GDP produced per unit of energy consumed. Rühl et al. (2011: 11) note that more generally between 1970 and 2009 the share of non-OECD manufacturing output rose by 7 percent, while energy intensity declined by 23 percent over that same period (here they are referring to the amount of energy consumed per unit of output, which has the opposite signal to figure 5.4). As they also point out, these numbers include the impact of the post-socialist transitional recession that was discussed in the previous chapter. Setting that aside, they maintain that while China accounted for most of the increase in the share of the industrial sector in non-OECD growth, it also contributed to the improvement in energy intensity through the growth of high valued-added production in its export industries. They suggest that globalization is driving a process of convergence whereby economic growth is not requiring as much energy as it has in the past, and the developments in China and India are a major part of this process. More generally, this has major implications for projections of future energy demand and carbon emissions, as they are based on an understanding of the relationship between energy demand and economic growth in the OECD economies.

As with economic growth rates, changes in per capita levels of energy consumption in the CIBS economies place the region in global perspective. Equally, it is necessary to look at the absolute increases in energy demand in the CIBS economies. The data used to calculate table 5.2 show that total energy use in CIBS increased by 69.0 percent from 1,855,638 KT of oil equivalent in 2000 to 3,135,132 in 2008, and that China alone accounted for 80 percent of that increase. However, because of the high rates of population change in both India and China per capita levels of energy consumption remain relatively low. Table 5.5 presents comparative data on energy consumption per capita in the CIBS economies with the average for middle income economies, the OECD, and the global average serving as benchmarks. Again, we see a familiar pattern of China showing a substantial increase in consumption, followed by India, with Brazil and South Africa being relatively stable. The higher level of consumption in South Africa reflects the dominance of the extractive sector in its economic structure. India's growth rates are in line with the average for middle-income economies, while the growth in China seems to have surged in the past decade. That said, China's level of per capita energy consumption in 2009 was still below the global average. In 1980, China's level of consumption was only 14.7 percent of the OECD average, but in 2009 it had increased to 29.2 percent. China's surge in energy consumption to date has been driven in large part by its export-oriented

TABLE 5.5 Trends in per capita energy consumption in CIBS, 1980–2009 (kg of oil equivalent)

	1980	1990	2000	2009	Change 1980–2000	Change 2000–09
Brazil	935.5	937.2	1084.5	1242.8	15.9	14.6
China	609.9	760.2	867.1	1695.3	42.2	95.5
India	298.5	372.9	450.0	585.0	50.8	30.0
South Africa	2368.2	2666.9	2599.8	2920.5	9.8	12.3
Middle income	603.3	1025.5	958.0	1268.0	58.8	32.4
OECD	4146.7	4245.3	4590.7	4261.6	10.7	−7.2
World	1457.1	1669.3	1649.0	1802.6	13.2	9.3

Source: World Bank Development Indicators Database.

industrial expansion, rather than personal consumption. But as personal incomes increase so there is huge potential for an additional surge in energy demand. The key issue then becomes how that demand can be met and what that will mean for GHG emissions.

The final issue to consider here is the carbon intensity of energy use. Again, there are significant differences between the countries in the CIBS group. Table 5.6 shows total primary energy consumption by fuel in 2011. Renewable production of electricity is included, but not biofuels as they are a secondary source.

From table 5.6 it is clear that Brazil is an outlier in terms of the structure of its energy mix. First, it has the highest level of reliance upon oil, but it is a significant producer of crude oil, with 90 percent of production coming from deep-water offshore fields in the Campos Basin. Oil-consumption growth is flat and with increasing domestic production Brazil became a net exporter of oil in 2009. Natural gas plays a modest role, with domestic production associated with oilfields and imports coming by pipeline from Bolivia and, most recently, from LNG with two regasification terminals being constructed in the last few years. Brazil also has two nuclear power plants with plans to build more; however, it is hydroelectric power that dominates the power-generation mix. In 2008, Brazil had 104 GW of installed electricity-generating capacity with 84 percent of production coming from hydroelectricity, and two new large plants are planned. Brazil is also the world's second largest producer of ethanol, after the United States. Although Brazil does export ethanol, most of its sugarcane-based production is used domestically and is blended with gasoline to fuel the vehicle fleet. More than half of the vehicles on the road are flexi-fuel which means that they can run on 100 percent ethanol or an ethanol-gasoline mixture (20–25 percent ethanol). The EU is already a market for biofuel exports and with the US market now open to imported ethanol, there are plans to expand exports. A combination of reliance upon hydroelectric power and the use of ethanol means that the

TABLE 5.6 CIBS total primary-energy consumption by fuel, 2011 (percentage of total consumption)

	Oil	Natural gas	Coal	Nuclear energy	Hydro-electricity	Renew-ables
Brazil	45.2	9.0	5.2	1.3	36.4	2.8
South Africa	20.7	3.0	73.6	2.3	0.3	0.1
China	17.7	4.5	70.4	0.7	6.0	0.7
India	29.0	9.8	52.9	1.3	5.3	1.6

Source: BP (2012b), *BP Statistical Review of World Energy June 2011*, London: BP, p. 41.

level of carbon emissions from fuel combustion is relatively low and Brazil only accounts for 1.2 percent of global CO_2 from fuel combustion (IEA 2011e: 20). The carbon intensity of energy use is also low at 1.59 tCO_2/toe (CAIT). There are also plans to produce electricity from sugarcane biomass waste, providing another source of low-carbon energy. In sum, it seems that Brazil plans to meet future energy demand through a combination of expanded hydroelectric power, more nuclear power, an expansion of ethanol and biomass production, and an increase in natural gas, both from domestic sources and LNG. This suggests that future increases in oil production will be aimed at satisfying export markets in the US and Europe, a model that is very similar to that of Norway. Thus, domestic-energy demand growth should not be a source of substantial emissions growth; the problem for Brazil is that it is the third largest GHG emitter because of its agriculture, land-use and forestry activities that are resulting in significant land-use change in the Amazon region.

The other three CIBS countries have far more in common with each other when it comes to their energy mix and the carbon intensity of energy use. In all three cases, fossil fuels dominate the energy mix and coal plays a particularly important role in China and South Africa. China is now the second largest oil importer after the United States, having surpassed Japan in 2009. It is also the largest producer and consumer of coal in the world. India is the fourth largest energy consumer in the world and the third largest producer and consumer of coal. South Africa cannot match the standing of these two energy giants, but as a legacy of the apartheid period and the associated trade in embargo it does have a highly developed synthetic fuels industry and has the world's largest gas-to-liquids plant at Mossel Bay in the Western Cape. The synthetic fuels industry uses imported pipeline gas from Mozambique and domestic coal as its feedstock, and its refining industry is designed to handle heavy oils; all of which results in a high level of carbon intensity of energy use. In China, in 2008, the carbon intensity of energy use was 3.40 tCO_2/toe, up from 2.41 in 1990, in India it was 2.44, up from 1.47 in 1990, but in South Africa it was 2.56 in 2008, which was actually down from 3.35. This likely reflects improvements in the quality of imported oil as a result of the end of the trade embargo. In all three instances the national energy system is struggling to keep up with rapidly growing demand for energy, particularly electricity and domestic fossil-fuel production that has been unable to match demand, resulting in growing import dependence. In South Africa domestic coal dominates the power-generation mix, with 94 percent of electricity being generated from coal in 2009. At present, South Africa accounts for 40 percent of total CO_2 emissions from fuel combustion from energy in Africa, but only 1 percent of the global total (IEA 2011e: 25). However, to meet future demand growth without substantially increasing emissions will require the application of CCS technologies to its thermal power stations and the development of nuclear and renewable power-generation capacity. The current level of electrification is 75 percent, by far the highest in sub-Saharan Africa, but this is a combination of 88 percent penetration in urban areas, with only 55 percent of rural areas having access to electricity (IEA 2011e: 26). Thus, energy poverty remains a barrier to economic prosperity. Similar problems exist in India, but on a much larger scale. Today, India emits more than 5 percent of global CO_2 emissions from fuel combustion and the level of emissions more than tripled between 1990 and 2009. The electricity and heat sector accounted for 54 percent of emissions in 2009, and in that year 69 percent of electricity came from coal, a further 12 percent from natural gas, and 3 percent from oil (IEA 2011e: 23). That said, a large share of India's population do not have access to modern energy services and still rely on traditional renewable and biomass sources. According to the EIA's (2011d: 1) *Country Analysis Brief of India*, more than 800 million Indian households are still using traditional biomass sources for cooking. According to World Bank data, in 2009 only 66.3 percent of households in India had access to electricity, compared to 99.4 percent in China (this is an issue that is discussed in greater detail in the next chapter).

South Africa has very limited domestic reserves of oil and gas and is thus heavily reliant on imports. In 2010, it imported 67 percent of its oil consumption, mainly from OPEC countries (EIA 2011e: 3). Both China and India are substantial oil and gas producers in their own right, the problem being that domestic demand far outstrips production and is growing more quickly than domestic production, which results in increasing levels of import dependence. This means that energy security is a major concern of national energy strategy and every measure is being taken to expand domestic production, as well as secure privileged access to foreign reserves. This is an issue that is explored in more detail below. China even has to import coal because soaring demand has outstretched the capacity of the railway system to deliver coal from producing regions to the centers of demand. In such circumstances, it is no surprise that both China and India have ambitious plans to develop renewable power generation, but these can only make a modest contribution given the rate of demand growth. In both countries, natural gas currently plays a modest role and it is likely that gas imports will increase in the future, both by pipeline from neighboring states and as LNG. The latter is a more expensive option that faces stiff competition from established consumers such as Japan and South Korea. It is also possible that unconventional gas production, both from coal-bed methane and shale gas, could increase domestic production. Given the pressure to increase energy production to fuel continued economic growth, it is unlikely that the consumption of carbon-intensive fossil fuels will actually decline any time soon, but what is necessary is that as much as possible of the future incremental growth should be met by low-carbon sources, otherwise the carbon intensity of energy use and the absolute levels of carbon emissions will continue to increase.

Given all that has been said about the trends in both total energy demand and the carbon intensity of energy use in the CIBS countries, it is not surprising that they pose a major challenge for the global climate-change policymakers. For the national governments of these countries, providing secure and affordable access to modern energy services is essential to their continued economic growth, which in turn is essential to meet the expectations of their people who wish to benefit from their country's growing economic prosperity. The energy-exporting countries face a particular challenge as their economic prosperity is currently tied to securing an acceptable price for their hydrocarbon exports. Longer term, the global-demand destruction associated with the transition to a low-carbon energy system could compromise their current economic-growth model. For all of the economies in this group, the dilemma then is how to sustain economic growth, which is essential for political stability, without further aggravating social and environmental problems at both a national and global scale.

China: Securing Energy for the Workshop of the World

For China's ruling elite in the Communist Party, securing access to energy supplies is critical to keeping the social contract between themselves and the Chinese people. This is because continued economic growth is essential to deliver the improvement in living standards and that growth is dependent upon secure and reliable access to ever-increasing levels of energy services. As discussed above, over the last 20 years China has experienced a dramatic societal transformation, as rapid economic growth has been fueled by industrialization and urbanization; this in turn has resulted in the Chinese economy outstripping the ability of the domestic-energy system to satisfy demand. Like the United States, China is a major energy producer; according to the IEA (2011d), in 2010 it ranked fifth in terms of oil production with 5.0 percent of global output, seventh in terms of gas production with 3.0 percent of global output, and first in terms of coal output, with 51 percent global hard-coal output. China has substantial coal reserves and, as noted earlier, coal accounts for the majority of its primary energy consumption. The domestic coal industry has been subject to significant restructuring which has sought to close or consolidate small inefficient mines and improve the productivity, environmental, and safety records of mining (Shen et al. 2012). Efforts are also being made to improve the efficiency of coal-fired power generation. As noted earlier, the sheer scale of domestic coal consumption and the location of production relative to demand requires China to import coal to supply the coastal regions. China became a net coal importer in 2009, but coal imports are not considered a threat to China's energy security, as they are modest – accounting for 6 percent of total coal consumption in 2011 (BP 2012a: 37) – and there are multiple sources of supply in relative proximity to China. At present, Indonesia, Australia, Vietnam, and Russia are the major sources of coal imports. In 2009, China imported 126 million tons of coal and this accounted for 15 percent of the global coal trade. Since then, there has been a surge in China's coal imports, which reached 182 million tons in 2011, making China the world's top coal importer ahead of Japan. Increasing imports are seen as a means of closing down inefficient and environmentally damaging domestic production, but the growth of Chinese coal imports will also have a significant impact on the global coal industry (Tu and Johnson-Resier 2012).

By comparison, natural gas is relatively underdeveloped in China, although the government has plans to increase its share in the energy mix to 10 percent by 2020. To do this, the domestic price of gas will have to be increased to stimulate production and it will be necessary to encourage households to switch to gas. The pipeline infrastructure will also need to be expanded to create a larger market. An import pipeline has already been constructed to move gas from Turkmenistan, and its capacity is being doubled to supply 60 bcm a year, while a pipeline is also being completed from Myanmar to supply 17 bcm a year. At the same time, a series of LNG terminals has been built to supply the coastal regions with gas for power generation and more are planned. There is also the possibility of significant imports of pipeline gas from Russia, but the two sides cannot agree a price, among other things (Jakobson et al. 2011; Paik et al. 2012). The Chinese government does not see gas as presenting an energy security problem; this is because gas is largely used in the power-generation sector and there are other fuels that can substitute should supplies be interrupted. However, the increased use of gas is an important part of the strategy to reduce the carbon intensity of energy use because if increased gas consumption can reduce the growth of coal in power generation it can contribute to the decarbonization of the power sector, along with nuclear power and renewables. Gas consumption in China quadrupled between 2000 and 2010, and current estimates suggest that gas demand in China will grow at 6 percent a year over the next 25 years (O'Hara and Lai 2011: 504). Meeting this demand will require a substantial increase in domestic production from both conventional sources and unconventional sources – coal-bed methane and shale gas; it will also require substantial imports such as LNG from the Asia-Pacific and Middle East, and by pipeline from Central Asia, Myanmar, and potentially Russia. For the moment, it seems that China has contracted sufficient imports to meet its immediate needs, so the scale of future imports, and thus China's impact on global gas markets, will be determined by the rate of growth of domestic gas demand and the development of domestic gas production.

It is oil that is seen as the Achilles' heel when it comes to China's energy security. China became a net importer of crude oil in 1993, and since then demand has grown much faster than production as China's major oil-producing fields have passed their peak and the domestic industry has struggled to develop new production (see figure 5.5). It is hoped that new offshore

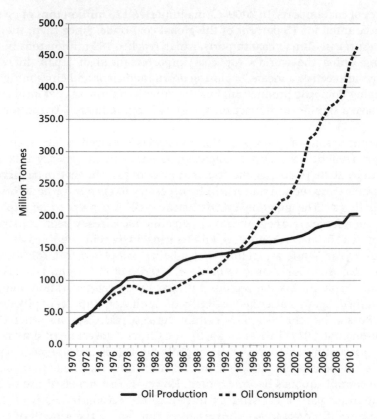

Source: BP (2012) *BP Statistical Review of World Energy June 2012*. London: BP, pp. 9–10.

Figure 5.5 China's oil production and consumption, 1970–2011

production will compensate for falling onshore production. China is also aggressively asserting its territorial claims in the South China Sea, as the contested regions have considerable oil and gas potential. However, China has had no alternative but to increase its level of oil imports. Rapid demand growth has come mainly from the transportation sector as a result of the dieselization of the railway system, the growth of internal air travel, and the growth in car ownership and urban transportation systems (Leung et al. 2011: 485–6). Thus, it is the increased mobility of China's population, plus the expectation of growing car ownership that make it difficult to slow the growth of oil demand. China is now the largest car market in the world and private ownership is seen as a symbol of growing prosperity. Not surprisingly, the Chinese government wants to ensure that most of these new cars are built in China and that they are as energy efficient as possible.

China's "Going out Strategy"

The focal point of China's energy-security strategy is ensuring a "reliable and adequate supply of oil," recognizing that national policy cannot determine the global price of oil. Jian (2011: 6) suggests that it is possible to identify four phases in the development of China's oil industry since the late 1970s. The first phase, from 1978 to 1992, is one of self-reliance and self-sufficiency when domestic production is able to meet demand and there is limited engagement with international energy markets. The second phase is 1993 to 1999, during which time domestic oil production can no longer meet demand and the government starts to reform the state-owned oil companies to improve their competitiveness, and these NOCs start to seek oil in foreign markets. The third phase, from 2000 to 2003, is a period of very rapid growth in domestic-energy demand and increasing import dependence, with imports accounting for 27.5 percent of consumption in 2000, but by 2008 that had increased to 49.4 percent, and in 2011 import dependence had reached 55.9 percent (BP 2012a: 73). During this period, the international ambitions of China's NOCs – China National Petroleum Corporation (CNPC), China Petroleum & Chemical Corporation (Sinopec), and China National Offshore Oil Corporation (CNOOC) – matched the Chinese government's strategy that they should "go global" and secure access and equity ownership of oil reserves abroad (Ma and Andrews-Speed 2006). Jian (2011: 6) maintains that since the global financial crisis we have been in a fourth phase, where the strategy has been to "go abroad and buy." The financial turmoil has enabled China to use its substantial financial reserves to purchase additional access to oil production. A case in point would be the agreement in 2009 between the China Development Bank (CDB) and the state-owned Russian oil company Rosneft and the oil pipeline monopoly to build a pipeline from East Siberia to Daqing in northeast China. A loan of $25 billion has been provided to complete the pipeline (including a line to the Pacific coast) and develop new oilfields in East Siberia; in return, China will receive 300 thousand barrels a day of oil a year for 20 years (Jiang and Sinton 2011). Downs (2011) estimates that between 2009 and late 2011, the China Development Bank extended lines of credit in large-scale and long-term loans totaling almost $75 billion to national oil companies and government entities in Brazil, Ecuador, Russia, Turkmenistan, and Russia. Analysis by Jiang and Sinton (2011: 7) concludes that Chinese oil companies are now operating in 31 countries and have equity production in 20 of these countries, although those equity shares are concentrated in four countries: Kazakhstan, Sudan, Venezuela, and Angola. So what impact has this activity had on China's oil-import security?

China has pursued an explicit policy of diversifying its sources of oil imports. Data for 2012 (Jian 2011: 17) show that the majority of China's oil imports were spread between 11 countries, with Saudi Arabia (19 percent) and Angola (16 percent) being the only two countries to command more than

TABLE 5.7 The changing geography of China's oil imports

Region	1990	1997	2005	2006	2008	2010
Middle East	39	48	46	44	46	46
Russia/C. Asia	n/a	n/a	11	11	10	10
Atlantic Basin	n/a	n/a	23	5	3	3
Asia-Pacific	60.0	26.2	8.0	4.0	n/a	n/a
Africa	0.0	16.7	n/a	32.0	23.0	22.0
Others	0.0	9.6	12.0	4.0	18.0	19.9

Source: Jian, Z. (2011), *China's Energy Security: Prospects, Challenges and Opportunities*. Washington, DC: The Brookings Institution Center for Northeast Asian Policy Studies, p. 17.

10 percent of total imports. As table 5.7 shows, there have been some changes in the geography of China's imports. The Middle East remains dominant, but imports from Africa have become increasingly important. The routes taken by these imports expose China to two maritime choke points: the Straits of Hormuz in the case of imports from the Persian Gulf, and the Straits of Malacca in the case of both Middle Eastern and African imports, which together account for 70–80 percent of total oil imports. One response to the so-called "Malacca dilemma" has been to expand China's naval capacity to enable it to patrol the sea lanes and contribute to international efforts to protect crude-oil traffic. A second response has been to seek sources of oil from neighboring states that can be delivered by pipeline. A pipeline from Kazakhstan was completed in 2006, and another from Russia in 2011.

The actions of China's NOCs, supported by the CDB, have been criticized in the West (Downs 2006; Taylor 2006). There are accusations that China's NOCs are able to outbid the IOCs when seeking access to oil reserves in developing economies. Often the deals struck by the NOCs are part of wider packages of financial assistance, which is something that the IOCs can't match (Mohan and Power 2008). Equally, China's NOCs are accused of investing in regimes with questionable human rights records or, as in the case of Sudan, that are prosecuting armed conflict. It is certainly the case that China's NOCs have invested in countries where the IOCs are unwilling or unable to invest, either because of the foreign policy of their home states and/or because of concerns about reputation risk. Sudan is the most obvious example, but China also continues to invest in Hugo Chavez's Venezuela. However, in places such as Nigeria and Angola, where both IOCs and China's NOCs are operating, the Chinese companies seem no more successful in negotiating the complex domestic politics and the lack of transparency that often hinder development. Both Downs (2006) and Leung (2011: 135) suggest that there is limited evidence that this "going out" strategy has made a significant contribution to China's energy security. This is due to several factors: first, because equity ownership of oil will not protect Chinese consumers against price shocks as the NOCs will trade this oil at world price, which is set by market interactions; second, because equity oil from Africa will face the same transportation barriers as non-equity oil from the Middle East and Africa; and third, because the reality at the moment is that most of China's equity oil is not shipped directly to China. Leung (2011: 1335) suggests that it is often more profitable to sell oil from Sudan on international markets – Japan is a ready market – and purchase imports from elsewhere; equally, it is more economic to sell production from West Africa to consumers in the Atlantic basin and then purchase oil from the Middle East. In 2010, China's total oil consumption was 9.25 mb/d, and domestic production was 4.08 mb/d, making imports 5.17 mb/d (BP 2012b: 8–9). Jiang and Sinton (2011: 7) report that in the first quarter of 2010 China's NOCs total equity shares were 1.36 mb/d or 26.3 percent of China's total imports, a significant amount, but not sufficient to provide security of supply. A fourth consideration is that if neither the growth of NOC equity oil nor that of domestic-oil production is able to keep up with the growth of domestic-oil demand, this non-equity oil-import dependence is bound to increase. Finally, China has been accused by the likes of US President George Bush of "locking in" oil production and aggravating energy-security concerns (Downs 2007). This misunderstands the nature of the global oil market; if China is unable to secure oil from the fields in which it has an equity share, it must go on to the international markets to access that oil, which would result in less oil being available for other buyers. In fact, one could argue that by developing production in countries such as Sudan, where the IOCs cannot operate, China's NOCs are actually putting more oil into the market. Equally, the NOCs, in combination with the CDB, are providing capital to finance the development of new oil production. Thus, on balance, one might conclude that the actions of China's NOCs are not aggravating energy security at a global scale, the real problem being the pace of demand growth in China and the other emerging markets that are challenging the capacity of the global oil industry to match supply with demand. As Mitchell et al. (2012: xiv) aptly summarize the situation: "The oil security problem has moved to Asia."

China now faces three energy-security challenges: the first is to secure the supply of energy resources to satisfy growing domestic demand; the second is to improve the energy intensity of the economy and accelerate the decoupling of economic growth from energy demand; and the third is to reduce the carbon-energy intensity of energy use, and thus CO_2 emissions, through the promotion of low-carbon sources of energy supply. Fortunately, these three challenges are mutually reinforcing as the improvements in energy efficiency needed to reduce energy intensity can reduce the absolute demand for fossil fuels, thus reducing the amount of oil, gas, and coal that is imported. Equally, meeting a greater share of future energy demand from low-carbon sources – nuclear and renewables – not only curbs fossil-fuel demand, but also reduces the carbon intensity of energy use. Chinese policymaking in relation to energy and climate-change issues is fragmented and uncoordinated (Kong 2011); nonetheless, since the 2000s, there has been an extensive set of policy measures and programs aimed at enhancing energy security and improving energy efficiency (Hallding et al. 2009). The Chinese government's Copenhagen Pledge sets the following targets: to reduce CO_2 emissions intensity (per unit of GDP) by 40–45 percent by 2020 relative to 2005, and to increase the share of renewable energy to around 15 percent by 2020 (Kuby et al. 2011: 803). As carbon intensity is a ratio, it is difficult to determine an absolute level of carbon reduction that will be delivered, but China was the first developing economy to agree to a reduction target. China is also using the need to increase the share of renewable energy in total energy consumption to develop an industrial base from which to export low-carbon technology to the world. This move is already proving positive in improving energy access in the developing world, but is generating trade frictions with the OECD states that also wish to develop their low-carbon industries as part of a green recovery. The current high-energy and high-carbon growth model is not sustainable – economically, socially, and ecologically – and the Chinese leadership recognizes this; however, a failure to develop a new growth strategy will have implications for the entire planet as China's current surging energy demand and associated carbon emissions are now driving global change.

MENA, Saudi Arabia and the Challenges to "Autocratic Oil"

This final section considers the energy dilemma facing Saudi Arabia, the world's most important oil exporter. Events across the Middle East and North Africa (MENA) during 2011, the so-called "Arab Spring," have drawn attention to the growing social tensions that exist in many of the region's energy-exporting states. The MENA countries are home to 5 percent of the world's population, have 66 percent of its oil reserves, and 45 percent of its gas reserves (Anoun 2009). The MENA region can be divided into two groups: the oil (and gas) exporters, which includes the Six Gulf Cooperation Countries (Bahrain, Kuwait, Qatar, Oman, Saudi Arabia, and the UAE), plus Algeria, Libya, Iraq, and Iran; and the net-oil importers: Egypt, Jordan, Lebanon, Morocco, Syria and Tunisia. Even before the Arab Spring that was triggered by events in Tunisia, the region was far from stable and fraught with growing social and political tensions. For the energy-exporting countries, oil and gas account for 70 percent of total exports and 75 percent of budget revenues (Ianchovichina 2011). The concept of the "rentier state" has been applied to describe the political economy of these states whereby the ruling elite exerts autocratic control over the distribution of rents earned by oil and gas exports

(Yates 1996). The "rentier state" receives substantial rents from foreign individuals, companies, or governments, in this case rents from payment for oil and gas. According to Beblawi (1987: 57), the distinguishing factor in the Middle East is that such rents accrue directly to the state and "only a few are engaged in the generation of this rent (wealth), the majority being only involved in the distribution and utilization of it." Such societies are seldom transparent (Ross 2001), but there is an implicit social contract between the ruling elite, who control the apparatus of the state, and the wider population that requires they benefit from the distribution of rent provision by meaningful employment and consistent improvements in the standard of living (Eifert et al. 2002). The problem is that these states are vulnerable to the volatility associated with being an energy exporter and they face ever-increasing pressure to deliver improved living standards, a situation that is strained by high rates of population growth (Fattouh and El-Katiri 2012). Table 5.8 provides information on the demographic characteristics of the oil-exporting states of MENA. This makes clear the distinction between the very small populations of some of the Gulf Cooperation Countries' members that enables them to maintain a sizeable exportable surplus and amass huge sums in their Sovereign Wealth Funds. It is the large MENA states that face the greatest challenge, particularly those whose energy wealth is spread thinly and who face significant development challenges; this is made clear in the final column that shows oil income per capita. The other factor apparent from table 5.8 is the pent-up demand for new employment that exists when more than 25 percent of the population is currently less than 15 years old. The challenge of providing work for this population is all the more challenging when one considers the relatively poor economic performance of many of the MENA states. Thus, we can conceive of the energy-exporting states of MENA, and particularly those of the GCC, as facing a particular form of "resource curse" that is distinct from the problems facing energy-exporting states in sub-Saharan Africa, discussed in the next chapter. Here we are most concerned about developments in Saudi Arabia, which in 2011 was responsible for 25.7 percent of global oil production and which currently holds 29.9 percent of the world's oil reserves.

The very existence of modern Saudi Arabia is a product of the age of oil (Yergin 2008). In a short period of time oil wealth has dramatically transformed Saudi society, but current trends suggest that domestic energy profligacy is in danger of compromising the country's key source of export earnings. The importance of Saudi Arabia to global energy security lies not just in its absolute contribution to global oil production, but also in its role as a "swing producer" that has spare capacity that can compensate when exports are compromised elsewhere in the world. The full extent of Saudi Arabia oil reserves and its capacity to sustain production are unknown and are the subject of constant speculation. A recent report (Tottie et al. 2012: 10) suggests that Saudi Arabian oil production will remain in the region of

TABLE 5.8 The demographic characteristics of the MENA's oil-exporting states

	Population mid-2012 Millions	Rate of natural increase %	Projected by mid-2025 Millions	% less than 15 years old	Oil and gas income per capita (2009 dollars)
GCC					
Bahrain	1.2	1.3	1.6	20	3,720
Kuwait	2.9	1.5	4.8	32	19,500
Oman	3.1	2.0	4.0	24	7,950
Saudi Arabia	28.7	1.8	36.2	30	7,800
Qatar	1.9	1.0	2.2	14	24,940
UAE	8.1	1.2	9.9	17	14,100
Others					
Algeria	37.4	2.0	42.0	28	1,930
Libya	6.5	1.9	7.5	31	6,420
Iraq	33.7	2.9	48.9	43	1,780
Iran	78.9	1.3	90.5	24	1,600

Sources: Population Reference Bureau (2012), *World Population Data Sheet.* Washington, DC: Population Reference Bureau, pp. 6–12, and Ross (2012), *The Oil Curse: How Petroleum Wealth Shapes the Development of Nations.* Princeton, NJ: Princeton University Press, pp. 20–1.

12 mb/d until 2015, with spare capacity of at least 2 mb/d. Saudi Arabia also plays a key "moderating" role in OPEC as it understands that there is a balance to be struck between a "fair" price that meets the expectations of the oil-exporting states and a level of oil price that is not so high that it provokes economic crisis and demand destruction. The problem is that what constitutes a fair price is constantly increasing as the oil-exporting states require more and more "rent" to balance their budgets, and some states, such as Russia, require a higher price than others. This also reflects the higher production costs of the non-MENA oil exporters. Most oil-exporting states understand the need to manage their rents and to diversify their economies, but they now face the longer prospect of demand destruction as climate-change policies serve to reduce global demand for fossil fuels. That situation is still some way off, and the most immediate concern for both exporting and importing states is the ability to match supply with demand at a price that does not damage the prospects for economic recovery.

While there may be some certainty that Saudi Arabia can sustain current levels of oil production, the concern is that growing domestic demand for energy services will substantially reduce the size of the country's exportable service. Darbouche and Fattouh (2011: 16) maintain that this is part of a wider problem across MENA. Although in 1980 the region's share of global oil production was less than 4 percent, in 2010 it had increased to 10 percent. They suggest four reasons for this growth in domestic consumption, all of which are relevant to the situation in Saudi Arabia: first, the expanding population; second, general improvements in the standard of living; third, industrialization policies that are geared toward diversification through the development of energy-intensive industries, such as petrochemicals; and, fourth, the provision of energy at low prices to domestic consumers that encourages excessive consumption. The net result of all this is that levels of energy intensity in the oil-exporting states of MENA have actually been increasing, that is to say they are now consuming more energy per unit of GDP than they did in the past, which also results in higher CO_2 emissions as the energy mixes in all of these economies are fossil-fuel dominated. Put another way, their energy consumption is growing faster than their GDP growth. Not surprisingly, the members of OPEC more generally do not have a positive attitude toward setting carbon-reduction targets, despite the fact that the MENA states are especially likely to feel the negative consequences of climate change in terms of increased temperature and an even greater stress on water supplies (Luomi 2010).

A study by Lahn and Stevens (2011: 1–2) reveals that Saudi Arabia's demand for its own oil and gas is growing at around 7 percent a year and that unless things change this will "jeopardize the country's ability to export to global markets." On a "business as usual" trajectory they predict that the country could be a net oil importer by 2038. Saudi Arabia currently has a production capacity of around 12.5 mb/d and produces around 10 mb/d, but current domestic consumption is 2.8 mb/d, over a quarter of current production. Saudi Arabia is now the world's sixth largest oil consumer. As discussed above, the reasons for the growth in domestic demand are well understood and Saudi government policy has reserved gas production for domestic-power production and as feedstock for the petrochemical industry (Fattouh 2011). One of the problems is that domestic-gas production has faltered and more oil has had to be used to compensate. At present, oil and gas account for all domestic-energy consumption and one solution is to promote further diversification through the development of nuclear power and solar power. However, such a policy is difficult to implement while domestic-energy prices remain so low; for example, gas prices need to rise to encourage new development. Again, this is well understood, but the current social and political situation makes it very difficult to increase domestic-energy prices. The low cost of energy is one way that "rent" is distributed to the population. All of these factors result in a very high level of energy intensity. Lahn and Stevens (2011: 6) report that in 2007, Saudi Arabia's energy intensity was nearly twice that of Malaysia, which has a comparable population and level of development. An ABB (2012) report on energy efficiency in Saudi Arabia reports that between

2000 and 2010, the energy intensity of GDP rose by 2.3 percent a year and the carbon intensity by 2.0 percent a year; the lower rate of increase in carbon intensity reflects the switch from oil to gas in the power-generation sector. Lahn and Stevens (2011: 26) point out that this high level of energy intensity is a consequence of the inefficient use of energy, rather than economic development and improved living standards. In other words, it is possible for Saudi Arabia to become far more energy efficient without reducing living standards, and what is required is the political will to introduce economy-wide measures. Such a change is in the long-term interest of Saudi citizens and official government policy is to reduce electricity by 30 percent between 2005 and 2015, and to halve the peak demand growth rate by 2015, compared to the 2000–5 period. At current production levels, the Saudi government needs a price of about $90 dollars a barrel to balance its budget. However, the state's social commitments are only likely to increase in the near term as the country has the fastest-growing labor market in the world. Providing meaningful employment will require increased government expenditure. If domestic-energy consumption continues to erode the country's exportable surplus, a price well above $100 will be required that will have a damaging effect on global economic prospects. This means that Saudi Arabia's soaring levels of domestic-energy consumption are a matter of global concern, not just in environmental terms in relation to carbon dioxide emissions, but also in economic terms in relation to the supply of oil at affordable prices.

Conclusions: Decarbonizing Demand Growth

This chapter has adopted a broader definition of emerging economies than that usually associated with BRICS, BASIC, and CIBS. This is not because the narrower grouping is not important; rather, it is because there is a wider group of countries that are experiencing rapid rates of economic growth. Some have small populations and thus their cumulative impact is modest, but others, such as Indonesia and the Philippines, have large populations and have the potential to make a big impact. For most of these countries, with the notable exception of India, it is not population growth that is now the key driver of rising energy demand; rather, it is improving living standards and rising levels of consumption that are driving demand. In some energy-exporting economies, such as Indonesia, the growth of domestic demand has already resulted in a substantial reduction in gas exports. Thus, from an energy-security perspective, it is a cause for concern not just because growing demand for energy services in this group of countries is seen as contributing to the possibility that supply will not be able to keep up with growing demand, but also because growing domestic demand will reduce energy exports themselves, Saudi Arabia being a significant example. Thus, energy efficiency and the development of alternative sources of energy should be key components of energy strategy in fossil-fuel exporting economies.

Looking back to the 1990s, it is clear that over the past decade there has been a rapid acceleration in the rate of economic growth and a surge in energy demand in the emerging economies. China has seen remarkable growth since the turn of the century and others are now following in its wake. The energy-security and climate-change consequences are clear for all to see, and it is understandable that the developed world wish to see the fastest-growing emitters amongst the emerging economies included in any future global climate-change agreement. Already there has been a substantial shift in the center of gravity of energy demand in the global economy, but the key issue concerns what happens over the next 20–30 years. All the projections suggest that as living standards continue to improve, so demand for energy services will increase. The experience of the developed world suggests that over time the relationship between economic growth and energy consumption changes, but this is unlikely to happen quickly enough to constrain the growth of energy demand over the next 20–30 years. In such a context, it is the way that future demand growth is satisfied that is critical. The key issue is how much of that future energy demand will be met by coal-fired power generation versus lower-carbon fuels (natural gas) and low-carbon sources – nuclear and renewables. The reality is that the rate of growth is such that all energy sources will experience growth, but what really matters is that the carbon intensity of energy use should be constrained as much as possible. Investment in energy efficiency is also important, as it will help to slow the growth of demand and improve the overall energy efficiency of the economy. It will also ease energy-security concerns by reducing the level of imports. The transportation sector presents a particularly intractable challenge, as improvements in living standards are bound to result in higher levels of car ownership. Clearly, the energy efficiency of the vehicle sector will be significant and alternative fuels – biofuels, gas-to-liquids and compressed natural gas – can help to reduce the need to consume conventional oil and associated products. For oil-importing economies, this is important because of the high cost and volatility associated with oil imports; it is also important for oil-exporting countries because it helps to maintain the volume of oil available for export. The removal of subsidies on gasoline also has a part to play, as this would drive efficiency and reduce demand (notwithstanding the possibility of the rebound effect resulting in high demand).

The dynamism of the emerging economies is such that their ability to overcome their energy dilemmas will be critical to the success or failure of global climate-change policy. The processes of globalization have contributed to their economic success, and those same processes mean that consumption in the developed economies is directly implicated in the rapid growth of energy demand and carbon emissions in the emerging economies. Given this interdependence, a much more constructive relationship needs to be shaped between the two groups of economies. The same technological solutions are required by both groups to improve energy intensity and reduce the carbon intensity of energy use; thus, there should be ample opportunity for trade investment and cooperation, rather than aid and assistance. Equally, both groups have a common interest in secure, affordable, and equitable access to energy services. The current stalemate over a post-Kyoto agreement reflects a focus on climate change as an air-pollution problem whereby the solution is to get parties to agree to reductions in emissions; instead, what is needed is an approach based on ensuring that future energy-demand growth is met by the most sustainable means possible, which includes substantial improvements in energy intensity and reductions in carbon intensity. Such an approach would have a better chance of constraining the emissions growth of the emerging economies without being seen as a threat to their future development prospects. Equally, it needs to be understood by politicians in these countries that a failure to constrain emissions would result in catastrophic climate change that would threaten the economic prosperity of all on the planet.

CHAPTER SIX

Energizing Development
Energy Dilemmas in the Developing World

Introduction

This chapter deals with the final group of countries of the four identified in the global energy dilemmas typology, the "developing countries." Finding the most appropriate way to describe this group of countries is in itself problematic, the term "global South" is often used, while others prefer the notion of the "majority world," which has a certain logic to it given the discussion that follows below. However, I have decided to stick with the terms "developing world" and "developing economies," while recognizing that it is not entirely satisfactory to do so as it suggests a particularly material notion of human progress. Although this group of countries is the residual left once the other three groups are identified – high-energy, post-socialist and emerging economies – this is not an arbitrary outcome. As explained in chapter 2, each group is defined by the relationship between energy security, globalization (the level and dynamics of economic development), and their contribution to energy-related carbon emissions – a consequence of the level of energy intensity and the carbon intensity of energy use (both the absolute levels and recent dynamics being key considerations). This final group is defined by its low levels of economic development (measured as GDP per capita); limited engagement with the global economy (often through the export of primary commodities); low levels of commercial primary-energy consumption (and access to modern energy services); and very modest amounts of carbon dioxide emissions per capita. In other words, a group of countries that has not – to date at least – contributed to the current problems of energy security and climate change in any significant way (see table 6.1). The structure of this chapter is somewhat different from the previous three, for reasons that are explained later, and is based around key issues, rather than key countries or regions. The first part of the chapter focuses on the key "Kaya driver" in much of the developing world, namely, population growth. This is then followed by a more general review of the Kaya characteristics of the group that highlights its diversity. The remainder of the chapter then focuses on two issues: the problem of "energy access" and the "resource curse." In both instances the analysis considers the nature of the problem, its causes and consequences,

TABLE 6.1 Share of key indicators by macro-region

	CO_2 emissions		Energy use		GNI (PPP)		Population	
	1990	2007	1990	2008	1990	2009	1990	2010
Developed	41.7	39.0	48.6	42.2	58.6	47.6	16.1	14.1
Post-socialist	18.8	9.1	19.7	10.7	8.9	7.6	7.8	5.9
Emerging	23.7	38.6	22.1	34.5	17.9	29.9	50.5	50.0
Developing	6.8	8.5	8.2	10.8	12.0	12.7	25.3	29.6
Unclassified*	9.0	4.8	1.4	1.8	2.6	2.2	0.3	0.4

*The residual when all the country-specific data are deducted from the world data.

Source: World Bank Development Indicators Database.

and possible solutions. The chapter concludes by placing the energy dilemmas of the developing world in a global context.

The Critical Role of Population Change

Many of the countries in the developing world are characterized by high levels of population growth. This is made clear in table 6.1 where their share of total global population has increased to almost 30 percent, while the other three groups are either stagnant or declining. As discussed in chapter 2, population is a key driver of energy-related GHG emissions; as noted then, the more people there are on the planet the greater the demand for energy and other resources, such as land, water, food, and habitation. Global demographic trends were discussed in chapter 2 and it was made clear that the geography of future trends was a key driver of the global shift in energy demand now under way. To refresh our memory, the United Nations, Department of Economic and Social Affairs and Population Division (2011: xii–2) medium variant forecasts that the world's population will increase to 9.3 billion by 2050 and 11 billion by 2100. However, the vast majority of the additional population will be in the less-developed economies (the term used by the UN to describe the developing world) and their population will increase from 5.7 billion to 8 billion by 2050. In 1950, the less-developed economies accounted for 68 percent of the global population, but by 2050 that share will have increased to 85.6 percent, with Asia accounting for 55.3 percent and Africa 23.6 percent. At present, the populations of the 48 least-developed economies are still the fastest growing in the world. The total population of these countries was 0.85 billion in 2011, and under the medium variant it will reach 1.7 billion by 2050. We should also remember that HIV/AIDs prevalence is highest in sub-Saharan Africa and this is having a significant impact on population size, characteristics, and well-being (Ashford 2006). As we shall see below, it is mainly these countries facing the greatest problems of energy access, and they are also the most vulnerable to the impacts of climate change. All of these figures are based on the UN's medium variant, although it is possible that future population growth could be higher or lower; the UN's high variant predicts a population of 10.6 billion by 2050 and a low variant of 8.1 billion. The population in the developing world is still young; at present the under-15-year-olds account for 29 percent and the 15–24-year-olds a further 18 percent, and it is their reproductive choices that will dictate how many people there will be on the planet in 2050.

Given the significance of the population size and dynamics in determining demand for energy services and the level of anthropogenic GHG emissions, it is surprising that demographic analysis plays such a limited role in discussions of climate-change mitigation. Climate-change modeling does factor in population, but it tends to be a crude analysis based on the total population, with no allowance being made for the composition and dynamics of that population at a global or regional level (Jiang and Hardee 2011). Equally, it is not the number of people that is the most important determinant of their energy demand and carbon emissions, but their level of consumption (Satterthwaite 2009). As noted in chapter 2, there is a world of difference between the environment impact of the average American and the average Kenyan. The Kaya Identity captures this factor by including both income per capita levels and population. Fortunately, there is a significant body of literature that deals with the relationship between population and climate change that makes a strong case for a more sophisticated analysis of the role of demographic processes in driving GHG emissions (Dietz and Rosa 1997; O'Neill 2010; O'Neill et al. 2001, 2010). This work suggests, for example, that it is the number of households that matters more than the number of people when looking at future demand for energy and the associated GHG emissions. The number of households is increasing faster than the rate of population growth and the number of people per household is declining, so the result is a reduction in economies of scale in terms of provision of heating, lighting, and so on. The age composition of the population is also significant and the evidence suggests that as the population ages the per capita demand for energy declines (Dalton et al. 2006). At the same time, the nature of the demand for energy services changes as individuals leave the workforce, as their demand for transportation services declines and their demand for residential services increases (Cohen 2010). Urbanization is seen as a driver of higher energy demand and GHG emissions, but this is a complex relationship as cities are more efficient at delivering such services and they are also engines of economic growth, a factor that drives future demand. O'Neill (2010: 88) states that "Urbanization implies greater productivity, faster economic growth and more emissions." Thus, the fact that the majority of future population growth in the developing world will be in cities is an important factor to consider in modeling future energy demand and GHG emissions. The OECD (Pezzini 2012) estimates that the size of the "global middle class" will increase from 1.8 billion in 2009 to 3.2 billion in 2020, and could reach 4.9 billion by 2030, with the bulk of the growth being in Asia. We also know that where people on the planet are born has a significant impact on their demand for energy and their carbon emissions. Research by Murtaugh and Schlax (2009) has sought to quantify the "carbon legacies of individuals." As part of this analysis, they estimate the average per capita emissions from fossil fuels in 2005 for one person, the emissions of their ancestors, and the emissions that will be added by each child that they have. The average US citizen produced 20.18 tons of CO_2 per year, their ancestors produced 1,644 tons in their lifetime, and each of their children will produce 9,441 tons. By comparison, the average citizen of Bangladesh produced 0.27 tons of CO_2, their ancestors produced 18 tons, and each of their children will produce 56 tons. However, the figures for China illustrate the impact that rising living standards can have on future emissions. In 2005, the average Chinese citizen produced 3.62 tons of CO_2, their ancestors 311 tons, but each child will produce 1,384 tons. Thus, one of the key factors to consider here is the future living standard of the growing population in the developing world, as this is likely to determine their per capita emissions. As an aside, this analysis also concluded that the impact of a woman in the United States forgoing an additional child would generate a level of emissions reductions far greater than she could ever hope to achieve by adopting an energy-efficient low-carbon lifestyle through the remainder of her lifetime. The implication is that the falling population of the developed world will deliver significant emissions reductions despite the higher carbon footprints of each child born compared to children in the emerging and developing world.

Analysis by O'Neill et al. (2010: 17525) concludes that "reduced population growth could make a significant contribution to global emissions reductions." This raises the question of why population policy is not considered a relevant lever for climate-change mitigation. Demographers and philosophers working on these issues suggest that it is because the social processes underlying demographic change are complex and difficult to predict, and because any notion of "population control" raises ethical and religious concerns (Cohen 2010: 158). Cafaro (2012: 45) makes a powerful argument for including measures to slow population growth in climate-change mitigation policymaking. He notes: "Over the past three and half decades, improvements in energy and carbon efficiency have been overwhelmed by increases in population and wealth." Furthermore, he points out that 40 percent of what he calls "excessive greenhouse gas emissions" over the rest of this century (in BAU) will come from population growth, thus a reduction in the number of people is an "environmental gift that keeps giving," as fewer people means fewer children. Both Cafaro (2012) and Cohen (2010) focus on "non-coercive measures" to curb population growth. These are: free or low-cost birth control; making abortion safe, legal, and freely available; other policies that improve women's lives such as educational opportunities (and one can add increased employment opportunities); and, finally, media campaigns to promote teenage pregnancy prevention and to extol the benefits of small families. Clearly, these policy prescriptions would chime with the interests of those promoting the improvement of women's rights, but they would be controversial in many developing countries, as well as costly to provide. What Cafaro is advocating is an acceleration of what some might call the "benefits of modernization," to complete the demographic transition more rapidly in the developing world. Undoubtedly, keeping the world's population below 8 billion by 2050 would make a significant contribution to reducing the growth of GHG emissions (O'Neill 2010); but reducing the consumption levels of the wealthiest billion would likely have an even great impact.

At present, the low levels of income and consumption dampen the Kaya consequences of high population growth in the developing world; however, if this group of countries succeeds in raising their standards of living, then there is the potential for them to contribute to increasing levels of demand for energy and increasing levels of GHG emissions. At the same time, we should also recognize that the energy systems in these countries are notoriously inefficient and that substantial gains could be made to improve efficiency. But we also know that efficiency improvements often result in higher levels of absolute energy demand. This raises an important ethical question, which lies at the heart of the energy dilemma facing the developing world: none would deny the people of the developing world the right to improve their living standards, but how can that be done without further aggravating the energy security and climate-change challenges that the world already faces?

Big Issues rather than Key Countries

The approach adopted in this chapter is somewhat different from the previous three. In the previous three cases, the number of countries that fell into a particular group was in the range of 20 to 30. At the same time, there were a few key countries or groups of countries that dominated the scene: the United States, the EU, Russia, and the CIBS economies. The situation in the developing world is very different: it is a large heterogeneous group with countries facing very different development, energy-security, and climate-change challenges, and the sheer number of countries makes it very difficult to identify key or representative countries. Equally, the literature on energy and climate change in the developing world is drawn between quantitative cross-country comparisons and more qualitative country- and local-level cases studies, the latter being particularly true of work on sustainable energy. Thus, the approach adopted in this chapter focuses on big issues rather than key countries.

The list of countries in Annex 1 identifies 195 "states," some of which are dependencies and others which are very small islands or city-states. By comparison, the World Bank's country classification contains 215 economies, the UNDP's Human Development Index is calculated for 187 states, and there are currently 192 parties to the Kyoto Protocol, and 193 member-states in the UN. A comparison of the regional groupings in Annex 1 with the World Bank's classification of low income, middle income (subdivided into lower-middle and upper-middle income) and high income reveals that the majority of the developing economies group fall within the low (a GNI per capita of $ 1,006 or less) and lower-middle income groups ($1,006 to $3,975), with some in the upper-middle income groups ($3,976 to $12,275).

The developing economies group as listed in Annex 1 contains 110 countries; it is not feasible to analyze the Kaya characteristics of all of them, and instead a sample of 20 percent is included in table 6.2 (this is a simple stratified sample based on every fifth country on the list). The list covers a range of world regions – Central and Latin America, sub-Saharan Africa and Asia – and income levels within the group, and its purpose is to illustrate the wide variation as well as the significantly lower levels of economic development that characterize these countries. The fact there is a degree of missing data also highlights the problem of obtaining reliable information on the energy and climate-change status of some of the world's least-developed economies. A further issue to consider is that sources such as BP's *Statistical Review* focus on commercially traded primary-energy sources and do not include the subsistence use of biomass, which – as we shall see below – is a very significant factor in the developing world. Thus, as noted in chapter 1, the actual level of energy consumption and thus energy intensity, and also carbon intensity, is understated, as is the level of economic activity, as GNI measures do not capture the informal sector. The net effect is likely that these omissions cancel one another out and the important factor is that the absolute and relative levels of energy consumption and carbon emissions are very low by comparison to the other three groups of countries. The geopolitical implications of this are that the majority of the states in the global political system consume very small amounts of energy and emit very modest levels of GHGs; yet because they are the countries most vulnerable to the impacts and face the greatest challenges in terms of adaptation, they expect equal standing when it comes to discussions aimed at resolving the problem of climate change.

The relationship between the level of economic development and the level of energy consumption in the developing world is plotted in figure 6.1. The level of GDP (or GNI) per capita is a key driver of energy-related carbon emissions and, as discussed in chapter 2, there is a positive relationship between the level of economic development and the level of energy consumption; however, such measurements are based on a particular material understanding of what equates to development, as opposed to quality of life. That said,

TABLE 6.2 Kaya characteristics for selected developing economies

	CO_2 per capita 2007	Population (,000s) 2010	GNI per capita 2009	Energy intensity 2008	Carbon intensity of energy use 2007	Access to electricity
Argentina	4.6	40,665.7	14,030	6.90	2.31	97.2
Belize	1.4	344.7	6,030	na	na	91.7
Central African Republic	0.1	4,505.9	750	na	na	5.1
Costa Rica	1.8	4,639.8	10,870	9.57	1.52	99.1
Dominican Republic	2.1	10,225.5	8,080	9.15	2.62	95.9
Gambia	0.2	11,750.7	1,260	na	na	8.3
Jordan	3.8	6,093.0	5,700	4.19	2.94	99.9
Liberia	0.2	4,101.8	330	na	na	3.3
Mali	0.1	15,368.8	990	na	na	17.4
Morocco	1.5	32,381.3	4,380	8.44	3.23	97.0
Nepal	0.1	29,852.7	1,170	3.00	0.35	43.6
Pakistan	1.5	173,383.0	2,670	4.68	2.36	57.6
Peru	1.0	29,496.1	8,300	15.41	1.79	76.9
Sao Tome and Principe	0.8	165.4	1,830	na	na	48.5
Somalia	0.1	9,358.6	na	na	na	na
Swaziland	0.9	1,201.9	4,550	na	na	29.7
Tonga	1.7	104.3	4,650	na	na	92.3
Uruguay	0.1	3,356.6	12,800	9.31	1.97	99.5
Zambia	0.2	12,926.4	1,300	2.15	0.36	18.8

na = not available.
See table 3.1 for an explanation of the indicators.

Sources: World Bank Development Indicators Database; CAIT; and UNDP-WHO (2009), *The Energy Access Situation in Developing Countries.* New York: UNDP, p. 66.

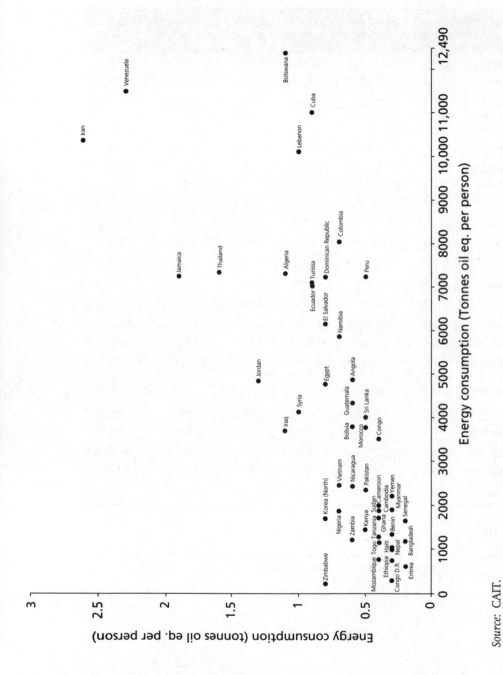

Source: CAIT.

Figure 6.1 The relationship between energy consumption and GDP per capita in the developing economies, 2007

there is also strong correlation between the HDI status of a particular country and energy consumption, and the relationship is even stronger for electricity consumption per capita. This is not surprising given the need to access modern energy services to provide education and healthcare.

If one returns to the thresholds between low-income, lower-middle income and upper-middle income, used by the World Bank, obviously the low-income group represents the very poorest economies, but they are also characterized by very low levels of commercial energy consumption. The group between $1,000 and $4,000 includes a number of energy (Nigeria and Sudan) and other-mineral exporting economies (Zambia), some of which are discussed in more detail below. The upper-middle-income group with a GDP of $4,000 and above shows a greater degree of variation in relation to the link between energy consumption and development and the two extreme outliers – Iran and Venezuela – are both significant oil exporters (Libya is another example). As noted at the beginning of this chapter, when it comes to energy and development, there are two issues that are of particular significance to this group of countries. The first issue is the lack of access to basic modern energy services. This is a particular challenge for the least-developed economies, but some of the energy-rich economies, such as Nigeria, still have major problems with energy access. It is also the case that some of the largest emerging economies considered in the previous chapter – China and India – have energy access problems in their rural regions akin to those faced by the least-developed countries. The second issue relates to energy-rich developing countries, as a subset of resource-rich economies, and is often described as the "resource curse" – that is, the range of economic, political, and environmental pathologies that cumulatively mean that in many instances these economies seem unable to benefit from the income (rent) generated by energy exports. In our wider discussions of energy security, the issue of energy access can be seen as a particular interpretation of "access to affordable energy services," with emphasis on physical access and economic affordability. In a more traditional sense, the political instability associated with many oil-exporting countries in the developing world is an energy-security concern for importing states and is also a major cause of the price volatility prevalent in the global oil market. The rest of this chapter is structured around these two key issues and their resolution.

Energy Access: The Missing Millennium Goal

In 2000, the United Nations Millennium Declaration set out eight "Millennium Development Goals" (MDGs) to be achieved by 2015 to eradicate extreme poverty. The eight goals were aimed at: ending poverty and hunger; providing universal education; reducing gender inequality; improving child health; combating HIV/AIDs; promoting environmental sustainability and global partnership. Since then considerable progress has been made, though it is uneven both in terms of progress on individual targets and in particular regions – sub-Saharan Africa and South Asia are singled out as particularly problematic (the UN produces an annual review of progress toward the achievement of the MDGs).

Providing universal access to modern energy services was not defined as a specific MDG. The reasons for this are unclear, but it may be that promoting increased energy consumption did not sit well with the wider notion of sustainable development. However, it soon became clear that because of the clear relationship between energy consumption and economic development, and also because of the centrality of energy services such as heating, cooling, lighting, mechanical power, and transportation to poverty alleviation, many of the MDGs could not be achieved without improvements in energy access. At the same time, it was clear that the high degree of reliance on biomass for cooking was both a threat to the health of billions and a challenge to sustainable development. Consequently, starting at the World Summit for Sustainable Development in Johannesburg in 2002, the last decade has seen the gradual promotion of access to modern energy services to the status of the "missing MDG." Various international agencies are now active in assessing the scale of the problem and promoting possible solutions.

Before examining the scale of the problem, it is necessary to define the key terms. The IEA (2011f: x) has defined "energy access" as "a household having reliable and affordable access to clean cooking facilities, a first connection to electricity and then an increasing level of electricity consumption over time to reach the regional average." The UNDP (Gaye 2007: 4) defines the related concept of "energy poverty" as "inability to cook with modern cooking fuels and the lack of a bare minimum of electric lighting to read or for other household and productive activities at sunset." A report by the UNDP-WHO (2009: 13) has defined "modern fuels" as "electricity, liquid fuels (such as Kerosene) and gaseous fuels (such as liquefied petroleum gas) and natural gas." This definition explicitly excludes traditional biomass and coal, but it has nothing to say about renewable sources of energy. Clearly, energy access based on increased consumption of hydrocarbon fuels increases the exposure of energy-poor developing countries to fossil-fuel price volatility; the combustion of these fuels is a source of GHGs. Thus, there is also a policy imperative on the part of the international agencies and developed economies to promote improved energy access in the developing world by promoting "sustainable energy," which the UNDP (2012: 11) define as: "encompassing renewable sources of energy (e.g. based on solar, wind, hydro, geothermal and sustainably grown biomass) as well as efficiency improvements in the use of energy carriers." Notwithstanding the additional level of complexity that is added by the sustainability dimension, the problem of energy access is now focused on two separate issues, the provision of clean cooking fuels and the access to electricity. The first issue relates to replacing traditional biomass and coal as a cooking fuel with cleaner fuels, but it also involves initiatives to improve the efficiency of cooking stoves. The second issue is about providing access to additional energy services, such as lighting, communication, and motive power, to promote employment and economic development; here improved access to electricity is seen as the key policy goal.

Over the past decade, two stylized facts have emerged about the level of access to electricity and to clean cooking fuels. In this statement on "Sustainable Energy for All," the UN General Secretary, Ban Ki-Moon (2011: 2) states: "More than 1.3 billion people lack access to electricity, and at least 2.7 billion people are without clean cooking facilities. More than 95 percent of these people are either in sub-Saharan Africa or developing Asia." These figures seem to have changed little over the past decade as the regions are also characterized by high rates of population growth. Thus, just standing still represents a policy challenge and it is possible that the number of energy poor could actually increase over the next decade or so. That said, real progress has been made in increasing access to electricity, particularly in Central and South America and in Asia more generally. Table 6.3 provides more detailed information on regional variation in the level of access to electricity and reliance upon traditional biomass for cooking. In addition, table 6.1 also has additional information on electricity access. Both sources of information highlight the variation in the level of access and that a lack of basic access to modern fuels and electricity is a problem that is concentrated in particular parts of the developing world.

It is no coincidence that the regions and countries suffering the most from a high degree of reliance on traditional cooking fuels and low access to electricity are the same as the places where slow progress is being made in relation to the MDG. It is well understood that reliance on traditional biomass fuels and inefficient stoves is both a source of health problems – particularly respiratory diseases related to indoor air pollution – and a major drain on the time of individual households. It is also understood that the burden of collecting fuel and cooking falls disproportionately on women and girls. A report by the UNDP-WHO (2009: 17) notes that: "almost 3 million deaths per year are attributable to solid fuel use, with more than 99 percent of the deaths occurring in developing countries." Thus, providing access to cleaner and more efficient cooking stoves would bring obvious health benefits, and would also free up women to undertake other tasks while allowing girls to attend school and attain higher education levels. UN-Energy (2005: 7) states unequivocally that "Access to electricity contributes to the empowerment of women." The positive feedbacks include increased labor productivity and potentially a reduction in population growth rates, as we know that high levels of female education and employment depresses fertility rates. Thus, there is a virtuous circle between energy access, demographics, and economic development (Modi et al. 2005). The alternative is a "vicious circle of poverty, poor health, low productivity and household food security" (Gaye 2007: 8).

TABLE 6.3 Number and share of people without access to modern energy services in selected countries, 2009

	Without access to electricity		Relying on traditional use of biomass for cooking	
	Population (million)	Share of population (percent)	Population (million)	Share of population (percent)
Africa	587	58	675	65
Nigeria	76	49	104	67
Ethiopia	69	49	77	93
DR of Congo	59	89	62	94
Tanzania	38	86	41	94
Kenya	33	84	33	83
Other sub-Saharan Africa	310	68	335	74
North Africa	2	1	4	3
Developing Asia	675	19	1921	54
India	289	25	836	72
Bangladesh	96	59	143	88
Indonesia	82	36	124	54
Pakistan	64	38	122	72
Myanmar	44	87	48	95
Rest of Developing Asia	102	6	648	36
Latin America	31	7	85	19
Middle East	21	11	0	0
Developing Countries	1314	25	2662	51
World	1317	19	2662	39

Source: IEA (2011f), *Energy for All: Financing Access for the Poor*. Paris: IEA, p. 11.

To highlight the centrality of energy access to the development agenda, the United Nations General Assembly declared 2012 the year of "Sustainable Energy for All," and energy was identified as one of seven critical issues at the Rio+20 Summit in July 2012. The Sustainable Energy for All initiative has set three objectives for 2030: ensuring universal access to modern energy services; doubling the rate of improvement in energy efficiency; and doubling the share of renewable energy in global energy use. The last two objectives sit well with the Kaya approach adopted in this analysis as they focus on efficiency and decarbonization, but these are not necessarily the priority in the least-developed countries in sub-Saharan Africa and developing Asia; nor in the rest of the developing world for that matter.

Beyond Basic Energy Access

The emphasis so far has been on the least-developed countries where access to modern energy services is the key issue, but there are large parts of the developing world where this is no longer the problem; rather, it is the need to improve the level of energy service provision to promote economic development that is the pressing issue (Wilson et al. 2012). Figure 6.2 presents a framework that identifies three levels of energy-service provision.

What figure 6.2 makes clear is that meeting basic human needs should be seen as the beginning of an incremental process that recognizes a gradual improvement in the quantity and quality of energy services as essential to the process of economic development. An examination of data on electricity and income per capita by the World Bank's regional groups shows a clear step change between the lower- and middle-income groups. In 2009, the average level of electricity consumption for the lower-income group was 646.8 kWh, while for the upper-middle-income groups it was 2,695.6 kWh (World Bank, Development Indicators Database). The problem with this "energy ladder" approach, like any stage-based approach to economic development, is that it suggests a single linear path to progress associated with a transition from traditional biomass to fossil fuels in various forms. However, this can be overcome by separating the energy services that are required from the ways in which those services are provided. This avoids the assumption that the only way to improve energy-service provision is to follow the centralized, grid-based, fossil-fuel development path of the developed world. Furthermore, given the heterogeneous nature of the countries of the developing world, it is also important to avoid a "one size fits all" approach to energy and development. It is evident from the sizeable literature on these issues (see Bhattacharyya 2012, and Sovacool 2012, for recent reviews) that there is a clear urban–rural divide in many developing economies, with the urban and peri-urban regions benefiting from a higher level of energy service provision than rural regions, where most of the energy poor reside. One final warning is the need to recognize that traditional energy sources still have a

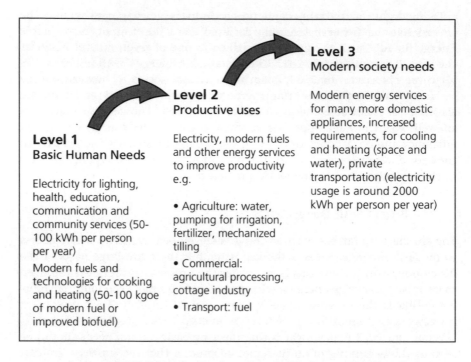

Level 3
Modern society needs

Level 2
Productive uses

Level 1
Basic Human Needs

Modern energy services for many more domestic appliances, increased requirements, for cooling and heating (space and water), private transportation (electricity usage is around 2000 kWh per person per year)

Electricity, modern fuels and other energy services to improve productivity e.g.

Electricity for lighting, health, education, communication and community services (50-100 kWh per person per year)

Modern fuels and technologies for cooking and heating (50-100 kgoe of modern fuel or improved biofuel)

• Agriculture: water, pumping for irrigation, fertilizer, mechanized tilling

• Commercial: agricultural processing, cottage industry

• Transport: fuel

Source: AGECC (2010) Energy for a Sustainable Future. UN, New York, 13

Figure 6.2 Incremental levels of access to energy services

role to play. As Practical Action's (2012) *Poor People's Energy Outlook 2012* makes clear, the biomass energy system is an important source of employment in many countries and, if its efficiency can be improved and its environmental impacts reduced, it can be part of the solution. It also has significant cultural value. Macqueen and Korhaliller (2011) make a case for "renewable biomass energy" as part of the solution to the energy dilemma in the developing world. They point out that if managed properly biomass can enhance energy security, constrain carbon emissions, boost rural employment, and reduce poverty (see Openshaw 2010). However, many of these renewable biomass solutions are now being advocated in the developing world and there is a danger that developing economies will export biomass, thus aggravating their domestic-energy access challenges (Wunder et al. 2012).

To arrive at a better understanding of the energy-development nexus, it is necessary to develop an approach to measuring access that moves beyond the provision of basic needs. The IEA has developed an Energy Development Index that seeks to mirror the UNDP's Human Development Index.

The index has been calculated on an annual basis since 2004 and is based on four indicators: per capita energy consumption, which serves as an indicator of the overall development of a country; per capita electricity consumption in the residential sector, which serves as an indicator of the reliability of services and the ability of consumers to pay; share of modern fuels in total residential sector use, which serves as a measure of access to clean cooking services; and share of population with access to electricity. A separate index is created for each indicator and the four indexes are then combined to create a single index, with each indicator having equal weighting. The IEA maintains that this index is a measure of a country or region's transition to the use of modern fuels. Figure 6.3 shows the Energy Development Index for 2011 for the majority of the countries considered as "developing" in this study. All indexes have their limitations, but this analysis does help to differentiate between those countries at the bottom of the ladder and those "progressing" in relation to access to modern energy services. Figure 6.3 also includes some of the countries that were considered earlier as part of the post-socialist group or the emerging economies group. This highlights the blurring of the boundaries between these groups when it comes to energy. The graph divides the group into quintiles on the basis of their EDI score. There is a clear "energy underclass" that comprises the energy poor in sub-Saharan Africa and developing Asia; but beyond that there are further degrees of differentiation. Not surprisingly, the literature on energy access tends to focus on the bottom level of provision, which explains why the international development agencies suggest that providing universal access to modern energy services will only increase global electricity generation by 2.5 percent, that oil demand would grow by less than 1 percent, and that CO_2 emissions would only increase by 0.8 percent (IEA, UNDP, and UNIDO 2010: 7). Furthermore, they estimate that to achieve universal access will require an investment of $48 billion a year between now and 2030, which is only 3 percent of anticipated total investment in energy. A further $4–5 billion a year would be required to provide universal access to clean cooking fuels (Ban Ki-Moon 2011: 4). But, in 2009, the total amount invested in extending energy access was $9.1 billion, of which 34 percent came from multilateral institutions, 30 percent from domestic governments, 22 percent from private investors, and 14 percent from bilateral aid (IEA 2011f: 7). However, this is only addressing the first part of the problem; it is the step from level 1 to levels 2 and 3 that presents the pressing energy challenge for the majority of developing economies. Here, the focus is on the improvement of both the quantity and quality of energy services available to both households and entrepreneurs to promote employment and economic development. Both Practical Action (2012) and the UNDP (2012) have explored the interrelationship between energy, employment, and economic development in more detail. Practical Action (2010) identified the basic connections between energy access and earning a living as being: the creation of new earning opportunities, improving existing earning activities, and reducing opportunity costs. In their 2012 Report, they stress that entrepreneurs seek more than just access:

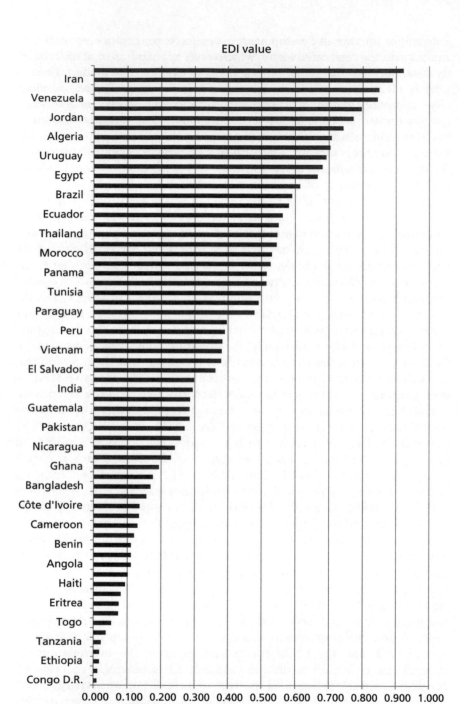

EDI value

Iran
Venezuela
Jordan
Algeria
Uruguay
Egypt
Brazil
Ecuador
Thailand
Morocco
Panama
Tunisia
Paraguay
Peru
Vietnam
El Salvador
India
Guatemala
Pakistan
Nicaragua
Ghana
Bangladesh
Côte d'Ivoire
Cameroon
Benin
Angola
Haiti
Eritrea
Togo
Tanzania
Ethiopia
Congo D.R.

0.000 0.100 0.200 0.300 0.400 0.500 0.600 0.700 0.800 0.900 1.000

Source: IEA (2012a), available at: <www.iea.org>

Figure 6.3 The Energy Development Index, 2011

"Reliability, quality and cost of energy supplies are critical success indicators to enterprises – but only when coupled with access to markets, social networks and a business proposition that has sufficient demand" (Practical Action 2012: x). Here we are moving beyond energy access to the development agenda more generally, but the lesson is that energy access – and improved energy services – is a means to an end, economic development, not an end in itself. This brings us back to the MDG and the fact that it is now clearly understood that "without access to energy services, it is not possible to achieve the millennium development goals" (Ban Ki-Moon 2011: 2).

Energy in the Service of Development

How you define the energy access problem determines the measures that need to be taken to address it. If, on the one hand, the emphasis is upon the issue of access to basic energy services and clean cooking fuels in the least-developed countries, which is the focus of the international agencies, then the solutions are likely be based upon financial and technical assistance and less on market-based solutions. If, on the other hand, the emphasis is upon energy for productive uses and modern energy services, then the emphasis is likely to be on more market-based provision. At the level of basic need it is necessary to break out of the poverty trap whereby people simply lack the ability to purchase a more efficient stove or invest in a solar panel and batteries to provide access to lighting and telecommunications. The literature is rich in case studies of micro-scale solutions, often using renewable energy technologies, but Practical Action (2012) warn that there are numerous examples where such projects proved unsustainable and the equipment was quickly abandoned as the local community lacked the expertise to maintain it once the donor organization had left. Clearly, community involvement is essential from the very outset if such initiatives are to provide long-term solutions (Wilson et al. 2012: 24–5). In fact, it might even be better if local organizations were responsible for their implementation, but donor agencies are usually unwilling to hand over the cash to local actors. At the same time, it is important that external initiatives do not undermine local capacity. For example, the influx of more efficient stoves from abroad as part of an assistance program could undermine local capacity to provide such stoves. Kuik et al. (2011: 628–9) observe that discussions around poverty, development, and energy security have two dimensions. First, at the national level, governments acknowledge the link between increased access to energy services and development, but this often translates into increased access for the industrial, service, and urban sectors. The second dimension of access for the poor and the marginalized attracts far less concern on the part of national governments that have insufficient resources to deal with all the demands they face. Consequently, Kuik et al. (2011: 629) see national governments facing three types of trade-off: first, because of a lack of resources, they tend to favor urban areas first, which are also more cost-effective to supply; second, there is a trade-off in relation to environmental sustainability that favors fossil fuels over renewable technologies that are seen as expensive and harder to obtain; and, third, as a result of the dominant policy turn toward privatization and liberalization, there is a tendency to favor return on investment rather than improving access. The net result is that national energy policies tend to focus on providing access to urban areas and to established industrial and service consumers on a commercial basis, rather than supporting improvements in access for the rural poor.

Experience to date suggests that there are three ways in which a country or region can improve access to electricity. The first way is to extend the existing grid. Most countries have some form of electricity grid based on the major urban areas; they may not be interconnected, but they do provide access to a large number of people. Often this infrastructure is based on antiquated and inefficient fossil-fuel generating capacity, and there are obvious efficiency and environmental gains to be had from upgrading the capital stock. Improved energy access can be provided by extending the grid to the surrounding peri-urban areas and by improving the quality of supply within the gird. A second way is to develop mini-grids around particular energy sources, such as a hydroelectric facility or a coalfield, or to connect a series of settlements within a region to a power-generation system using fossil fuel and/or renewable power generators – such as wind farms and solar arrays. The third way is to develop micro-level systems at the household and community level, often using renewable energy technologies such as solar panels, modern biomass, wind power, or small-scale hydroelectricity. The reality is that all of these alternatives are part of the solution as the development of a nationwide grid with large-scale power stations is beyond the financial capacity of most developing economies. The net result is that the level of access and the quality of energy service provision will vary greatly across each country, producing a distinct and uneven energy landscape that reinforces the urban–rural divide. Prasad (2011: 2) describes such a situation in sub-Saharan Africa: "The major problems of the electricity sector are low levels of consumption, unreliable power supply, power shortages, high electricity costs and unequal electricity access."

Recent analysis by the World Bank, Deichmann et al. (2010), supports this spatially disaggregated approach to improve access to electricity in sub-Saharan Africa. Their research concludes that "stand alone renewable energy technologies will be the lowest-cost option for a significant minority of households in African countries" and most of them will be in rural and remote areas. Furthermore, they conclude that "the economics of grid-supplied electricity in more densely populated areas remain compelling." This analysis suggests that scaling-up local-level renewable energy solutions is not really the way forward as it is unlikely to be the most cost-effective way of addressing the growing demand for energy. In such a context, the more significant energy-security and climate-change challenges relate to expanding grid-supplied capacity to the urban and peri-urban areas and other densely populated high-energy enclaves, such as mining and agri-industrial districts. To reduce fossil-fuel dependence and limit GHG emissions, the challenge here is for renewable and low-carbon technologies to contribute to grid-base electrification, a situation that parallels that in the developed and emerging economies.

The differentiated approach discussed above also suggests particular challenges in relation to financing improvements in energy access. Energy service provision in developing countries was initially a function of the state, but in the 1980s and 1990s the international development agencies promoted neoliberal policies that favored the privatization and liberalization of the power sector. By their own admission, this has had very mixed results (IEA 2011f). State ownership is commonly associated with inefficiency, corruption, and waste, but private owners seek a return on their investment and require paying customers to justify the provision of services and investment in infrastructure. The lack of sufficient paying customers often results in a lack of investment and poor-quality services, characterized by frequent supply disruptions. Thus, a catch-22 situation emerges whereby the private utility companies lack a sufficiently large paying market to justify investing in new capacity, while many potential customers either refuse to pay or seek local solutions – like petrol and diesel-powered generators – to provide security of supply for their businesses. One possible way out is for the state to subsidize the cost of power generation, thus providing the generator with the income needed to supply power and the customer with access to energy services at a price they can afford. In the developing world, governments often subsidize the direct cost of fossil fuels to consumers, which improves the affordability of modern fuels but also distorts the market. It is commonplace in energy-exporting countries for domestic fuel prices to be very low. Not surprisingly, the likes of the World Bank, IEA, and the G20 are not in favor of energy subsidies as a means of reducing energy poverty and promoting energy access. The G20 has launched an initiative to eradicate fossil-fuel energy subsidies. While it is acknowledged that well-targeted subsidies can be critical in ensuring access to modern energy services, subsidies to consumption are seen as encouraging increased energy use and reducing incentives to conserve energy. The legacies of the centrally planned economies discussed in chapter 4 illustrate the consequences of cheap energy to consumers; similar problems of wasteful consumption are now commonplace in the energy-exporting states of the Middle East where domestic fuel prices are very low. In a developing world context, subsidies on consumption reward those who use the most energy, which, by definition, is not the energy poor. Furthermore, fossil-fuel subsidies can lock consumers into "inefficient consumption and production paths" and undermine the introduction of cleaner sources of energy (IEA, OPEC, OECD, and World Bank 2010: 9). With the rising costs of fossil fuels, subsidies have become more important for consumers in the developing world, but more expensive for their governments to finance, and many countries are now seeking to remove subsidies. However, attempts to remove such subsidies can result in violent protests, as witnessed in Nigeria (Bazilian and Onyeji 2012). Beyond subsidies to consumers, governments everywhere subsidize energy in a variety of different ways, through trade instruments, regulations, taxation, provision of credits, direct finance, insurance, and provision of energy-related services. Trying to measure the level of energy subsidies in a given country is thus a challenging task that is complicated by the fact that many subsidies favor vested interests and are hidden by a lack of transparency. In a developing world context there is a complex trade-off between using subsidies on consumption to promote energy access and poverty alleviation, on the one hand, and seeking to remove market distortions to encourage private investment and investment in cleaner fuels and energy efficiency, on the other hand. There are no easy solutions, but it is clear that well-targeted policies that benefit the most needy can be a positive force. However, a balance needs to be struck to create the conditions for commercial energy service providers to thrive. Again, this suggests that addressing the problem of basic energy access requires one set of policy prescriptions, while creating the financial basis to meet productive demand and supply modern energy services requires a different set of policy prescriptions.

In sum, the literature on access to energy services is dominated by a discussion of the lack of access to clean cooking fuels and basic energy services in sub-Saharan Africa and developing Asia. These are clearly important issues as the cumulative consequences of these development failings are that nearly 20 percent of the world's population – one in five – lacks access to electricity, and nearly 40 percent lacks access to modern cooking fuels. However, for the majority of countries in the developing world, the issues of energy access have moved beyond basic needs and relate to improved energy services for productive uses and the development of modern energy services. Thus, we can conclude that there are two distinct energy challenges to be overcome in the developing world: one is to provide universal access to basic modern energy services (level 1 in figure 6.1); the second is to increase the quantity and quality of energy services to promote further economic development in the lower-middle income economies (levels 2 and 3 in figure 6.1), without aggravating existing energy-security and climate-change concerns. Here the current policy emphasis on trying to scale-up local decentralized renewable energy solutions may be misplaced. Instead, expanding the capacity and coverage of the existing grid-based system, while improving its efficiency and reducing its carbon emissions may be a more cost-effective way of climbing the energy ladder. The danger here is that meeting this demand will lead to a dash for fossil-fuel-based power generation across the developing world. One would have thought that this challenge presented an opportunity for initiatives like the Kyoto Protocol's Clean Development Mechanism (CDM) to finance lower-carbon solutions, but so far the vast majority of CDM projects have been located in emerging economies, predominantly China and India. This dimension of energizing development requires far greater attention than is currently being afforded it by policymakers and researchers alike.

The Curse of the Oil-Rich Developing Economies

In the context of our discussions above, one would have thought the developing economies that are endowed with an abundance of energy resources would have an advantage over the energy poor; for many, though not all, this has not turned out to be the case. There is a large literature devoted to explaining the so-called "resource curse" whereby resource-rich developing economies as a group are observed to have grown at a slower rate than resource-poor economies. However, the literature goes beyond GDP growth rates to suggest that resource-rich economies also tend to be less democratic and are more likely to be involved in conflict, particularly civil wars. The following statement from a recent World Bank publication sums up what the authors see as being generally accepted: "nations that are dependent on natural resources tend to grow slower than those that are resource poor," and "they also suffer from weak accountability and institutions, poor social capital, and increased likelihood of conflict" (Barma et al. 2012: 1). The authors of this book talk about the "political economy of natural resource-led development," which is a good way to think about the challenges facing resource-rich development economies as there is a complex interrelationship between the economic consequences of having easy access to large amounts of "rent" from natural resource exports, and the political pathologies that emerge as a consequence of that abundant rent. A reading of the literature makes clear that this is not a deterministic relationship; rather, the resource curse results from the way that those "rents" are mismanaged and misappropriated by the ruling elites in resource-rich developing economies. Not all resource-rich economies fall prey to the curse – looking back through history, some of today's most successful developed economies, such as the United States, followed an early path of resource-led development, and some remain relatively dependent on resource exports, for example, Australia, Canada, and Norway (Wright and Czelusta 2004).

We have also already encountered a number of resource-rich post-socialist economies and Russia's current energy dilemmas are in large part a consequence of the way that it manages its resource rents. Finally, the "rentier states" of the GCC represent a particular model of resource-abundant economy and although they face many of the same economic development challenges, for historical and cultural reasons they are distinct from the resource-rich developing economies. In the case of the latter, there is something about the way that they (mis)manage their resource wealth that, in many cases, results in underperformance, autocracy, and conflict.

In the context of our analysis of energy security, globalization, and climate change, the contemporary plight of the energy-rich developing economies is relevant in at least two ways. The first reason for this is because they are a major source of petroleum exports to the rest of the world and the trends suggest that there will be more energy-exporting developing economies in the future, and their share of global oil and gas trade will increase. Table 6.4 provides information on the current status of the oil-exporting developing economies. Unfortunately, complete data on domestic oil consumption are unavailable; some countries, such as Egypt, consume the bulk of the oil that they produce, but most export the majority of their production. In the case of the oil-producing states in the MENA and sub-Saharan Africa, the list of countries reads like a "who's who" of conflict zones over the past two decades, spanning from the first Gulf War in 1990 to the civil war in Syria in 2012. Thus, the fact that over a quarter of the world's oil production and 45 percent of known oil reserves are accounted for by states that are prone to economic failure and instability should be a major cause of concern for the oil-importing states. At present, a large part of the short-term volatility in the global oil market is a consequence of this instability. In some instances intervention by oil-importing states has also been a cause of disruption of supply to the world market. A final point here is to note that the resource-curse literature is about a wider range of resources, but oil seems to be particularly problematic (Bridge and Le Billion 2013: 125–52). There is a tendency to lump oil and gas together, but relatively few developing economies are gas exporters and, while there has been no research to verify this claim, I suspect that the nature of the gas supply chain makes gas-exporting states far less susceptible to the resource curse – this is certainly a supposition that warrants further research.

The second reason that a consideration of the resource curse is relevant is that in the case of sub-Saharan Africa there seems to be a connection between those states experiencing rapid population growth, the problem of basic energy access, and resource abundance. It is striking that a country like Nigeria, which accounted for nearly 3 percent of world oil production in 2011 and has a population of over a 150 million, should have 50.2 percent of its population living on less than $2 a day (2010 data from World Bank Database) and only 46.8 percent with access to electricity (see table 6.5). Thus, one of the "paradoxes of plenty" associated with some oil-exporting developing economies is that they have failed to provide universal energy access to their own people. In a wider context, the resource curse can be seen as one type of development failure that compounds the problems facing the "bottom billion" that live in the world's least-developed economies. Collier (2008: 39) calculates that about 29 percent of the people in the bottom billion live in countries in which resource wealth dominates the economy. He also notes that the payments made to oil-exporting developing economies by oil-importing states are far more substantial than the finance provided as development assistance. This is particularly true at present, and if that

TABLE 6.4 Oil-producing developing countries in 2011

	2011 production (million tonnes)	End of 2011 reserves (thousand million tonnes)	2011 R/P ratio (years)
Argentina	30.3	0.3	11.4
Columbia	48.7	0.3	5.9
Ecuador	27.1	0.9	33.2
Peru	7.0	0.2	22.2
Trinidad & Tobago	5.9	0.1	16.7
Venezuela	139.6	46.3	*
Iran	205.8	20.8	95.8
Iraq	136.9	19.3	*
Syria	16.5	0.3	20.6
Yemen	10.8	0.3	32.0
Algeria	74.3	1.5	19.3
Angola	85.2	1.8	21.2
Chad	6.0	0.2	36.1
Rep of Congo	15.2	0.3	18.0
Egypt	35.2	0.6	16.0
Eq. Guinea	12.5	0.2	18.5
Gabon	12.2	0.5	41.2
Libya	22.4	6.1	*
Nigeria	117.4	5	41.5
Sudan	22.3	0.9	40.5
Tunisia	3.7	0.1	15.0
Vietnam	15.9	0.6	36.7
Total	1050.9	106.6	
World	3995.6	234.3	54.2
% World	26.3	45.5	

*More than 100 years.
R/P ratio: Reserves-to-production ratio – if the reserves remaining at the end of the year are divided by the production that year, the result is the length of time that those remaining reserves would last if production were to continue at that rate.

Source: BP (2012b), *BP Statistical Review of World Energy June 2012*. London: BP, pp. 8 and 10.

TABLE 6.5 Oil- and gas-dependent developing economies

Country	Population (million)	GDP per capita (US$ 2010)	Electricity access (% 2008)	Oil & gas share of exports (% 2007–2009)	Oil & gas share of total public revenues (% 2007–2009)
Algeria	34.4	4,460	99.3	98.5	68.6
Angola	18.0	3,960	26.2	95.6	83.6
Bolivia	9.7	1,790	77.5	44.4	26.0
Cameroon	18.9	1,160	29.4	33.3	38.2
Chad	11.1	1,284	3.5	84.3	57.1
Colombia	44.5	1,142	93.6	23.9	na
Congo DR	64.2	2,345	11.1	25.0	na
Congo Rep.	3.6	2,310	30.0	87.7	86.0
Ecuador	13.5	4,510	92.2	Na	49.0
Eq. Guinea	0.2	14,680	*27.0	98.9	93.5
Gabon	1.5	7,760	**36.7	77.3	65.7
Guinea	9.8	380	**20.2	89.9	24.5
Iran	72.0	4,530	98.4	75.8	69.2
Iraq	31.2	2,320	85.0	97.5	81.0
Libya	6.3	12,020	99.8	97.5	89.7
Mauritania	3.2	1.060	**30.1	Na	11.0
Nigeria	151.3	1,180	46.8	97.5	83.7
Sudan	41.4	1,270	31.4	90.2	55.7
Syria	21.2	2,640	92.7	39.7	29.6
Timor-Leste	1.1	2,220	22.0	97.3	98.2
Trinidad & Tobago	1.3	15,380	99.0	87.0	57.8
Venezuela	27.9	11,590	99.0	81.2	46.3
Vietnam	86.2	1,100	89.0	17.5	31.0
Yemen	23.1	1.060	38.3	98.9	68.1

* = 2006.
** = 2005.

Sources: Adapted from Barma et al. (2012), *Rents to Riches? The Political Economy of Natural Resource-Led Development.* Washington, DC: World Bank, pp. 260–2, and UNDP-WHO (2009), *The Energy Access Situation in Developing Countries.* New York: UNDP, pp. 66–71.

massive flow of financial resources was more effectively used it could do much to address the millennium development goals discussed earlier in this chapter.

Rather than reviewing the literature on the resource curse for its own sake, our principal concern here is with the resource curse as a challenge to energy security, in relation to both the security of oil exports and energy access. There are a number of seminal publications and review articles that provide access to the wider literature (Stevens 2003; Rosser 2006), and the purpose here is to present some of the key claims and underlying drivers of the problems facing oil-exporting developing economies. The next section focuses on the impact of oil rents on economic performance; it is then followed by a discussion of the political dimensions. It is important to note that this is a body of research that has evolved over the last 20–30 years, and one of the criticisms that is leveled at some of the seminal works is that they focus on the 1970s and 1980s when the resource-rich economies did underperform; however, a longer-term perspective reveals that their performance was no better or no worse than the resource-poor states. As Michael Ross (2012) notes, the question really should be why the resource-rich states have not performed better than the resource-poor, when they have the benefit of substantial amounts of financial capital easily earned from their resource sectors.

In their seminal article, Sachs and Warner (2001: 828) noted that the "empirical support for the curse of natural resources is not bullet proof, but it is quite strong," and go on to insist that "high resource intensity tends to correlate with slow growth." They also note that there is no universally accepted theory of the natural-resource curse, but suggest that most explanations have a crowding-out logic. That is, the dominance of natural resources in an economy crowds out "x" and it is "x" that drives sustainable economic growth. For them, "x" is traded manufacturing activities. Thus "one explanation of the resource curse is that resource abundance tended to render the export sector uncompetitive and that as a consequence resource-abundant countries never successively pursued export-led growth" (Sachs and Warner 2001: 835). The concept of "Dutch disease" provides one mechanism by which the non-resource sector is rendered uncompetitive. The term refers to the experience of the Dutch economy as a consequence of gas exports that resulted in an appreciation of the Dutch currency. This made domestic production more expensive and reduced its export competitiveness. At the same time, the increased purchasing power of the Dutch currency made it more affordable to import goods, thus the domestic non-resource sector declined. The idea of "Dutch disease" seems to be generally accepted by academics and policymakers alike, but the empirical evidence in support of it is rather limited (Davis and Tilton 2005: 239). That said, oil-exporting states do seem to be susceptible to both exchange-rate appreciation and high inflation rates. Another reason why a dominant resource sector might hinder the development of the non-resource sector is that its rents are not produced in the same way as manufactured goods (more on this below). Furthermore, oil production, for example, tends to be capital rather than labor intensive. Thus, it does not promote economic diversification through the payment of a large workforce. Though the rents do drive domestic consumption, this often tends to be concentrated within the ruling elite, serving to drive inequality with a small element of society being very rich. At the same time, the oil sector operates as an "enclave" that is relatively isolated from the host economy. Linkages tend to be internalized within the oil industry, which reduces the domestic multiplier effect. One way of addressing this is to impose local content requirements on the oil companies to promote the development of local service companies; thus, there are tactics that can be employed to get a better deal for the host economy. However, this form of development does not isolate the oil-exporting economy from another major challenge, that of price volatility. As table 6.5 reveals, many of the oil-exporting developing economies are highly dependent upon oil revenues, which dominate their exports and are by far their largest source of public revenues. Oil prices, and resource prices more generally, are volatile, and thus oil-exporting states in times of plenty need to hedge against future falls in revenues. Falling revenues from oil exports are part of a wider problem of declining terms of trade for exporters of primary commodities, because as the revenues from exports fall they have to import less or face a growing trade deficit. The sheer scale and volatility of oil revenues presents a challenge to even the most competent government, but, as we shall see below, the very nature of oil revenue often undermines the capacity or willingness of the ruling elite to make the right decisions. The economic geographer Richard Auty (1993, 2001; Auty and Gelb 2001) coined the term "resource curse" and developed a "staple trap" model to explain why resource-abundant economies seem unable to promote sustained economic growth. According to Auty (2001: 83), prolonged reliance on primary exports has three adverse consequences: economic diversification initially occurs in other primary commodities, it retards urbanization, and results in surplus rural labor, which raises income inequalities and social tensions. There is also a tendency to use resource rent to protect inefficient infant industries that are often also protected by trade barriers. Furthermore, rents are often invested in large white-elephant projects that do nothing to promote economic growth that are really a mechanism for rent distribution among the ruling elite. Finally, governments in resource-abundant economies tend to be larger, as the state uses rent to finance a large state apparatus to provide employment and co-opt potential sources of opposition. In short, the staple trap describes a situation whereby the governments of resource-rich economies make poor decisions and fail to promote competitive industrialization that promotes diversification and provides meaningful employment for the masses. To do this, Auty maintained that it required what he called the "developmental state." The staple trap is not a forgone conclusion and states can avoid it by pursuing policies that use resource rent to finance diversification and sustainable economic growth; however, analysis of the politics of resource-abundant states suggests that the nature of oil rents, in particular, makes it easy to fall into the staple trap. In an economic sense, it is the way that rent is captured and then spent that is critical to understanding the performance of oil-exporting states (Karl 1997; Barma et al. 2012: 10). Ross (2012) suggests that the wave of privatizations during the 1970s and 1980s placed the rents under the direct control of the oil-exporting states, and that this was the origin of many of the problems they have subsequently encountered. Jones Luong and Weinthal (2008) support this view through their analysis of the post-Soviet states and maintain that "oil is not a curse"; rather, mineral-rich states are cursed by the structure of ownership they choose to manage their mineral wealth. What this suggests is that the economic and political dimensions of the resource curse are inextricably linked and, as noted at the onset, it really is a problem of political economy.

The political science literature explores the reason why oil-exporting states tend to be less democratic and more conflict prone than other types of resource-rich or resource-poor economies. Like the literature on economic performance, much of this analysis is too reductionist – seeking out one or two variables to explain the level of autocracy or incidence of civil war – and seems blind to the importance of history and geography (see Watts 2009; and Le Billion 2005). The most extreme case is Friedman's (2006) idea of the "First Law of Petropolitics," which makes a causal link between the oil prices and the pace of freedom. Nonetheless, it does seem that oil wealth can be a cause of political instability. The problems seem to stem from the nature of oil wealth and evolve out of the idea of the "rentier state," developed to explain the polity of the oil-rich states of the Middle East. The argument goes that because oil wealth is not earned and its rents are easily captured (and hidden) by the state, the state does not have to tax the population to obtain its revenue. This makes the state less accountable to the people and the people less concerned about what happens to state revenues, as these have not come from taxing their income (Humphreys et al. 2007: 11). Consequently, there is a lack of connection between the people and the state. This lack of transparency and accountability is also a breeding ground for the misappropriation of rents and corruption. Furthermore, the literature suggests that the rents controlled by the state are used to finance oppression and militarization, or, in a more benevolent situation, the rents are used to placate the citizenship, thus reducing the likelihood that they will challenge the legitimacy of the state. Often these autocratic rulers are supported by oil-importing states in the interest of maintaining political stability. Ross's (2001) seminal work on oil and democracy identified three causal mechanisms: the "rentier effect" and the "repression effect," both of which were discussed above. The third mechanism, which he calls the "modernization effect," provides a link to the staple-trap model; here a failure to modernize the economy limits the educational level and professional specialization of the workforce, thus retarding the development of a democratic opposition to a ruling elite. His subsequent analysis suggested that oil does hinder democracy (but so does non-fuel wealth) and there was tentative support for a link between oil wealth and authoritarianism through the rentier and modernization effects. A decade later Ross (2012: 1) extended his analysis to 50 years of data and 170 countries, and he concludes that "Today, the oil states are 50 percent more likely to be ruled by autocrats and more than twice as likely to have civil wars as non-oil states." He suggests that the cause of the problem is the unusual nature of petroleum revenues (he fails to distinguish between oil and gas), which have four distinctive qualities: their scale, their source, their stability, and the secrecy surrounding them. He notes (Ross 2012: 6): "the most important political fact about oil . . . is that the revenues it bestows on governments are usually large, do not come from taxes, and can easily be hidden." One of the most interesting findings suggested by Ross is the impact that oil wealth has on the status of women and on population growth. He maintains that petroleum wealth tends "to choke off opportunities for women" and that one of the consequences of this is higher levels of fertility and population growth, with slower per capita economic growth (Ross 2012: 202). This statement resonates with our earlier discussion of the relationship between population growth and climate change, and the differential gender consequences that stem from a lack of access to basic energy services. Ross (2012: 205) states unequivocally: "If not for oil's damaging effects on women's work, the petroleum-rich countries would have outperformed the non-oil states, improving the lives of women and men alike."

The political science literature on resource-abundant economies also claims that oil wealth promotes civil war and conflict. This analysis is divided, on the one hand, into studies using large data sets and multiple variables to explain the incidence of civil war, and being oil rich is seen as an important explanatory variable (work by Michael Ross and Paul Collier and colleagues being the most significant); and, on the other hand, detailed studies of particular regions and countries that are conflict prone. Michael Watts's (2004, 2009) work on Nigeria is an excellent example. A simple way of looking at this work is that it highlights that oil rents are clearly something worth fighting over. Equally, the development failure associated with the staple trap may generate social tensions that generate conflict (Auty 2004). The literature makes a distinction between separatist struggles that revolve around the right to control the revenues from oil-producing regions within a state (the Niger Delta being the most obvious case, though there are many others), and general civil unrest created by the failure of the state to meet the needs of the people (the recent Arab Spring may be an example). Undoubtedly, each conflict is different with its own geography and history and many conflicts have a just cause with the state being culpable, which does not lend itself to the use of correlation and regression to explain greed and grievance. Equally, oil may be a contributory factor, rather than the cause of much of the conflict, repression, and violence found in the oil-rich economies of the developing world. Ross (2012: 178) concludes that "the production of oil tends to further heighten the danger of civil war, especially in low- and middle-income countries, and especially since 1989." But he notes: "Petroleum is never the only source of conflict, and it never makes conflict inevitable."

In sum, we can conclude that oil wealth presents a particular economic and political challenge for developing economies and their political elites. The literature suggests a wide range of problems that an oil-exporting developing economy may encounter: poor economic growth and exposure to price volatility; low standards of living and associated poverty and social inequality; high levels of corruption; authoritarianism and poor governance, as well as the risk of civil war. It is no wonder that discovery of oil wealth is seen by some as a curse, rather than a blessing. However, it is important to stress that none of these problems are a forgone conclusion. The dangers that come with oil wealth are now well understood and there are clear policy prescriptions to maximize the benefits that should come from the wealth and opportunity provided by oil rents. At the heart of the problem is what happens to the oil rents, thus the policy prescriptions revolve around making the management of those rents transparent and more effective in terms of promoting sustainable growth. According to Stevens (2003), based on a review of the literature, there are a number of measures that can be taken to avoid the resource curse. First, it could be left in the ground, the aim being to manage the pace of exploitation and thus the rate of production and depletion. However, as table 6.4 reveals, many oil-exporting developing countries have modest levels of production and limited reserves, so it would be difficult to resist the desire to produce as much as possible as quickly as possible. There are also economic arguments in favor of realizing resource wealth early and investing it wisely. Second, the economy could be diversified to reduce vulnerability to volatility. The problem here is that the lack of a positive business environment – corruption, the lack of clear property rights and the rule of law – discourages investment in the wider economy. Furthermore, the wider problems of poverty and inequality depress the purchasing power of the domestic market. Third, revenue sterilization could be undertaken, which involves macroeconomic policy aimed at reducing the negative impacts of large windfall revenues, such as exchange-rate appreciation (Dutch disease) and inflation. One way that this can be achieved is through a fourth measure, the creation of a stabilization or oil fund. This also reduces the problem associated with volatility and enables funds to be set aside for future generations. As Stevens (2003: 21–2) suggests, there are both advantages and disadvantages in relation to the creation of such funds and they are no substitute for sound macroeconomic policy. The fifth possibility is investment policy, which is really an extension of the diversification strategy as the aim is to strengthen the non-resource sectors of the economy. In the context of our earlier discussion, one aim of the investment strategy could be to provide universal access to modern energy services, as this is critical to the development of the manufacturing and service sectors. If domestic energy strategy focused on the development of sustainable energy sources, as well as the promotion of energy efficiency, it would also help to preserve the amount of oil for export. Norway, and in the future Brazil, provide examples where domestic energy needs are met from renewable and low-carbon sources, with oil (and gas) being exported. This strategy could serve as a model for new oil-exporting countries. It also has the added benefit of isolating domestic energy provision from fossil-fuel price volatility. Unfortunately, the data in table 6.5 suggests that attention to energy access has not been a priority in many oil-exporting developing economies. In relation to the political dimensions of the resource curse, Stevens (2003: 22–3) suggests that "in the literature two strands emerge as desirable to encourage a 'blessing' rather than a 'curse.' The first is to develop democracy . . . The second is the need to remove corruption and contain rent seeking." The reasons for this are clear from the discussion above, but so are the barriers. Why should the ruling elite in an oil-exporting economy be persuaded that the best course of action is to promote the rule of law, increase transparency, and enter into democratic elections? In that respect, it would seem that the timing of when a country became oil rich is critical. If a country is a functioning democracy before it finds oil it is better equipped to manage its resource wealth. Although some of the newly emerging oil-exporting countries in sub-Saharan Africa are more democratic and more stable – Ghana, for example – only time will tell how well they manage their new-found wealth. In too many instances, the discovery of oil only serves to aggravate pre-existing tensions and failures. International efforts such as the Extractive Industries Transparency Initiative (EITI) and "Publish What You Pay" can encourage greater transparency in relation to the collection and management of rents; yet it is hard to reconcile Nigeria's status as an "EITI Compliant Country" with the continuing poverty and violence in the Niger Delta. In the final analysis, the reality is that the oil-importing states and their associated oil companies, whether it is the IOCs of the OECD countries, or the NOCs of the emerging countries, are most interested in a continued flow of oil on the world market. Thus, at present, the demands of global energy security trump the needs of the people who live in the oil-exporting countries of the developing world. However, if things fail to improve it is likely that the economic and political instability that results from the development failures associated with the resource curse will impede the flow of oil on to the world market. In some senses, the Arab Spring was a precursor of just such a situation. What this means is that the future energy security of the importing countries is best served by assisting the oil-exporting countries of the developing world to manage, and in the case of new producers avoid, the resource curse, rather than turning a blind eye to the actions of the autocrats.

Conclusions: Energy for Development

At present the headline issue in relation to energy and development is the need to achieve universal access to basic modern energy services. The UN makes it clear that this can be achieved at minimal cost and with minimal impact on energy demand and carbon dioxide emissions. It is now widely accepted that universal energy access is essential to the achievement of the MDG. Nobody would disagree that this is an important objective that deserves priority on the part of international organizations and donor states; but it oversimplifies the energy challenges that face the developing world. The relationship between population growth, energy access, and economic development is far more complex than the provision of more efficient cooking stoves and small-scale off-grid solutions. Such initiatives are a good place to start in terms of providing improved energy services to the bottom billion, but they will not address the issue of energy for development. By this, I mean the step change in energy service provision required to power sustainable economic development (level 3 in figure 6.2). This requires the expansion of existing grids and the development of regional and mini-grids to provide reliable and affordable access to modern energy services (specifically electricity). It is this challenge that faces the majority of developing economies, even those that are energy rich. At present many of these countries are following fossil-fuel-based solutions that expose them to the rising cost of fuel imports and the problems of volatility. In such a context the pursuit of more sustainable energy solutions brings with it the dual benefits of reducing reliance on fossil fuels and reducing carbon emissions. Furthermore, more sustainable solutions can include modern biomass energy that could provide employment in rural areas. Such an approach should be attractive to international organizations and donor countries seeking to support energy access in the developing world, particularly as many of the same solutions – wind power, solar power, biomass, and small-scale hydropower – are being developed in their home economies. Of course, the danger here is that the focus will be on trade as aid, rather than on building local capacity to develop domestic manufacturing, installation, and servicing capacity. But there is also ample scope for South–South cooperation in sustainable energy technologies. In sum, the issue is not scaling-up the solutions provided to address basic energy access; instead it is about provision of modern energy services to power economic development, which in turn will help to constrain population growth and reduce both gender and rural–urban inequality, potentially slowing the pace of urbanization.

This chapter has shown that resource-rich economies face particular challenges, yet they have the opportunity to use the rents generated by fossil-fuel exports to finance sustainable energy solutions for their domestic economies. Such an approach could contribute to the diversification of the economy by providing jobs and economic opportunity in the non-fossil-fuel sector, and by creating the conditions to support economic development. Meeting domestic energy demands from sustainable sources also has the added benefit of preserving the exportable surplus of fossil fuels and isolates the domestic economies from price volatility without having to resort to expensive subsidies. Again, the international community should see benefit in such a proposition as the current instability of many energy-exporting economies in the developing world is a growing source of energy insecurity. What is clear is that a last-gasp fossil-fuel-based development of energy services is not a sustainable solution for anyone; instead, energizing development must be achieved through the provision of sustainable low-carbon energy services. In sum, the energy dilemma in the developing world is not just about providing energy access to those who have none; it is about providing modern energy services to power economic development without compromising the environment, locally or globally.

CHAPTER SEVEN

Conclusions

The purpose of this analysis has been to demonstrate that the relationship between energy, economy, and environment is complex and varies greatly across the globe. Furthermore, globalization processes are critical to understanding the interplay between two of the greatest challenges that society faces today: energy security and climate change. This final chapter has two tasks: first, to pull together the results of the analysis of the global energy dilemmas facing each of the four regions by identifying the key "Kaya drivers," and, second, to consider the global governance and policy challenges posed by the global energy dilemma. This analysis has drawn from a wide range of literature from many disciplines, and it is not my intention here to complicate matters further by seeking to locate the concluding discussion in the voluminous literatures on energy security, globalization, and climate-change policy. Rather, the aim is to focus on the insights gained from the deployment of the global energy dilemmas nexus.

Global Energy Dilemmas

This book is organized around the proposition that the world currently faces a global energy dilemma: *can we have secure, affordable, and equitable supplies of energy that are also environmentally benign?* When the research project on which this book is based started, the notion of equity was missing from the definition, but as the project proceeded it became increasingly apparent that issues of access, equity, and justice are central to the global energy dilemma. As Ulrich Beck (2010: 256) suggests, social inequalities and climate change are two sides of the same coin; and issues of inequality and justice are at the center of the current impasse over a global climate-change agreement. It is not just a matter of providing access to energy services in the developing world; it is also about the social and economic consequences of higher energy prices across the globe. If future energy supplies are to be environmentally benign, the chances are that they will be more expensive to deliver. This is the cost of correcting Stern's market failure and including environmental externalities of energy production in the cost of energy services to the consumer. The term "environmentally benign" is used to capture a broad range of environmental impacts. Clearly, the focus of the current analysis is on climate change and the major role that fossil-fuel combustion plays in increasing atmospheric concentration of GHGs. However, it is important to understand that all forms of energy supply come with environmental impacts. As we have depleted the more accessible sources of oil and gas, we are starting to exploit inaccessible and unconventional sources of supply – shale gas, shale oil, oil shale, oil sands, deep-water offshore production, Arctic oil and gas – all of which have potentially significant environmental impacts. Equally, low-carbon sources of energy supply come with their own environmental impacts; nuclear power is the most obvious example, but renewables such as wind, solar, and tidal power have environmental impacts too. The message is now clear: we can no longer afford to ignore the environmental costs of satisfying our expanding demand for energy services. The difference between climate change and the other forms of environmental impact is that it is global in scope; thus, no single country or region can provide a solution as this requires global cooperation and compromise.

The starting point in this analysis was an examination of the evolution of the current fossil-fuel energy system and its contribution to the problem of anthropogenic climate change. The concept of "energy transitions" was introduced to explain how the energy system has evolved since the Industrial Revolution. Today, the term "low-carbon transition" is used to describe the changes that are now needed to reduce GHG emissions from energy consumption. The term "transition" was also used to describe the process of change after the collapse of the Soviet Union, a transition from plan to market. In that context, the notion of transition was widely criticized as it suggested a straightforward change from one system to another. The reality was far more complex as market-based economic relations had to be grafted on to an economy that was the product of a different logic. As a result, many favored the term "transformation" as it recognized the path-dependent nature of systemic change and also allowed for multiple outcomes, some more reminiscent of the socialist past, others closer to the Western notion of a market economy. There is a lesson to be learnt here in relation to the low-carbon transition. First, is it more of a transformation than a transition? It will take a long time to achieve and for many years fossil fuels will remain the dominant source of primary energy supply. This means that, in the short term at least, we ignore the current challenges facing fossil-fuel production at our peril, as they are the contemporary guarantors of energy security. Second, there will be multiple pathways to a low-carbon energy future. This is particularly important in relation to the current analysis and is explained in more detail below. Third, the future is not one of an energy transition whereby a particular energy source becomes dominant, as was the case in the past; rather, there will be a greater diversity of energy sources at a national, regional, and global level. This differentiation is already apparent in the relative importance of natural gas and nuclear power, both of which are predominantly found in the energy mix of developed economies. This diversity means that different regions will find different solutions to the global energy dilemma; thus, policymakers should avoid prescribing a single-policy solution.

This analysis has used the "Kaya Identity" as a heuristic device to identify the key drivers of carbon dioxide emission from energy use. To remind us, the Kaya Identity suggests emissions are the product of population size, multiplied by GDP per capita, by energy intensity, and by the carbon intensity of energy use. Thus, there are four potential drivers of emissions: the size of the population and its rate of growth, the level of economic activity and its rate of growth, energy intensity – which is the relationship between energy consumption and economic output – and the carbon intensity of energy use, which is largely determined by the energy mix in a particular economy or region. Clearly, these four factors are not the only things that influence energy-related carbon emissions and each driver itself comprises a number of processes. However, the intent here has been to use the Kaya Identity as an analytical framework to examine how the relative importance of each driver differs geographically. The global energy dilemmas nexus was used to divide the world on the basis of the type of energy dilemma that they face. Each of those regions has been subjected to substantive analysis and, in the case of the first three regions, this has been supplemented by detailed examination of the key countries or regional groupings. The analysis also introduced the notion of the triple challenge that combines the issues of climate change and global energy security. Thus, the triple challenges are:

- To improve *energy intensity*, that is, to reduce the amount of energy used per unit of economic output.
- To reduce the *carbon intensity* of energy supply, that is, the amount of CO_2 produced per unit of energy supplied.
- To achieve the above in ways that are *secure, affordable, and equitable* (and that does not threaten economic growth).

We can now use the global energy dilemmas nexus and the notion of the triple challenge to present the key Kaya drivers and policy issues for each of the four regions. For the high-energy societies of the developed world, it is their high levels of economic development (and personal consumption) and associated energy demand that are the key drivers of energy-related emissions. In the current economic climate, the suggestion that constraining economic growth and reducing personal consumption should be used as policy levers clearly has no traction, though it is the position of some environmental groups and academics. Rather, energy policy has focused on policies to improve energy intensity, that is, improvements in energy efficiency and demand reduction, on the one hand, and policies to reduce the carbon intensity of energy use, on the other hand. However, there is a growing tension between the climate-change imperative of decarbonization via the expansion of low-carbon energy and the energy-security imperative in terms of the need to provide affordable supplies of energy. At the same time, the more conventional energy-security concerns relating to fossil-fuel security remain significant, though in some policy contexts the expansion of domestic low-carbon energy supplies is seen as an antidote to reliance on imported fossil fuels. The rapid expansion of shale gas production presents an additional level of complexity as it provides the possibility of cheap, abundant, and relatively low-carbon source of energy. However, the reality is that natural gas is a fossil fuel and a substantial expansion of natural gas in the global energy mix will not reduce the level of carbon dioxide emissions to the level required to avoid catastrophic climate change. For the developed world, the policy prescription is clear: rapid decarbonization of energy supply, coupled with demand reduction and improved efficiency. The challenge is how to achieve this in a manner that does not threaten economic recovery and competitiveness.

The post-socialist states have been identified as a distinct group in this analysis; first, because of the particular relationship of energy, economy, and environment propagated by the central-planned economy; and, second, because the collapse of the Soviet Union had a dramatic impact on energy consumption and carbon dioxide emissions in the so-called "transition economies." Thus, from a Kaya perspective, the collapse of the Soviet system impacted on all four drivers, the population in many post-socialist states fell and in most is now stable, the level of economic activity fell dramatically as a consequence of "transitional recession," and with it the level of energy intensity fell as energy consumption also declined. The carbon intensity of energy use also declined as some of the more carbon-intensive elements of the energy system collapsed, though this was not a universal process. Thus, as noted earlier, the collapse of the Soviet system delivered a windfall carbon dioxide emissions reduction, but at considerable social and economic cost. As discussed in chapter 4, the key issue for these economies is what happens next. Prior to the global financial crisis, the majority of these economies were experiencing economic growth, levels of personal consumption were increasing, and, with these, energy demand. In short, these economies were on the road to joining the ranks of the high-energy societies. Thus, for them to avoid a significant rebound, their carbon emissions policies need to focus on improving energy efficiency – there are substantial gains to be made here – and developing low-carbon sources of energy supply. Both demand reduction and the expansion of indigenous renewable energy production have the added benefit of reducing the reliance on imported fossil fuels (such as Russian gas). A focus on energy efficiency and the development of low-carbon energy also has benefits for the energy-exporting economies amongst this group as it helps to preserve hydrocarbon exports without having to resort to investment in expensive new production. For this group, the bottom line is that at present they have benefited from improving levels of energy intensity (as their economies have grown faster than the growth of energy demand) and low levels of carbon emissions; the danger is that they rely on fossil fuels to satisfy future energy demands, which will then compound the problems created by the high levels of consumption in the high-energy economies and the surging demand of the emerging economies.

The emerging economies are by far the most dynamic group and it is largely they who will shape the future in terms of energy security and climate change. In most instances, the key Kaya drivers relate to the rapid rate of economic growth experienced over the last decade and the carbon-intensive nature of their energy supply. Much of this growth has been driven by the expansion of their exports sectors and the developed economies have been the major markets for those goods. However, increasingly, economic growth and consumption are now being driven by domestic demand. Thus, as living standards increase so does demand for white goods, vehicles, and all the other trappings of consumer society. Therefore, for this group of countries, the key imperative is securing sufficient energy to continue to fuel economic growth and the improvement of living standards. For many political regimes this is part of an implicit social contract; thus, energy security is a matter of short-term survival and climate change is far less significant a concern. In such a context the physical challenge of matching supply with growing demand takes precedence over concerns about emissions. Consequently, many countries in this group see the idea of emission-reduction targets as a threat to their economic prosperity and prefer to talk in terms of reductions in energy intensity. This can be achieved by ensuring that their economies grow more rapidly than their demand for energy grows. However, they are not immune to the consequences of climate change or the other environmental costs of the energy system – such as air pollution and competing demands for water. The rapid growth in energy demand also makes them sensitive to more traditional energy-security concerns, such as price volatility and scarcity. In the case of the energy-exporting emerging economies, the rapid growth of domestic demand also threatens their ability to export, which not only presents a massive opportunity cost, but also contributes to global energy insecurity by constraining supply. In the current context, many of these emerging economies are not going to be persuaded to sign up to binding emissions-reduction targets; but some are persuaded that improving energy efficiency, managing demand growth, and developing indigenous low-carbon sources of energy can help them to sustain economic growth, improve energy intensity, and meet the demands of their population. Thus, what is required here is an alternative growth model based on a more sustainable energy system, which brings with it a reduction in the rate of growth of carbon emissions and a reduced reliance upon imported fossil fuels.

The final group of countries in the developing world face yet a different set of dilemmas. At present, their low levels of economic development and energy consumption mean that they are not major contributors to energy-related carbon emissions. In a Kaya context, the key driver here is population growth that also presents a major development challenge. Over the past decade, it has been recognized that universal access to modern energy services is essential to poverty reduction. Thus, the current policy imperative is providing universal energy access. Achieving this is not costly; nor will it have a significant impact on the problems of climate change and energy security. It is a matter to be decided by the international institutions, donor countries, and the governments of the countries most affected by a lack of energy access. Furthermore, the provision of universal energy access can bring with it the benefits of reduced population growth and improvements in the living standards of women and children. However, universal energy access is only the beginning, as further economic development requires the provision of the level of energy services required to support new economic activity. Here, the imperative should be on the creation of sustainable energy systems to support economic growth. Such systems can include traditional sources of energy supply, fossil fuels where these are the most effective solution, and the development of new renewable sources of supply. They can also include the expansion of existing grid-based systems and the development of regional and off-grid solutions. Here, it is important to design systems that fit particular local, national, and regional contexts, and to include local people in the fabrication of equipment and the maintenance and management of the system. Simply providing equipment in the form of trade as aid will not result in sustainable solutions. Such an approach may allow these countries to leapfrog the risk of total reliance on centralized fossil-fuel grid-based systems by switching to a more diversified and sustainable energy system of the type that is the aspiration of the high-energy societies. The rapid growth of mobile phone usage provides a useful analogy, in that it enabled a dramatic increase in access to telecommunications without the need to first develop conventional phone lines. Thus, low-carbon off-grid solutions in more remote regions can develop at the same time as grid-based systems. This sustainable solution is equally applicable to the oil- and gas-exporting economies of the developing world, and would help them to maintain their exports, while promoting the diversification of the economy and meeting the needs of the population. It also reduces the need for costly fossil-fuel subsidies and isolates their domestic economy from some of the price volatility associated with fossil fuels, thus avoiding two of the pathologies associated with the resource curse. The alternative, an increasing reliance on fossil fuels, will prove economically unsustainable and environmentally disastrous as the countries of the developing world are the most vulnerable to the impacts of climate change. Thus, the energizing of development needs to be made part of the solution to climate change rather than part of the problem.

Global Policy and Governance Challenges

The Kaya Identity has provided a framework for identifying the key drivers of energy-related carbon dioxide emissions, and this final section considers the variety of policies that are required to reduce emissions and assesses the adequacy of the current global governance structures relating to energy security, globalization, and climate change. The analysis presented above made a number of policy prescriptions in relation to the energy dilemmas facing the four groups of countries; some features are common to all, while others are related to specific groups. Thus, the challenges faced by individuals and governments in high-energy societies, used to 24/7 access to reliable and affordable energy services, are naturally very different from individuals and governments where only a minority of the population has access to electricity. Table 7.1 presents a set of policy prescriptions devised by World Bank staff as part of the 2010 *World Development Report* on climate change and development. Although couched in the language of the low-carbon transition, they are useful because they map well on to the global energy dilemmas nexus and the discussion of policy imperative presented above. Thus, the high-income countries equate to our high-energy economies, the bulk of our post-socialist and emerging economies fall within the middle-income countries, and the developing countries into the low-income countries. Of course, the policy prescriptions reflect a particular market-oriented – some would say neoliberal – approach toward development, with a particular focus on the removal of fossil-fuel subsidies and the imposition of cost-recovery pricing.

TABLE 7.1 Policy prescriptions for a low-carbon energy transition

High-income countries (high-energy economies)
- Undertake deep emission cuts at home
- Put a price on carbon: cap and trade or carbon tax
- Remove fossil-fuel subsidies
- Increase research, development, and demonstration in new technologies
- Change high-energy consuming lifestyle
- Provide financing and low-carbon technologies to developing countries

Middle-income countries (post-socialist economies & emerging economies)
- Scale up energy efficiency and renewable energy
- Integrate urban and transport approaches to low-carbon use
- Remove fossil-fuel subsidies
- Adopt cost-recovery pricing including local externalities
- Conduct research, development, and demonstration in new technologies

Low-income countries (developing economies)
- Expand energy access through grid and off-grid options
- Deploy energy efficiency and renewable energy whenever they are least cost
- Remove fossil-fuel subsidies
- Adopt cost-recovery pricing
- Leapfrog to distributed generation, where grid infrastructure does not exist.

Source: World Bank (2010a), *World Development Report 2010*. Washington, DC: World Bank, p. 204.

However, they do provide an effective score card and a coherent set of policy prescriptions that address the energy elements of the Kaya Identity – energy intensity and the carbon intensity of energy use. Thus, they map well on to the discussion above.

If one takes the policy prescription for the high-income countries, it is clear that EU energy and climate policy ticks most of the boxes, but it is also apparent just how far short of the mark the United States currently is with its emphasis on technological solutions and its failure to adopt emission targets at the federal level, let alone acknowledge the environmental consequences of its high-energy consuming lifestyle. The policy prescriptions for middle-income countries recognize the need to address the key issue of mobility and also the role that these economies have to play in the research, development, and demonstration of new technologies. The policy prescription for low-income countries stresses the diversity of possible solutions, combining grid and off-grid options, and the possibility of leapfrogging to distributed generation. In all cases, energy efficiency, the development of renewable energy, and the removal of fossil-fuel subsidies are seen as essential. Thus, the policy prescriptions for a low-carbon transformation may be clear, but how do they relate to the challenge of energy security and who will implement them?

A central proposition of this analysis has been that the dual challenges of energy security and climate change need to be seen in combination within the context of globalization. Figure 7.1 identifies the major international organizations involved in these three arenas. A brief analysis of each arena reveals a different sense of purpose, internal conflicts and tensions, and a distinct lack of interconnection.

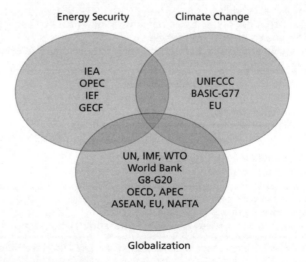

Figure 7.1 *The global governance challenge*

Starting with energy security, there are a host of international organizations that are concerned primarily with ensuring the efficient operation of the current fossil-fuel energy system (Goldthau and Witte 2010; Hirst and Frogatt 2012). The list in figure 7.1 is far from comprehensive, but the two principal organizations are the IEA, which represents the interests of the energy-importing states of the OECD, and OPEC, which represents the interests of many of the world's oil-exporting states. The IEA seeks to ensure security of supply and affordability, while OPEC seeks a steady income for producers and a fair return for those investing in the industry. The International Energy Forum (IEF) was created in 1991 and currently involves 89 countries which together account for 90 percent of oil and gas supply and demand. The aim of the IEF is to enable dialogue between producers and consumers, and to provide information and promote greater transparency. These three organizations are involved in the Joint Organizations Data Initiative (JODI) that provides monthly data on oil supply, demand, and stocks. It is fair to say that none of them currently represents the interests of the energy-importing emerging economies, though there has been the suggestion that IEA membership should be extended to China and India. The final organization in figure 7.1 is the Gas Exporting Countries Forum (GECF), which is a relatively new organization created in 2001 and has 12 members. The Forum seeks to increase coordination between member countries and improve communication between gas producers and consumers to ensure a stable and secure supply and demand in global markets (El-Katiri and Honoré 2012). The nature of global gas markets means that the GECF is unlikely to achieve the status of OPEC, but its membership includes most of the major reserve holders of conventional gas. As an OECD organization, the IEA has been increasingly involved in policy discussions relating to climate change, and its *World Economic Outlook* now presents various scenarios in relation to energy consumption and climate change, but it only advises member-states and has no policymaking power of its own. By comparison, OPEC sees climate-change policy as a threat to future fossil-fuel demand and seeks compensation for oil-producing states. Thus, OPEC's interests are at odds with most other emerging and developing countries. Overall, it is fair to say that the current energy-governance architecture is primarily concerned with the more traditional dimensions of energy security in relation to the fossil-fuel energy system – with a bias toward international trade in oil – and it is not well aligned with the challenges of climate change and energy access (Goldthau 2011; and Cherp et al. 2011).

The governance structure relating to climate change is dominated by the UNFCCC, which was adopted in 1992 and came into force in 1994. At present 195 countries (plus the EU) are parties to the Convention. The principal policy instrument of the UNFCCC is the Kyoto Protocol that currently 192 countries are party to. The Kyoto Protocol was agreed in 1997, but only came into force in 2005. It required the so-called Annex 1 countries to achieve binding targets over the 2008–12 commitment period, with the aim of reducing their cumulative emissions by 5 percent over 1990s levels. It expired at the end of 2012 and no new agreement is in place. Instead, the Durban Summit in December 2011 created a "roadmap" which will guide countries to reaching a new agreement by 2015, which will then come into effect after 2020. Meanwhile, at the Doha Summit in late 2012, most of the signatories to the Kyoto Protocol agreed to make new pledges under the existing mechanism to govern emissions until 2020 with the aim of reducing emissions by 18 percent over 1990 levels. As noted earlier, those committed to the extension of the Kyoto Protocol probably account for less than 15 percent of global emissions, so the UNFCCC's current efforts fall well short of a global agreement on emission reductions. The other groups identified in figure 7.1 represent particular interest groups within the climate change negotiations. BASIC was discussed in chapter 3, as was the Group of 77 that represents the interests of 131 developing countries and seeks to enhance their negotiating capacity. Together, they represent interests in opposition to those of the developed economies, and they expect the developed economies to agree to deep emission cuts and assist them by financing measures to mitigate and adapt to climate change. The EU is identified as a distinct group within the climate-change sphere as it has provided international leadership and has set emission-reduction targets that extend beyond the Kyoto Protocol, but the EU alone cannot solve the problem of global climate change. Furthermore, solidarity in relation to climate-change policy within the EU is being eroded by the eurozone crisis. The problem at the moment is that the governance architecture relating to climate change is focused on a top-down approach, based on binding commitments, and this has failed to deliver a global agreement beyond 2012. In this respect, the current structure is in danger of becoming part of the problem. It is clear that a bottom-up approach, based on the summation of national pledges, will not deliver the level of emissions reduction required to limit global warning to below 2°C and that a substantial "emissions gap" remains and is growing (UNEP 2012). Instead, some are suggesting a middle road, based on a "clean energy alliance," involving the developed economies and the BRICS (Nutall and Manz 2008), or a "building block approach" (Faulkner, Stephen, and Vogler 2010) that would provide a middle ground between an all-encompassing global agreement and a race to the bottom. What is clear is the current governance structure seems unlikely to deliver a global agreement any time soon.

The final policy area of globalization is by far the most crowded and it is populated by organizations that share a common purpose in promoting international trade and economic growth. There is not the need to examine all of them in detail; some, such as the IMF, WTO, and World Bank, operate at a global scale, while the rest represent the interests of particular groups – G8, G20, OECD, APEC – or are formal trade blocks, such as ASEAN, EU, and NAFTA (and others). As a study by the UNEP and WTO (2009: xi) acknowledged, the recent expansion of international trade has resulted in an increase in the level of global economic activity, which has driven increased demand for energy and with it increased CO_2 emissions. Of late, many of these organizations have become more involved in both the energy security and climate-change policy arenas. The World Bank is serving as the interim trustee for the Green Climate Fund agreed at the Cancun Climate Summit, and much of its activities now focus on climate-change mitigation and adaptation in the context of poverty alleviation. The UN is the one organization that spans across the energy, globalization, and climate-change arenas, with the 2012 Sustainable Energy for All campaign being a case in point. However, if one steps back from the detail of individual organizations and the lattice of cross-agency cooperation, we can conclude that we have an energy governance structure that is primarily concerned with traditional energy-security concerns in relation to fossil fuels and that is divided between the interests of energy-importing and energy-exporting states. We have a climate-change governance structure that is dominated by a particular top-down approach to emissions reductions, which seems incapable of reaching a new agreement because of entrenched differences between the developed and the developing countries. Finally, we have a globalization governance structure dedicated to maximizing the growth of international trade and economic activity that are known to be the key drivers of energy insecurity and increased carbon dioxide emissions. This is an obvious simplification of a very complex situation, but it explains why we are currently a long way from resolving the global energy dilemma. Thus, there appears to be a governance void at the interface between energy security, globalization, and climate change.

The emergence of so-called "nexus thinking" is one way of addressing the interconnected nature of the energy, climate, and economy challenges that the world currently faces. The energy dilemmas nexus analysis here is an example of such an approach. Other examples include Sir John Beddington's (2009) notion of the "perfect storm" that links energy, food, and water security challenges within the wider context of climate change. The Bonn 2011 Conference adopted a similar approach to the water, energy, and food security nexus. In a background paper for that conference, Hoff (2011: 9) notes that a nexus approach is one that "integrates management and governance across sectors and scales." Thus, the governance void identified above is not to be addressed by creating a new supranational environmental organization under the auspices of the UN, or by having yet another summit, but by adopting an integrated approach so that all actors consider the externalities created by their own actions and policy decisions. A policy brief for the Planet Under Pressure Conference in March 2012 also stresses the importance of interconnectedness, maintaining that we need to "Transform global governance to address the interconnected nature of today's challenges" (Gaffney et al. 2012: 2). The World Economic Forum (2012: 7) has also contributed to such an approach with its Global Energy Architecture Performance Index that seeks to assess national energy systems in terms of their ability to: "promote economic growth and development . . . in an environmentally sustainable way . . . while providing universal energy access and security." The challenge is how to promote this nexus thinking in the context of the current compartmentalized and disconnected global governance structure. Unfortunately, the Rio+20 Conference in 2012 fell well short of the mark and serves to demonstrate that such global summits are no longer the way forward. Instead, organizations such as the G20 may be more relevant, as they bring together those countries that are the key actors in the global economy, the major emitters and those that will have to finance the low-carbon transition. It is also their consumption that is at the origin of the perfect storm.

The final factor to consider is that the very nature of climate change means that it serves to multiply the risks and challenges within the nexus. Thus, as the climate changes so the existing energy system is put under new stresses (Pascal 2009), the problems of water security are exacerbated, and food security is further challenged. Therefore, it is not a matter of economic growth or climate change in the sense that we have a choice to make. Inaction on climate change will inevitably compromise economic growth and well-being. For some (Anderson and Bows 2012: 41), we are already on a track that will make constraining global warming to less than 2°C almost impossible; for others, time is fast running out if we are going to stabilize emissions by 2020 (Peters et al. 2013). This analysis started by quoting the IEA's 2008 *World Energy Outlook* Report; the analysis was completed just as the IEA (2012b: 1) warned that its New Policies Scenario now corresponds to a long-term average global temperature increase of 3.6°C. The IEA (2012b: 3) also points out that "No more than one-third of proven reserves of fossil fuels can be consumed prior to 2050 if the world is to achieve the 2°C goal, unless CCS is deployed." Just as this text was being completed, in early 2013, BP's (2013: 79) *Energy Outlook 2030* Report concluded that the world can secure the energy – largely fossil fuels – needed to fuel continued economic growth, but that it will come with a 26 percent increase in carbon emissions between 2011 and 2030. Shell's (2013) latest scenarios – mountains and oceans – also result in a level of global warming well above the 2°C threshold. This puts our current obsession with fossil-fuel security in a very different context and highlights the fact that sooner, rather than later, environmental scarcity, as discussed in chapter 2, must become a major source for fossil-fuel demand destruction, particularly in the case of coal. The IEA suggests that the current emphasis should now be on energy efficiency and demand reduction, as only that can buy sufficient time to enable a global agreement on emissions reductions compliant with the 2°C goal. Only time will tell, but it should be clear to all that new thinking and new approaches are required if we are to resolve the global energy dilemma. It is also clear that the global energy dilemmas nexus is part of a wider configuration of global challenges that together comprise the perfect storm.

My intention in this analysis has been twofold: first, to highlight the ways in which the global energy dilemma plays out across the different regions and countries of the world; and, second, to demonstrate the interrelationships between energy security, globalization, and climate change. My hope is that those in the research and policymaking communities will acknowledge that climate change is far more than an air-pollution problem resolved by agreements to reduce emissions, but must be seen as a key challenge to energy security and globalization (development), and that energy security is about more than secure and affordable supplies of fossil fuels and must be seen in the wider context of climate-change mitigation, the globalization of demand and equitable access. Finally, that the continued expansion of international trade and the pursuit of economic growth must confront the adverse environmental consequences of globalization. Therefore, to start to resolve the global energy dilemma we urgently need to adopt an integrated approach to policymaking and governance that encompasses the interrelationships between the three "E's" of energy, environment, and economy.

Appendix: Country Classification

Developed	Post-socialist	Emerging	Developing
Andorra	Albania	Brazil	Afghanistan
Australia	Armenia	Brunei-Darussalam	Algeria
Austria	Azerbaijan	Chile	Angola
Belgium	Belarus	China	Antigua and Barbuda
Canada	Bosnia &	Hong Kong	Argentina
Channel Islands	Herzegovina	India	Bahamas
Cyprus	Bulgaria	Indonesia	Bahrain
Denmark	Croatia	Kuwait	Bangladesh
Finland	Czech Republic	Malaysia	Barbados
France	Estonia	Mexico	Belize
Germany	FYR Macedonia	Philippines	Benin
Gibraltar	Georgia	Qatar	Bhutan
Greece	Hungary	Saudi Arabia	Bolivia
Greenland	Kazakhstan	Singapore	Botswana
Iceland	Kyrgyz Republic	South Africa	Burkina Faso
Ireland	Latvia	Taiwan	Burundi
Isle of Man	Lithuania	Thailand	Cambodia
Israel	Moldova	Turkey	Cameroon
Italy	Mongolia	UAE	Cape Verde
Japan	Montenegro		Central African Republic
Korea	Poland		Chad
Lichtenstein	Romania		Colombia
Luxembourg	Russia		Comoros
Malta	Serbia		Congo
Monaco	Slovak Republic		Costa Rica
Netherlands	Slovenia		Cote D'Ivoire
New Zealand	Tajikistan		Cuba
Norway	Turkmenistan		Djibouti
Portugal	Ukraine		Dominica
San Marino	Uzbekistan		Dominican Republic
Spain			DPR of Korea
Sweden			DR of the Congo
Switzerland			Ecuador
United Kingdom			Egypt
United States			El Salvador
			Eritrea
			Ethiopia
			Fiji

Developed	Post-socialist	Emerging	Developing
			Gabon
			Gambia
			Ghana
			Guatemala
			Guinea Bissau
			Guyana
			Haiti
			Honduras
			Iran
			Iraq
			Jamaica
			Jordan
			Kenya
			Lao DPR
			Lebanon
			Lesotho
			Liberia
			Libya
			Madagascar
			Malawi
			Maldives
			Mali
			Marshall Islands
			Mauritania
			Mauritius
			Micronesia (Federated states of)
			Morocco
			Mozambique
			Myanmar
			Namibia
			Nauru
			Nepal
			Nicaragua
			Niger
			Nigeria
			Oman
			Pakistan
			Palau
			Panama
			Papua New Guinea
			Paraguay
			Peru
			Rwanda
			Saint Kitts and Nevis
			Saint Lucia
			Samoa
			Sao Tome and Principe
			Senegal
			Seychelles
			Sierra Leone

Continued

Developed	Post-socialist	Emerging	Developing
			Solomon Islands
			Somalia
			South Sudan
			Sri Lanka
			Sudan
			Suriname
			Swaziland
			Syria
			Tanzania
			Timor-Leste
			Togo
			Tonga
			Trinidad and Tobago
			Tunisia
			Tuvalu
			Uganda
			Uruguay
			Vanuatu
			Venezuela
			Viet Nam
			Yemen
			Zambia
			Zimbabwe

Bibliography

ABB (2012) *Saudi Arabia: Energy Efficiency Report.* Zurich: ABB.

Advisory Group on Energy and Climate Change (2010) *Energy for a Sustainable Future.* UN, New York.

Alberta Department of Energy (2012) *Policy Review Jacobs Consultancy: EU Pathway Study (2112).* Edmonton: Government of Alberta.

Aleklett, K., Höök, M., Jakobsson, K., Lardelli, M., Snowden, S., and Söderbergh, B. (2010) The peak of the oil age: analyzing the world oil production. Reference scenario in the World Energy Outlook 2008. *Energy Policy* 38: 1198–414.

Anderson, K. and Bows, A. (2012) Beyond "dangerous" climate change: emission scenarios for a new world. *Philosophical Transactions of the Royal Society* 369: 20–44.

Anoun, M.-C. (2009) Oil and gas resources in the Middle East and North Africa: a curse or a blessing? In J.-M. Chevalier (ed.), *The New Energy Crisis: Climate, Economics and Geopolitics.* Basingstoke: Palgrave Macmillan, pp. 143–72.

Arnal, E. and Förster, M. (2010) Growth, employment and inequality in Brazil, China, India and South Africa: an overview. In Organisation for Economic Co-operation and Development (ed.), *Tackling Inequalities in Brazil, China, India and South Africa: The Role of Labour Market and Social Policies.* Paris: OCED, pp. 13–55.

Ashford, L. S. (2006) *How HIV and AIDs Affect Populations.* Washington, DC: Population Reference Bureau.

Auty, R. M. (1993) *Sustaining Development in Mineral Economies: The Resource Curse Thesis.* London: Routledge.

Auty, R. M. (2001) The political economy of resource driven growth. *European Economic Review* 45: 839–46.

Auty, R. M. (2004) Natural resources and civil strife: a two-stage process. *Geopolitics* 9: 29–49.

Auty, R. M. and Gelb, A. H. (2001) Political economy of resource-abundant states. In R. M. Auty (ed.), *Resource Abundance and Economic Development.* Oxford: Oxford University Press, pp. 126–44.

Bachman, J. (2010) Special report: Oil and ice: worse than the Gulf spill, *Reuters Business and Financial News*, 8 November, at: <http://www.reuters.com/article/2010/11/08/us-russia-oil-idUSTRE6A71IL20101108>; date accessed: July 21, 2011.

Baev, P. K. (2010) Russia abandons the energy super-power idea but lacks energy for "modernisation." *Strategic Analysis* 34: 885–96.

Bahgat, G. (2005) Energy security: the Caspian Sea. *Minerals and Energy* 20: 3–15.

Ban Ki-Moon (2011) *Sustainable Energy for All.* New York: UN.

Barma, N. H., Kaiser, K., Minh Le, T., and Viñuela, L. (2012) *Rents to Riches? The Political Economy of Natural Resource-Led Development*. Washington, DC: World Bank.

Barnett, J. (2007) The geopolitics of climate change. *Geography Compass* 1: 1361–75.

Barnett, J. (2008) The worst of friends: OPEC and G-77 in the climate regime. *Global Environmental Politics* 8: 1–8.

Baumert, K., Herzog, T., and Pershing, J. (2005) *Navigating the Numbers: Greenhouse Gas Data and International Climate Policy*. Washington, DC: World Resources Institute.

Bazilian, M. and Onyeji, I. (2012) Fossil fuel subsidy removal and inadequate public power supply: Implications for businesses. *Energy Policy* 45: 1–5.

Beblawi, H. (1987) Introduction: the rentier state in the Arab world. In H. Beblawi and G. Luciani (eds), *The Rentier State*, London: Croom Helm, pp. 1–22.

Beck, U. (2010) Climate for change, or how to create a green modernity? *Theory, Culture & Society* 27: 254–66.

Beddington, J. (2009) *Food, Energy, Water and the Climate: A Perfect Storm of Global Events?* London: Government Office for Science, at: <http://www.bis.gov.uk/assets/goscience/docs/p/perfect-storm-paper.pdf>; date accessed: January 15, 2013.

Beeson, M., Mills, S., and Yong, W. (2011) The new resource politics: can Australia and South Africa accommodate China? *International Affairs* 87: 1365–84.

Bellona (2011) Comment: Russia stands firm on abandoning Kyoto, kills hopes for legally binding climate deal, at: <http://www.bellona.org/articles/articles_2011/kyotono_russia>; date visited: November 22, 2011.

Bhattacharyya, S. C. (2012) Energy access programmes and sustainable development: a critical review and analysis. *Energy for Sustainable Development* 16: 260–71.

Bolton, P. (2012) *Oil prices*. House of Commons Library, Standard Note 2106. London: House of Commons.

Boussena, S. and Locatelli, C. (2011) Gas market developments and their effect on relations between Russia and the EU. *OPEC Review* 35: 27–46.

Bouzarovski, S. (2009) East-Central Europe's changing energy landscapes: a place for geography. *Area* 41: 452–63.

Boykoff. M. T. and Smith, J. (2010) Media presentations of climate change. In C. Lever-Tracy (ed.), *Routledge Handbook of Climate Change & Society*. London: Routledge, pp. 210–18.

Bradshaw, M. J. (2001) The post-socialist states in the world economies: transformation trajectories. *Geopolitics* 6: 27–46.

Bradshaw, M. J. (2007) The greening of global project finance: the case of the Sakhalin-II oil and gas project. *The Canadian Geographer* 51: 255–79.

Bradshaw, M. J. (2009a) The geopolitics of global energy security. *Geography Compass* 3: 1920–37.

Bradshaw, M. J. (2009b) The Kremlin, national champions and international oil companies: the political economy of the Russian oil and gas industry. *Geopolitics of Energy* 31: 2–14.

Bradshaw, M. J. (2012) Russian energy dilemmas: energy security, globalization and climate change. In P. Aalto (ed.), *Russia's Energy Policies: National, Interregional and Global Dimensions*. Cheltenham: Edward Elgar, pp. 206–29.

Bridge, G. (2011) Past peak oil: political economy of energy crises. In R. Peet, P. Robbins, and M. J. Watts (eds), *Global Political Ecology*. London: Routledge, pp. 307–24.

Bridge, G. and Le Billion, P. (2013) *Oil*. Cambridge: Polity.

British Petroleum (2009) *BP Statistical Review of World Energy 2009*. London: BP.

British Petroleum (2011) *BP Statistical Review of World Energy 2011*. London: BP.

British Petroleum (2012a) *BP Energy Outlook to 2030*. London: BP, at: <http://www.bp.com/sectiongenericarticle.do?categoryId=9035979&contentId=7066648>; date accessed May 16, 2012.

British Petroleum (2012b) *BP Statistical Review of World Energy 2012*. London: BP.

British Petroleum (2013) *BP Energy Outlook to 2030*. London: BP, at: <www.bp.com/.../bp...energy.../2030_energy_outlook_booklet.pdf>; date accessed: January 18, 2013.

Broderick, J. et al. (2011) *Shale Gas: An Updated Assessment of Environmental and Climate Change Impacts*. Manchester: Tyndall Centre, University of Manchester.

Bromley, S. (2005) The United States and the control of world oil. *Government and Opposition* 40: 225–55.

Buchan, D. (2010) *Eastern Europe's Energy Challenge: Meeting Its EU Climate Commitments*. Oxford: The Oxford Institute for Energy Studies, Working Paper EV 55.

Buchan, D. (2011) *Expanding the European Dimension in Energy Policy: The Commission's Latest Initiatives*. Oxford: Oxford Institute for Energy Studies, Working Paper SP 23.

Bulkeley, H. and Betsill, M. M. (2003). *Cities and Climate Change: Urban Sustainability and Global Environmental Governance*. London: Routledge.

Bush, G. W. President (2006) *President Bush Delivers State of the Union Address*, at: <http://www.whitehouse.gov/news/releases/2006/01/2006131-10/htm>; date accessed: December 15, 2008.

Buzar, S. (2007) *Energy Poverty in Eastern Europe: Hidden Geographies of Deprivation*. Aldershot: Ashgate.

Cafaro, P. (2012) Climate ethics and population policy. *WIREs Climate Change* 3: 45–61.

Campbell, C. J. and Laherrère, J. H. (1998) The end of cheap oil, *Scientific American;* reprinted in *Oil and the Future of Energy*. Guilford, CT: Lyons Press, pp. 1–7.

Carbon Dioxide Information Analysis Center (CDIAC) (2012) *Recent Greenhouse Gas Concentrations*, at: <http://cdiac.ornl.gov/pns/current_ghg_html>; date accessed: October 4, 2012.

Carter, J. President (1980) *Jimmy Carter State of the Union Address*, at: <http://www.jimmycarterlibrary.org/documents/speeches/su80jec.phtml>; date accessed: December 15, 2008.

CERES (2010) *Canada's Oil Sands: Shrinking Window of Opportunity*. Boston, MA: CERES.

Charap, S. (2010) Russia's lacklustre record on climate change. *Russian Analytical Digest* 79: 11–15.

Cherp, A., Jewell, J., and Goldthau, A. (2011) Governing global energy: systems, transitions, complexity. *Global Policy* 2: 75–88.

Chertow, M. R. (2011) The IPAT equation and its variants. *Journal of Industrial Ecology* 4: 13–29.

Chester, L. (2010) Conceptualising energy security and making explicit its polysemic nature. *Energy Policy* 38: 887–95.

Chevalier, J.-M. (2009) The new energy crisis. In J.-M. Chevalier (ed.), *The New Energy Crisis: Climate, Economics and Geopolitics*. Basingstoke: Palgrave Macmillan, pp. 6–59.

Clarke, D. (2007) *The Battle for Barrels: Peak Oil Myths and World Oil Futures*. London: Profile Books.

Cleveland, C. J. and Kaufmann, R. K. (2003) Oil supply and oil politics: Déjà vu all over again. *Energy Policy* 34: 485–9.

Climate Analysis Indicators Tool (CAIT) Washington, DC: World Resources Institute, at: <http://www.wri.org/tools/cait/>; date accessed: January 15, 2013.

Cohen, J. E. (2010) Population and climate change. *Proceedings of the American Philosophical Society* 154: 158–82.

Collier, P. (2008) *The Bottom Billion: Why the Poorest Countries are Failing and What Can Be Done about It*. Oxford: Oxford University Press.

Commission of the European Communities (CEC) (2008) *20 20 by 2020: Europe's Climate Change Opportunity*. Brussels: CEC.

Commission of the European Communities (CEC) (2010) *Energy 2020: A Strategy for Competitive, Sustainable and Secure Energy*. Brussels: CEC, COM(2010)639.

Commission of the European Communities (CEC) (2011) *The EU Energy Policy: Engaging with Partners Beyond Our Borders*. Brussels: CEC.

Committee on America's Climate Choices, National Research Council (2011) *America's Climate Choices*. Washington, DC: The National Academies Press.

Committee on America's Energy Future, National Research Council (2009) *America's Energy Future: Technology and Transformation: Summary Edition*. Washington, DC: The National Academies Press.

Commoner, B. 1972). A bulletin dialogue on: "The Closing Circle" – response. *Bulletin of Atomic Scientists* (May): 17–56.

Cornillie, J. and Fankhauser, S. (2004) The energy intensity of transition countries. *Energy Economics* 26: 283–95.

Council on Foreign Relations (2006) *National Security Consequences of U.S. Oil Dependency*. Washington, DC: Council on Foreign Relations, Independent Task Force Report No. 58.

Cranston, G. R. and Hammond, G. P. (2010) North and south: Regional footprints on the transition pathway towards a low carbon, global economy. *Applied Energy* 87: 2945–51.

Crutzen, P. J. and E. F. Stoermer (2000) The "Anthropocene." *Global Change Newsletter* 41: 17–18.

Dalton, M., O'Neill, B., Prskawetz, A., Jiang, L., and Pitkin, J. (2006) Population aging and future carbon emissions in the United States. *Energy Economics* 30: 642–75.

Darbouche, H. and Fattouh, B. (2011) *The Implications of the Arab Uprisings for Oil and Gas Markets*. Oxford: Oxford Institute for Energy Studies, Working Paper MEP 2.

Davis, G. A. and Tilton, J. E. (2005) The resource curse. *Natural Resources Forum* 29: 233–42.

Davis, J. D. (1984) *Blue Gold: The Political Economy of Natural Gas*. London: George Allen and Unwin.

Deffeyes, K. S. (2001) *Hubbert's Peak: The Impending World Oil Shortage*. Princeton, NJ: Princeton University Press.

Deichmann, U., Meisner, C., Murray, S., and Wheeler, D. (2010) *The Economics of Renewable Energy Expansion in Rural Sub-Saharan Africa*. Washington, DC: World Bank, Policy Research Working Paper 5193.

Department of Energy and Climate Change (2011) *Digest of United Kingdom Energy Statistics 2011*. Norwich: UK National Statistics Authority.

Diamond, J. (2005) *Collapse: How Societies Choose to Fail or Succeed*. London: Penguin.

Dicken, P. (2004) Geographers and "globalization": (yet) another missed boat? *Transactions of the Institute of British Geographers* 29: 5–26.

Dicken, P. (2011) *Global Shift: Mapping the Changing Contours of the World Economy*, 5th edn. London: Sage.

Dienes, L. and Shabad, T. (1979) *The Soviet Energy System: Resource Use and Policies*. Washington, DC: V.H. Winston and Sons.

Dietz, T. and Rosa, E. A. (1997) Effects of population and affluence on CO_2 emissions. *Proceedings of the National Academy of Science* 94: 175–9.

Dow, K. and Downing, T. E. (2007) *The Atlas of Climate Change: Mapping the World's Greatest Challenge*. London: Earthscan.

Downs, E. S. (2006) *The Brookings Foreign Policy Studies Energy Security Series: China*. Washington, DC: The Brookings Institution.

Downs, E. S. (2007) China's rise in Africa – the fact and fiction of Sino-African energy relations. *China Security* 3: 42–68.

Downs, E. S. (2011) China Development Bank's oil loans: pursuing policy and profit. *China Economic Quarterly*, December: 43–7.

Eifert, B., Gelb, A., and Tallroth, N. B. (2002) *The Political Economy of Fiscal Policy and Economic Management in Oil Exporting Countries*. Washington, DC: World Bank Policy Research, Working Paper 2889.

El-Gamal, M. A. and Jaffe, A. M. (2010) *Oil, Dollars, Debt, and Crises: The Global Curse of Black Gold*. Cambridge: Cambridge University Press.

Elias, R. J. and Victor, D. G. (2005) *Energy Transitions in Developing Countries: A Review of Concepts and Literature*. Stanford, CA: Stanford University, Program on Energy and Sustainable Development, Working Paper Number 40.

El-Katiri, L. and Honoré, A. (2012) The gas exporting countries forum: global or regional cartelization? In J. P. Stern (ed.), *The Pricing of Internationally Traded Gas*. Oxford: OIES/Oxford University Press, pp. 424–66.

Emberson, L., Rockström, J., He, K., Amann, J. M., Barron, J., Corell, R., Feresu, S., Haeuber, S. R., Hicks, K. F., Johnson, X., Karlqvist, A., Klimont, Z., Mylvakanam, I., Song, W. H., Vallack W., and Qiang, Z. (2012) Chapter 3 – Energy and Environment. In *Global Energy Assessment – Toward a Sustainable Future*. Cambridge, UK, and New York: Cambridge University Press, and Laxenburg, Austria: the International Institute for Applied Systems Analysis, pp. 191–254.

Emmerson, C. and Stevens, P. (2012) *Maritime Choke Points and the Global Energy System: Charting a Way Forward*. London: Chatham House.

Energy Information Administration (2009) *International Energy Outlook 2009*. Washington, DC: EIA.

Energy Information Administration (2010) *International Energy Outlook 2010*. Washington, DC: EIA.

Energy Information Administration (2011a) *International Energy Outlook 2011*. Washington, DC: EIA.

Energy Information Administration (2011b) *World Shale Gas Resources: An Initial Assessment of 14 Regions outside the United States*. Arlington, VA: Advanced Resources International Inc.

Energy Information Administration (2011c) *Annual Energy Outlook 2011*. Washington, DC: EIA.

Energy Information Administration (2011d) *Country Analysis Brief of India*. Washington, DC: EIA.

Energy Information Administration (2011e) *Country Analysis Brief of South Africa*. Washington, DC: EIA.

Energy Information Administration (2012a) *Energy Brief: How Dependent are We on Foreign Oil?* Washington, DC: EIA.

Energy Information Administration (2012b) *Annual Energy Outlook 2012 with Projections to 2035*. Washington, DC: EIA.

European Bank for Reconstruction and Development (EBRD) (2001) *Transition Report 2001: Energy in Transition*. London: EBRD.

European Bank for Reconstruction and Development (2012) *About the EBRD Factsheet*. London: EBRD.

European Environment Agency (2010) *Total Primary Energy Intensity* (CSI 028/ ENER017), European Environmental Agency, Brussels, at: <http://www.eea. europa.eu/data-and-maps/indicators/total-primary-energy-intensity/total-primary-energy-intensity-assessment-5>; date accessed: May 16, 2011

European Environment Agency (2012) *Greenhouse Gas Emission Trends and Projections in Europe 2012: Tracking Progress Towards Kyoto and 2020 Targets*. Copenhagen: EEA, EEA Report No.4/2012.

Exxon Mobil (2010) *The Outlook for Energy: A View to 2030*. Irving, Texas: Exxon Mobil.

Exxon Mobil (2012) *The Outlook for Energy: A View to 2040*. Irving, Texas: Exxon Mobil.

Fattouh, B. (2011) The Saudi gas sector and its role in industrialisation: developments, challenges and options. In B. Fattouh and J. P. Stern (eds), *Natural Gas Markets in the Middle East and North Africa*. Oxford: OIES and Oxford University Press, pp. 196–234.

Fattouh, B. and El-Katiri, L. (2012) *Energy and Arab Economic Development*. New York: UNDP Regional Bureau for Arab States, Arab Human Development Report, Research Paper Series.

Faulkner, R., Stephen, H., and Vogler, J. (2010) International climate policy after Copenhagen: towards a "building blocks" approach. *Global Policy* 1: 252–62.

Friedman, T. L. (2006) The first law of petropolitics. *Foreign Policy* 154: 28–39.

Froggatt, A. and Canzi, G. (2004) *Ending Wasteful Energy Use in Central and Eastern Europe*. Brussels: WWF European Policy Office.

Gaffney, O. et al. (2012) Interconnected risks and solutions for a planet under pressure. *Planet Under Pressure Rio+20 Policy Brief No. 5*, at: <http://www.icsu.org/ rio20/policy-briefs/interconnected-issues-brief>; date accessed: January 8, 2013.

Galkina, A. (2012) *Out in the Cold: Investor Risk in Shell's Arctic Exploration*. London: Platform, Fair Pensions and Greenpeace.

Gaye, A. (2007) *Access to Energy and Human Development*, New York: UNDP and Human Development Report Office, Occasional Paper 25.

Gény, F. (2010) *Can Unconventional Gas be a Game Changer in European Gas Markets?* Oxford: Oxford Institute for Energy Studies, Working Paper NG 46.

Giddens, A. (2012) *The Politics of Climate Change*, 2nd edition. Cambridge: Polity.

Goldman, M. I. (2008) *Petrostate: Putin, Power and the New Russia*, Oxford: Oxford University Press.

Goldthau, A. (2011) Governing global energy: existing approaches and discourses. *Current Opinion in Environmental Sustainability* 3: 1–5.

Goldthau, A. and Witte, J. M. (eds) (2010) *Global Energy Governance: New Rules of the Game*. Washington, DC: Brookings Institution Press.

Government of Alberta (2011) *Responsible Actions, Responsible Oil*. Edmonton: Government of Alberta.

Government of Russia (2010) *Energy Strategy of Russia for the Period up to 2030*. Moscow: Government of Russia.

Grace, J. D. (2005) *Russian Oil Supply: Performance and Prospects*. Oxford: Oxford University Press / OIES.

Gray, D. (1995) *Reforming the Energy Sector in Transition Economies: Selected Experience and Lessons*. Washington, DC: World Bank, Discussion Papers 296.

Grübler, A. (2004) Transition in energy use. *Encyclopaedia of Energy*, 6: 163–77.

Grübler, A., Johansson, T. B., Mundaca, L., Nakicenovic, N., Pachauri, S., Riahi, K., Rogner, H.-H., and Strupeit, L. (2012) Chapter 1 – Energy Primer. In *Global Energy Assessment – Toward a Sustainable Future*. Cambridge, UK, and New York: Cambridge University Press, and Laxenburg, Austria: the International Institute for Applied Systems Analysis, pp. 99–150.

Gustafson, T. (1989) *Crisis Amid Plenty – The Politics of Energy under Brezhnev and Gorbachev*. Princeton, NJ: Princeton University Press.

Gustafson, T. (2012) *Wheel of Fortune: The Battle for Oil and Power in Russia*. Cambridge, MA: The Belknap Press of Harvard University Press.

Hallding, K., Han, G., and Olsson, M. (2009) China's climate- and energy-security dilemma: shaping a new path of economic growth. *Journal of Current Chinese Affairs* 3: 119–34.

Hallding, K., Olsson, M., Atteridge, A., Vihma, A., Carson, M., and Román, M. (2011) *Together Alone: BASIC Countries and the Climate Change Conundrum*. Stockholm: Norden.

Happer, C., Philo, G., and Froggatt, A. (2012) *Climate Change and Energy Security: Assessing the Impact of Information and its Delivery on Attitudes and Behaviour*. London: UKERC.

The Hartwell Paper (2010) London: London School of Economics.

Harvey, D. (2003) *The New Imperialism*. Oxford: Oxford University Press.

Hedenskog, J. and Larsson, R. L. (2007) *Russian Leverage on the CIS and Baltic States*. Stockholm: Swedish Defence Research Agency.

Held, D., McGrew, A., Goldblatt, D., and Perraton, J. (1999) *Global Transformations: Politics, Economics and Culture*. Stanford, CA: Stanford University Press.

Helm, D. (2007) The new energy paradigm. In D. Helm (ed.), *The New Energy Paradigm*. Oxford: Oxford University Press, pp. 9–35.

Helm, D. (2009) EU climate-change policy – a critique. In D. Helm and C. Hepburn (eds), *The Economics and Politics of Climate Change*. Oxford: Oxford University Press, pp. 222–44.

Helm, D. (2011) Peak oil and energy policy – a critique. *Oxford Review of Economic Policy* 27: 68–91.

Helm, D. (2012) *The Carbon Crunch: How We're Getting Climate Change Wrong – and How to Fix It*. New Haven, CT: Yale University Press.

Hemmingsen, E. (2010) At the base of Hubbert's peak: grounding the debate on petroleum scarcity, *Geoforum* 41: 531–40.

Henderson, J. (2010) *Non-Gazprom Producers in Russia*. Oxford: Oxford University Press and OIES.

Henderson, J. (2011) *Domestic Gas Prices in Russia – Towards Export Netback?* Oxford: OIES, Working Paper NG 57.

Hirsch, R. L., Bezdek, R., and Wendling R. (2005) *Peaking of World Oil Production: Impacts, Mitigation and Risk Management*. Washington, DC: US Department of the Environment.

Hirst, G., Thompson, G., and Bromley, S. (2009) *Globalization in Question*, 3rd edn. Cambridge: Polity.

Hirst, N. and Frogatt, A. (2012) *The Reform of Global Energy Governance*. London: Imperial College, Gratham Institute for Climate Change, Discussion Paper No. 3.

Hoff, H. (2011) *Understanding the Nexus*. Background Paper for the Bonn 2011 Conference: The Water, Energy and Food Security Nexus. Stockholm: Stockholm Environment Institute.

Hoffman, G. W. and Dienes, L. (1985) *The European Energy Challenge: East and West*. Durham, NC: Duke University Press.

Homer-Dixon, T. and Garrison, N. (eds) (2009) *Carbon Shift: How Peak Oil and the Climate Crisis will Change Canada*. Toronto: Random House Canada.

Hosoe, T. (2012) Asia's post-Fukushima market for liquefied natural gas: a special focus on Japan. In P. Andrews-Speed, M. E. Herberg, T. Hosoe, J. V. Mitchell, and Z. Daojoing, *Oil and Gas in for Asia: Geopolitical Implications of Asia's Rising Demand*. Washington, DC: The National Bureau of Asian Research, NBR Special Report 41, pp. 43–56.

Howarth, R. W., Santoro, R., and Ingraffea, A. (2011) Methane and the greenhouse-gas footprint from shale formation. *Climatic Change Letters*, DOI 10.1007/s10584-011-0061-5.

Huber, M. (2009) Energizing historical materialism: Fossil Fuels, Space and the Capitalist Mode of Production. *Geoforum* 40: 105–15.

Hughes, G. (1991) The energy sector and problems of energy policy in Eastern Europe. *Oxford Review of Economic Policy* 7: 77–98.

Humphreys, M., Sachs, J. D., and Stiglitz, J. E. (2007) Introduction: what is the problem with natural resource wealth? In M. Humphreys, J. D. Sachs, and J. E. Stiglitz (eds), *Escaping the Resource Curse*. New York: Columbia University Press, pp. 1–20.

Ianchovichina, E. (2011) *The Middle East and North Africa and Dependence on the Capital-Intensive Hydrocarbon Sector*. Washington, DC: World Bank, MENA Knowledge and Learning, Quicknote Series, No. 38.

IHS-CERA (2009) *The Future of Global Energy Supply – Understanding the Building Blocks*. Cambridge, MA: Cambridge Energy Associates.

Independent Taskforce on Peak Oil and Energy Security (ITPOES) (2008) *The Oil Crunch: Securing the UK's Energy Future*. London: ITPOES.

Independent Taskforce on Peak Oil and Energy Security (ITPOES) (2010) *The Oil Crunch: A Wake-up Call for the UK Economy*. London: ITPOES.

Institute for Integrated Economic Research (2011) *Low Carbon and Economic Growth: Key Challenges*. Meilen, Switzerland: IIER.

Intergovernmental Panel on Climate Change (2007a) *Climate Change 2007: Synthesis Report, Summary for Policy Makers*. Geneva: IPCC.

Intergovernmental Panel on Climate Change (2007b) *Climate Change 2007: Synthesis Report*. Geneva: IPCC.

International Energy Agency (2007) *World Energy Outlook 2007*. Paris: IEA.

International Energy Agency (2008) *World Energy Outlook 2008*. Paris: IEA.

International Energy Agency (2009) *World Energy Outlook 2009*. Paris: IEA.

International Energy Agency (2010) *World Energy Outlook 2010*. Paris: IEA.

International Energy Agency (2011a) *World Energy Outlook 2011*. Paris: IEA.

International Energy Agency (2011b) *IEA Response System for Oil Supply Emergencies 2011*. Paris: IEA.

International Energy Agency (2011c) *Are We Entering a Golden Age of Gas?* Paris: IEA.

International Energy Agency (2011d) *2011 Key World Energy Statistics*. Paris: IEA.

International Energy Agency (2011e) *CO2 Emissions from Fuel Combustion: Highlights*. Paris: IEA.

International Energy Agency (2011f) *Energy for All: Financing Access for the Poor*. Paris: IEA.

International Energy Agency (2012a) *Golden Rules of a Golden Age of Gas*. Paris: IEA.

International Energy Agency (2012b) *World Energy Outlook 2012*. Paris: IEA.

International Energy Agency, Organization of the Petroleum Exporting Countries, Organisation for Economic Co-operation and Development, and the World Bank (2010) *Analysis of the Scope of Energy Subsidies and Suggestions for the G20 Initiative*. Paris: IEA.

International Energy Agency, United Nations Development Programme, and United Nations Industrial Development Organization (2010) *Energy Poverty: How To Make Modern Energy Access Universal*. Paris: IEA.

International Maritime Organization (IMO) (2009) *Prevention of Air Pollution from Ships – Second IMO GHG Study 2009*. Final Report MEPC 59/INF.10. London: IMO.

International Monetary Fund (IMF) (2012) *World Economic Outlook Update*. Washington, DC: IMF.

Jaccard, M. (2005) *Sustainable Fossil Fuels: The Unusual Suspect in the Quest for Clean and Enduring Energy*. Cambridge: Cambridge University Press.

Jaffe, A. and Manning, R. A. (1998) The myth of the Caspian "great game": the real geopolitics of energy. *Survival* 40: 112–29.

Jakobson, L., Holtom, P., Knox, D., and Peng, J. (2011) *China's Energy and Security Relations with Russia: Hopes, Frustrations and Uncertainties*. Sweden: Stockholm International Peace Research Institute, SIPRI Policy Paper No. 29.

Jhaveri, N. J. (2004) Petroimperialism: US oil interests and the Iraq War. *Antipode* 36: 2–11.

Jian, Z. (2011) *China's Energy Security: Prospects, Challenges and Opportunities*. Washington, DC: The Brookings Institution Center for Northeast Asian Policy Studies.

Jiang, J. and Sinton, J. (2011) *Overseas Investments by Chinese National Oil Companies: Assessing the Drivers and Impacts*. Paris: IEA Information Paper.

Jiang, L. and Hardee, K. (2011) How do recent population trends matter to climate change? *Population Research Policy Review* 30: 287–312.

Jiang, M., Griffin, W. M., Hendrickson, C., Jaramillo, P., VanBriesen, J., and Venkatesh, A. (2011) Life cycle greenhouse gas emissions of Marcellus shale gas. *Environmental Research Letters* 6, doi:10.1088/1748-9326/6/3/034014.

Jones Luong, P. and Weinthal, E. (2008) *Oil is Not a Curse: Ownership Structure and Institutions in Soviet Successor States*. Cambridge: Cambridge University Press.

Kalicki, J. H. and Goldwyn, D. L. (eds) (2005) *Energy and Security: Toward a New Foreign Policy Strategy*. Washington, DC: Woodrow Wilson Center Press.

Karl, T. L. (1997) *The Paradox of Plenty: Oil Booms and Petro-States*. San Francisco and Los Angeles, CA: University of California Press.

Kharecha, P. and Hansen, J. E (2008) Implications of "peak oil" for atmospheric CO2 and climate. *Global Biogeochemical Cycles* 22: GB3012, doi:10.1029/2007GB003142.

Klare, M. (2002) *Resource Wars: The New Landscape of Global Conflict*. London: Henry Holt and Company.

Klare, M. (2005) *Blood and Oil, the Dangers and Consequences of America's growing Petroleum Dependency*. London: Penguin.

Klare, M. (2008) *Rising Powers, Shrinking Planet: The New Geopolitics of Energy*. New York: Metropolitan Books.

Klare, M. (2009) The era of Xtreme energy: life after the age of oil, *Huffington Post*, at: <http://www.huffingtonpost.com/michael-t-klare/the-era-of-xtreme-energy_b_295304.html>; date accessed: October 11, 2011.

Klare, M. (2012) *The Race for What's Left: The Global Scramble for the World's Last Resources*. New York: Metropolitan Books.

Kong, B. (2011) Governing China's energy in the context of global governance. *Global Policy* 2: 51–65.

Kononenko, V. (2010) *Russia-EU Cooperation on Energy Efficiency*. Helsinki: Finnish Institute of International Affairs, FIIA Briefing Paper 68.

Kramer, G. J. and Haigh, M. (2009) No quick switch to low-carbon energy. *Nature* 465: 568–9.

Kramer, J. M. (1991) Energy and environment in Eastern Europe. In J. DeBardeleben (ed.), *To Breathe Free: Eastern Europe's Environmental Crisis*. Baltimore, MD: Johns Hopkins University Press, pp. 57–79.

Kuby, M., He, C., Trapido-Lurie, B., and Moore, N. (2011) The changing structure of energy supply, demand and CO2 emissions in China. *Annals of the Association of American Geographers* 101: 795–805.

Kuik, O. J., Bastos Lima, M., and Gupta, J. (2011) Energy security in a developing world. *WIREs Climate Change* 2: 627–34.

Kulagin, V. (2008) Energy efficiency and development of renewables: Russia's approach. *Russian Analytical Digest* 46: 2–8.

Ladislaw, S., Zyla, K., Pershing, J., Verrastro, F., Goodward, J., Pumphrey, D., and Staley, B. (2009) *A Roadmap for a Secure, Low-Carbon Energy Economy*. Washington, DC: CSIS and WRI.

Lahn, G. and Stevens, P. (2011) *Burning to Keep Cool: The Hidden Energy Crisis in Saudi Arabia*. London: Chatham House.

Le Billion, P. (2005) *Fuelling War: Natural Resources and Armed Conflict*. Adelphi Paper 373. London: Institute for Strategic Studies.

Le Billion, P. and El Khatib, F. (2004) From free oil to "freedom oil": terrorism, war and US geopolitics in the Persian Gulf. *Geopolitics* 9: 109–37.

Leichenko, R. M. and O'Brien, K. L. (2008) *Environmental Change and Globalization: Double Exposure*. Oxford: Oxford University Press.

Leung, G. C. K. (2011) China's energy security: perception and reality. *Energy Policy* 39: 1330–7.

Leung, G. C. K., Raymond, L., and Low, M. (2011) Transitions in China's oil economy, 1990–2010. *Eurasian Geography and Economics* 52: 483–500.

Levi, M. A. (2009) *The Canadian Oils Sands: Energy Security vs. Climate Change*. Washington, DC: Council for Foreign Relations, Centre for Geoeconomic Studies.

Locatelli, C. (1990) Energy and the restructuring of the economies of Eastern Europe and the USSR. *Energy Studies Review* 2: 133–43.

Lough, J. (2011) *Russia's Energy Diplomacy*. Russia and Eurasia Programme, Briefing Paper. London: Chatham House.

Lund, P. (2012) The European Union challenge: integration of energy, climate, and economic policy. *WIREs Energy and Environment* 1: 60–8.

Luomi, M. (2010) *Oil or Climate Politics? Avoiding a Destabilising Resource Split in the Arab Middle East*. Helsinki: The Finnish Institute of International Affairs, Briefing Paper 58.

Ma, X. and Andrews-Speed, P. (2006) The overseas activities of China's national oil companies: rationale and outlook. *Minerals and Energy* 21: 17–30.

McGlade, C., Spiers, J., and Sorrell, S. (2012) *A Review of Regional and Global Estimates of Unconventional Gas Resources*. London: UKERC.

McKeown, A. and Gardner, G. (2009) *Climate Reference Guide*. Washington, DC: WRI.

McNeil, J. (2000) *Something New Under the Sun: An Environmental History of the Twentieth Century*. London: Penguin Books.

Macqueen, D. and Korhaliller, S. (2011) *Bundles of Energy: The Case for Renewable Biomass Energy*. London: International Institute for Environment and Development.

Maddison, A. (2002) The West and the rest in the international economic order, *OECD Observer*, 235, at: <http://www.oecdobserver.org/news/fullstory.php/aid/884/The_West_and_the_Rest_in_the_International_Economic_Order.html>; date accessed: July 25, 2011.

Maddison, A. (2003) *The World Economy: Historical Statistics*. Paris: OECD.

Malm, A. (2012) China as chimney of the world: the fossil capital hypothesis. *Organization & Environment* 25: 146–77.

Maugeri, L. (2012) *Oil: The Next Revolution: The Unprecedented Upsurge of Oil Production Capacity and What it Means for the World*. Cambridge, MA: Belfer Center for Science and International Affairs, Harvard University, Discussion Paper 2012–10.

Medlock, K. B., Jaffe, A. M., and Hartley, P. R. (2011) *Shale Gas and U.S. National Security*. Houston, TX: James A. Baker III Institute of Public Policy, Rice University.

Melosi, M. (2010) Energy transitions in historical perspective: some thoughts. In L. Nader (ed.), *The Energy Reader*. Oxford: Wiley-Blackwell, pp. 45–60.

Metz, B., Davidson, O. R., Bosch, P. R., Dave, R., and Meyer, L. A. (eds) (2007) *Reports of the Intergovernmental Panel on Climate Change*. Cambridge: Cambridge University Press.

Miller, R. R. (2008) *Central Europe's Energy Security Schism*. Washington, DC: Centre for European Policy Analysis.

Mills, R. (2008) *The Myth of the Oil Crisis: Overcoming the Challenges of Depletion, Geopolitics and Global Warming*. London: Praeger.

Mitchell, J. (2010) *More for Asia: Rebalancing World Oil and Gas*. London: Chatham House.

Mitchell, J., Marcel, V., and Mitchell, B. (2012) *What Next for the Oil and Gas Industry?* London: Chatham House.

Modi, V., McDade, S., Lallement, D., and Saghir, J. (2005) *Energy Services for the Millennium Development Goals*. New York and Washington, DC: UNDP, World Bank, ESMAP.

Mohan, G. and Power, M. (2008) New African choices? The politics of Chinese engagement. *Review of African Political Economy* 115: 23–42.

Morse, E. L., Lee, E. G., Ahn, D. P., Doshi, A., Kleinman, S. M., and Yeun, A. (2012) *Energy 2020: North America, the New Middle East?* New York: Citi GPS.

Murray, W.E. (2006) *Geographies of Globalization*. London: Routledge.

Murtaugh, P. A. and Schlax, M. G. (2009) Reproduction and the carbon legacies of individuals. *Global Environmental Change* 19: 14–20.

Nayyar, D. (2008) *China, India, Brazil and South Africa in the World Economy*. Helsinki: United Nations University, UN-WIDER Discussion Paper No. 2008/05.

Noël, P. (2006) The new US Middle East Policy and energy security challenges. *International Journal* (Winter): 43–54.

Noël, P. (2008) *Beyond Dependence: How to Deal with Russian Gas*. London: European Council for Foreign Relations, Policy Brief.

Noël, P. (2009) *A Market Between Us: Reducing the Political Cost of Europe's Dependence on Russian Gas*. Cambridge: University of Cambridge, EPRG Working Paper 0916.

Noreng, O. (2006) *Crude Power: Politics and the Oil Market*. London: I.B. Tauris.

Novikova, A., Korppoo, A., and Sharmina, M. (2009) *Russian Pledge vs. Business as Usual: Implementing Energy Efficiency Policies can Curb Carbon Emissions*, Helsinki: UPI-Finnish Institute of International Affairs, Working Paper 61.

Nutall, W. J. and Manz, D. L. (2008) A new energy paradigm for the twenty-first century. *Technological Forecasting & Social Change*. 75: 1247–59.

Obama, B. (2006) *The Audacity of Hope*. New York: Canongate.

Obama, B. President (2009) *President Barack Obama's Inaugural Address*, at: <http://www.whitehouse.gov/blog/inaugral-address/>; dated accessed: January 21, 2009.

Obama, B. President (2013) *President Barack Obama's Inaugural Address*, at: <http://www.whitehouse.gov/the-press-office/2013/01/21/inaugural-address-president-barack-obama>; date accessed: January 21, 2013.

O'Brien, K. (2006) Are we missing the point? Environmental change as an issue for human security. *Global Environmental Change* 16: 1–3.

O'Brien, K. and Leichenko, R. M. (2000) Double exposure: addressing the impacts of climate change within the context of economic globalization. *Global Environmental Change* 10: 221–32.

O'Hara, S. and Lai, H. (2011) China's "dash for gas": challenges and potential impacts on global markets. *Eurasian Geography and Economics* 52: 501–22.

Olcott, M. B. (2009) *Russia, Central Asia and the Caspian: How Important is the Energy and Security Trade-off?* Houston, TX: James A. Baker III Institute for Public Policy, Rice University.

O'Neill, B. C. (2010) Climate and population growth. In L Mazur (ed.), *A Pivotal Moment: Population, Justice & the Environmental Challenge*. Washington, DC: Island Press, pp. 81–94.

O'Neill, B., Dalton, M., Fuchs, R., Jiang, L., Pachauri. S., and Zigova, K. (2010) Global demographic trends and future carbon emissions. *Proceedings of the National Academy of Sciences* 107: 17521–6.

O'Neill, B. C., MacKellar, F. L., and Lutz, W. (2001) *Population and Climate Change*. Cambridge: Cambridge University Press.

O'Neill, J. (2001) *Building Better Global Economic BRICs*. Global Economic Papers No: 66. New York: Goldman Sachs.

Openshaw, K. (2010) *Can Biomass Power Development?* London: Gate Keeper 144, International Institute for Environment and Development.

Organisation for Economic Co-operation and Development (OECD) (2005) *Structural Change and Growth: Trends and Policy Implications*. Paris: OECD.

Organisation for Economic Co-operation and Development (OECD) (2011a) *OECD Factbook 2010 – Economic, Environmental and Social Statistics*. Paris: OECD.

Organisation for Economic Co-operation and Development (OECD) (2011b) *OECD Economic Surveys: Russia 2011*. Paris: OECD.

Organization of the Petroleum Exporting Countries (OPEC) (2010) *OPEC Annual Statistical Bulletin 2010/2011*. OPEC, Geneva.

Ozturk, I. (2010) A literature survey on the energy-growth nexus. *Energy Policy*, 39: 340–9.

Paik, K.-W. (2012) *Sino-Russian Oil and Gas Cooperation-The Reality and Implications*. Oxford: OIES/Oxford University Press.

Paik, K.-W., Lahn, G., and Hein, J. (2012) *Through the Dragon Gate? A Window of Opportunity for Northeast Asian Gas Security*. London: Chatham House, Briefing Paper EER BP 2012/05.

Parks, B. C. and Roberts, J. T. (2008) Inequality and the global climate regime: breaking the north-south impasse. *Cambridge Review of International Affairs* 21: 621–48.

Pascal, C. (2009) *The Vulnerability of Energy Infrastructure to Environmental Change*. Chatham House. London: Chatham House, Briefing Paper EERG BP 2009/01.

Pearson, I., Zeniewski, P., and Zastera, P. (2012) The impact of unconventional gas on the European energy system. In *Unconventional Gas: Potential Energy Market Impact in the European Union*. Petten, The Netherlands: JRC Scientific Policy Report, Joint Research Centre, Institute for Energy and Transport, pp. 145–85.

Peters, G. P., Minx. J. C., Weber, C. L., and Ottmar, E. (2011) Growth in emission transfers via international trade from 1990 to 2008. *Proceedings of the National Academy of Science* 108: 8903–8.

Peters, G. P., Marland, G., Le Quéré, C., Boden, T., Canadell, J. G., and Raupach, M. R. (2012) Rapid growth in CO2 emissions after the 2008–2009 global financial crisis. *Nature Climate Change* 2: 2–4.

Peters, G. P., Andrew, R. M., Boden, T., Canadell, J. G., Ciais, P., Le Quéré, C. Marland, G., Raupach, M. R., and Wilson, C. (2013) The challenge to keep global warming below 2°C. *Nature Climate Change* 3: 4–6.

PEW Center on Global Climate Change (2011) *Climate Change 101: Federal Action*. Arlington, VA: PEW Center on Global Climate Change.

Pezzini, M. (2012) An emerging middle class. *OECD Observer*. At: <http://www.oec-dobserver.org/news/printpage.php/aid/3681/An_emerging_middle_class.html>; date accessed: September 22, 2012.

Pielke Jr., R. (2010) *The Climate Fix: What Scientists and Politicians Won't Tell You About Global Warming*. New York: Basic Books.

Pirani, S. (ed.) (2009) *Russian and CIS Gas Markets and their Impact on Europe*. Oxford: Oxford University Press and CIS.

Pirani, S., Stern, J., and Yafimava, K. (2009) *The Russo-Ukrainian Gas Dispute of January 2009: A Comprehensive Assessment*, Working Paper HG 27. Oxford: Oxford Institute for Energy Studies.

Podobnik, B. (2006) *Global Energy Shifts: Fostering Sustainability in a Turbulent Age*. Philadelphia, PA: Temple University Press.

Population Reference Bureau (2012) *2012 World Population Data Sheet*. Population Reference Bureau, Washington, DC, at: <http://www.prb.org/Publications/Datasheets/2012/world-population-data-sheet/data-sheet.aspx>; date accessed: August 2, 2012.

Practical Action (2010) *Poor People's Energy Outlook 2010*. Rugby: Practical Action.

Practical Action (2012) *Poor People's Energy Outlook 2012*. Rugby: Practical Action.

Prasad, G. (2011) Improving access to energy in sub-Saharan Africa. *Current Opinion in Environmental Sustainability* 3: 1–6.

Raupach, M. R., Marland, G., Ciais, P., Le Quéré, C., Canadell, J. G., Klepper. G., and Field, C. B. (2007) Global and regional drivers of accelerating CO2 emissions. *Proceeding of the National Academy of Sciences* 104: 10288–93.

Rees, J. (1991) Resources and environment: scarcity and sustainability. In R. J. Bennett and R. C. Estall (eds), *Global Challenge and Change: Geography for the 1990s*. London: Routledge, pp. 5–26.

Rice, S. and Tyner, J. (2011) Pushing on: *petrolism* and the statecraft of oil. *The Geographical Journal* 177: 208–12.

Riley, A. (2012) Commission v. Gazprom: The antitrust clash of the decade? *CEPS Policy Brief*. Brussels: Centre for European Studies.

Rivers, N. and Jaccard, M. (2009) Talking without walking: Canada's ineffective climate effort. In B. Eberlein and G. B. Doern (eds), *Governing the Energy Challenge: Canada and Germany in a Multi-Level Regional and Global Context*. Toronto: University of Toronto Press, pp. 285–313.

Ross, M. J. (2001) Does Oil Hinder Democracy? *World Politics* 53: 325–61.

Ross, M. J. (2012) *The Oil Curse: How Petroleum Wealth Shapes the Development of Nations*. Princeton, NJ: Princeton University Press.

Rosser, A. (2006) *The Political Economy of the Resource Curse: A Literature Survey*. Working Paper 268, Brighton: Institute of Development Studies.

Rowthorn, R. (2006) *The Renaissance of China and India: Implications for the Advanced Economies*. UNCTAD Discussion Paper No. 182, Geneva: UNCTAD.

The Royal Society of Canada (2010) *Environmental and Health Impacts of Canada's Oil Sands Industry*. Ottawa: The Royal Society of Canada.

Rubin, J. (2009) *Why Your World is About to Get a Whole Lot Smaller: What the Price of Oil Means for the Way We Live*. London: Virgin Books.

Rühl, C. (2008) *BP Statistical Review of World Energy 2008*. London: BP.

Rühl, C. (2009) *BP Statistical Review of World Energy 2009: What's Inside*. London: BP.

Rühl, C., Appleby, P., Fennema, J., Naumov, A., and Schaffer, M. (2011) *Economic Development and Demand for Energy: A Historical Perspective on the Next 20 Years*, at: <http://www.bp.com/liveassets/bp_internet/globalbp/STAGING/global_assets/downloads/R/reports_and_publications_economic_development_demand_for_energy.pdf>; date accessed July 31, 2012.

Rutledge, I. (2006) *Addicted to Oil: America's Relentless Drive for Energy Security*. London: I.B. Tauris.

Sachs, J. D. and Warner, A. M. (2001) The curse of natural resources. *European Economic Review* 45: 827–38.

Safonov, G. and Lugovoy, O. (2010) Economic development and emission projections in Russia. In A. Korppoo, G. Sakonov, and O. Lugovoy (eds), *Russia and the Post 2012 Climate Regime: Emission Trends, Commitments and Bargains*. Copenhagen: Nordic Council of Ministers, TemaNord, pp. 16–43.

Salay, J., Fenhann, J., Jaanimägi, K., and Kristoferson, L. (1993) Energy and environment in the Baltic states. *Annual Review of Energy and Environment* 18: 169–216.

Santos-Paulino, A. U. and Wan, G. (2010) *The Global Impact of the Southern Engines of Growth: China, India, Brazil and South Africa*. Helsinki: United Nations University UN-WIDER, Policy Brief, No.6.

Satterthwaite, D. (2009) The implications of population growth and urbanization for climate change. *Environment and Urbanization* 21: 545–67.

Schipper, L., Marie-Lilliu, C., and Lewis-Davis, G. (2001) *Rapid Motorisation in the Largest Countries in Asia: Implication for Oil, Carbon Dioxide and Transportation*. Paris: International Energy Agency.

Schmidt-Felzmann, A. (2011) EU member states' energy relations with Russia: conflicting approaches to securing natural gas supplies. *Geopolitics* 16: 574–99.

Secretary of Energy Advisory Board (SEAB) (2011) *Shale Gas Production Committee Second Ninety Day Report*. Washington, DC: US Department of Energy.

Selin, H. and VanDeveer, S. D. (2010) US climate change politics and policymaking. *WIREs Climate Change* 2: 121–7.

Shell (2008) *Shell Energy Scenarios to 2050*. The Hague: Shell International BV.

Shell (2013) *New Lens Scenarios: A Shift in Perspective for a World in Transition*. The Hague: Shell International BV.

Shen, L., Gao, T., and Cheng, X. (2012) China's coal policy since 1979: a brief overview. *Energy Policy* 40: 274–81.

Sheppard, E. (2002) The spaces and times of globalization: place, scale, networks and positionality. *Economic Geography* 78: 307–30.

Sieferle, R. P. (2001) *The Subterranean Forest: Energy Systems and the Industrial Revolution*. Cambridge: White Horse Press.

Simmons, M. R. (2005) *Twilight in the Desert: The Coming Saudi Oil Shock and the World Economy*. Hoboken, NJ: John Wiley and Sons.

Smil, V. (2003) *Energy at the Crossroads: Global Perspectives and Uncertainties*. Cambridge, MA: MIT Press.

Smil, V. (2008) Moore's curse and the great energy delusion. *The American*, November 19, at: <http://www.american.com/archive/2008/november-december-magazine/moore2019s-curse-and-the-great-energy-delusion/>; date accessed: May 16, 2011.

Smil, V. (2010) *Energy Transitions: History, Requirements, Prospects*. Denver, CO: Praeger.

Smil, V. (2011) America's oil imports: a self-inflicted burden. *Annals of the Association of American Geographers* 101: 712–16.

Smith, A. and Swain, A. (2010) The global economic crisis, Eastern Europe, and the former Soviet Union: models of development and the contradictions of internationalization. *Eurasian Geography and Economics* 51: 1–34.

Smith, A. and Timár, J. (2010) Uneven transformations: space, economy and society 20 years after the collapse of state socialism. *European Urban and Regional Studies* 17: 115–25.

Smith, L. C. (2011) *The New North: The World in 2050*. London: Profile Books.

Sorrell, S., Miller, R., Bentley, R., and Speirs, J. (2010) Oil futures: a comparison of global supply forecasts. *Energy Policy* 38: 4990–5003.

Sovacool, B. K. (ed.) (2011) *The Routledge Handbook of Energy Security*. London: Routledge.

Sovacool, B. K. (2012) The political economy of energy poverty: A review of key challenges. *Energy for Sustainable Development* 16: 272–82.

Sovacool, B. K. and Brown, M. A. (2010) Competing dimensions of energy security: an international perspective. *Annual Review of Environment and Resources* 35: 77–108.

Stern, N. (2007) *The Economics of Climate Change*. Cambridge: Cambridge University Press.

Stern J. (2009) *Future Gas Production in Russia: Is the Concern About Lack of Investment Justified?* Working Paper NG 35, Oxford: Oxford Institute for Energy Studies.

Stern, J. (ed.) (2012) *The Pricing of Internationally Traded Gas*. Oxford: Oxford Institute for Energy Studies and Oxford University Press.

Stevens, P. (2003) *Resource Impact – Curse or Blessing? A Literature Survey*. London: IPIECA.

Stevens, P. (2010) *The "Shale Gas Revolution": Hype or Reality*. London: Chatham House.

Stevens, P. (2012) *The "Shale Gas Revolution": Developments and Changes*. London: Chatham House.

Syvitski, J. (2012) Anthropocene: An Epoch of Our Making. *Global Change* 78: 12–15.

Taylor, I. (2006) China's oil diplomacy in Africa. *International Affairs* 85: 69–82.

Tertzakian, P. (2007) *A Thousand Barrels a Second: The Coming Oil Break Point and the Challenges Facing an Energy Dependent World*. New York: McGraw-Hill.

Tottie, J., Phillips, D., Pappu, S., and Cho, B. (2012) *Dawn in the Desert: Saudi Aramco's Transformation*. London: HSBC Global Research.

Tu, K. J. and Johnson-Reiser, S. (2012) *Understanding China's Rising Coal Imports*. Washington, DC: Carnegie Endowment for International Peace, Policy Outlook.

United Nations, Department of Economic and Social Affairs and Population Division (2010) *World Urbanization Prospects: The 2009 Revision Highlights*. New York: UN.

United Nations, Department of Economic and Social Affairs, Population Division (2011) *World Population Prospects: The 2010 Revisions, Highlights and Advance Tables*. New York: UN; available at: <http://esa.un.org/wpp/>.

United Nations Development Programme *Human Development Reports*; available at: <http://hdr.undp.org/en/>.

United Nations Development Programme (Russia) (2010) *National Human Development Report for the Russian Federation – Energy Sector and Sustainable Development*. Moscow: UNDP.

United Nations Development Programme (2012) *Integrating Energy Access and Employment Creation to Accelerate Progress on the MDGs in Sub-Saharan Africa*. New York: UNDP.

United Nations Development Programme and World Health Organisation (2009) *The Energy Access Situation in Developing Countries*. New York: UNDP.

United Nations Energy (2005) *The Energy Challenge for Achieving the Millennium Development Goals*. New York: UN.

United Nations Environment Progamme (2012) *The Emissions Gas Report 2012: A UNEP Synthesis Report*. Nairobi, Kenya: UNEP.

United Nations Population Fund (2010) *State of the World Population 2010*. New York: UNPF.

United States Department of Defense (US DoD) (2011) *Energy for the Warfighter: Operational Energy Strategy*. Washington, DC: US DoD.

United States Department of Energy (2008) *Energy Intensity Indicators: Economy-Wide Total Energy Consumption*, at: <http://www1.eere.energy.gov/ba/pba/intensityindicators/total_energy.html>; date accessed: April 13, 2011.

United States Department of Energy (2012) *Energy Intensity Indicators: Economy-Wide Total Energy Consumption*, at: <http://www1.eere.energy.gov/analysis/eii_total_energy.html>; date accessed: March 23, 2013.

United States Environmental Protection Agency (US EPA) (2012) *Inventory of U.S. Greenhouse Gas Emissions and Sinks 1990–2010: Executive Summary*. Washington, DC: US EPA.

Ürge-Vorsatz, D., Miladinova, G., and Paizs, L. (2006) Energy in transition: from the Iron Curtain to the European Union. *Energy Policy* 34: 2279–97.

US Geological Service (USGS) (2008) *Circum-Arctic Resource Appraisal: Estimates of Undiscovered Oil and Gas North of the Arctic Circle*. USGS, Fact Sheet 2008–3049. Menlo Park, CA: US Geological Service.

Valentine, S. V. (2011) The fuzzy nature of energy security. In B. Sovacool (ed.), *The Routledge Handbook of Energy Security*. London: Routledge, pp. 56–73.

Van Rompuy, H. (2011) *Challenges and Priorities for EU Energy Policy, President of the European Council*. Brussels: Speech to the European Council, May 11, 2011, PCE 0111/11.

Vatansever, A. (2010) *Russia's Oil Exports: Economic Rationale versus Strategic Gain*. Washington, DC: Carnegie Endowment, Energy and Climate Program Paper Number 116.

Venables, A. J. (2006) Shifts in economic geography and their causes. *Economic Review, Federal Reserve Bank of Kansas City*, 4th Quarter: 61–85.

Von Hirschhausen, C. and Waelde, T. W. (2001) The end of transition: an institutional interpretation of energy sector reform in Eastern Europe and the CIS. *MOCT-MOST: Economic Policy is Transitional Economies* 11: 91–108.

Wagner, H.-J. (2009) *Energy: The World's Race for Resources in the 21st Century*. London: Haus Publishing.

Watts, M. (2004) Resource curse? Governmentality, oil and power in the Niger Delta, Nigeria. *Geopolitics* 9: 50–80.

Watts, M. (2009) The rule of oil: Petro-politics and the anatomy of an insurgency. *Journal of African Development* 11: 27–55.

Wheeler, D. and Ummel, K. (2007) *Another Inconvenient Truth: A Carbon-Intensive South Faces Environmental Disaster, No Matter What The North Does*. Centre for Global

Development, Working Paper 134, Washington DC., at: <http://www.cgdev.org/content/publications/detail/14947/>, dated accessed: July 21, 2011.

The White House (2011) *Blueprint for a Secure Energy Future*. Washington, DC: The White House.

The White House (2012) *The Blueprint for a Secure Energy Future: Progress Report*. Washington, DC: The White House.

Wilson, D. and Purushothaman, R. (2003) *Dreaming with BRICs: The Path to 2050*. Global Economics Paper No. 99. New York: Goldman Sachs.

Wilson, E., Godfrey Wood, R., and Garside, B. (2012) *Sustainable Energy for All? Linking Poor Communities to Modern Energy Services*. Working Paper No.1, IIED Linking Worlds Series. London: International Institute of Environment and Development.

World Bank Development Indicators Database At: <http://data.worldbank.org/data-catalog/world-development-indicators>.

World Bank (2008a) *World Bank Development Indicators 2008*. Washington, DC: World Bank.

World Bank (2008b) *Energy Efficiency in Russia: Untapped Reserves*. Moscow: World Bank.

World Bank (2010a) *World Development Report 2010*. Washington, DC: World Bank.

World Bank (2010b) *Cities and Climate Change: An Urgent Agenda*. Washington, DC: The World Bank Urban Development Series, Knowledge Paper 10.

World Bank (2010c) *Lights Out? The Outlook for Energy in Eastern Europe and the Former Soviet Union*. Washington, DC: World Bank.

World Bank (2011a) *Global Development Horizons 2011: Multipolarity: The New Global Economy*. Washington, DC: World Bank.

World Bank (2011b) *Extreme Poverty Rates Continue to Fall*. At: <http://data.worldbank.org/news/extreme-poverty-rates-continue-to-fall>; date accessed: July 25, 2011.

World Bank (2011c) *World Bank Development Indicators 2011 Database*. Washington, DC: World Bank.

World Economic Forum (2012) *The Global Energy Architecture Performance Index Report 2013, Executive Summary*. Geneva: World Economic Forum.

World Energy Council (WEC) (2010a) *Energy Efficiency: A Recipe for Success*. London: WEC.

World Energy Council (WEC) (2010b) *Survey of Energy Resources: Focus on Shale Gas*. London: WEC.

World Resources Institute (WRI) (2010) *U.S. Climate Action in 2009–2010*. WRI, Washington, DC: WRI.

World Resources Institute (2011) *The Role of Driving in Reducing GHG Emission and Oil Consumption*. Washington, DC: WRI.

World Trade Organization (WTO) (2011) *World Trade Report 2011*. Geneva: WTO.

World Trade Organization (WTO) and United Nations Environment Programme (UNEP) (2009) *Trade and Climate Change*. Geneva: WTO.

World Wildlife Fund (WWF) and The Cooperative Bank (2008) *Unconventional Oil: Scrapping the Bottom of the Barrel*. Godalming: WWF UK.

Wright, G. and Czelusta, J. (2004) The myth of the resource curse. *Challenge* 47: 6–38.

Wrigley, E. A. (2010) *Energy and the English Industrial Revolution*. Cambridge: Cambridge University Press.

Wunder, S., Kaphengst, T., Timeus, K., and Berzins, K. (2012) *Impact of EU Bioenergy Policy on Developing Countries*. Brussels: Directorate-General for External Policies of the Union, European Commission.

Xuetang, G. (2006) The energy security in Central Eurasia: the geopolitical implications to China's energy strategy. *China and Eurasia Forum Quarterly* 4: 117–37.

Yafimava, K. (2011) *The Transition Dimension of EU Energy Security: Russian Gas Transit Across Ukraine, Belarus and Moldova*. Oxford: Oxford Institute for Energy Studies and Oxford University Press.

Yates, D. A. (1996) *The Rentier State in Africa: Oil Rent Dependency and Neocolonialism in the Republic of Gabon*. Trenton, NJ: Africa World Press.

Yeager, K., Dayo, F., Fisher, B., Fouquet, R., Gilau, A., and Rogner, H.-H. (2012) Chapter 6 – Energy and Economy. In *Global Energy Assessment – Toward a Sustainable Future*. Cambridge, UK, and New York: Cambridge University Press, pp. 385–422; and Laxenburg, Austria: International Institute for Applied Systems Analysis.

Yergin, D. (2008) *The Prize: The Epic Quest for Oil Money and Power*. New York: Simon and Schuster.

Yergin, D. (2009) It's still the one. *Foreign Policy* (September/October): 88–95.

Yergin, D. (2011) *The Quest: Energy, Security and the Remaking of the Modern World*. London: Allen Lane.

Index

Page references in *italics* denote a table/figure.